HOW THE WORKING-CLASS HOME BECAME MODERN, 1900–1940

HOW THE WORKING-CLASS HOME BECAME MODERN, 1900–1940

THOMAS C. HUBKA

Architecture, Landscape, and American Culture Series

University of Minnesota Press
Minneapolis
London

Original drawings by Thomas C. Hubka and Erik Larson

Published by the University of Minnesota Press
111 Third Avenue South, Suite 290
Minneapolis, MN 55401-2520
http://www.upress.umn.edu

Printed in the United States of America on acid-free paper

The University of Minnesota is an equal-opportunity educator and employer.

27 26 25 24 23 22 21 20   10 9 8 7 6 5 4 3 2 1

Library of Congress Cataloging-in-Publication Data
Hubka, Thomas C., author.
How the working-class home became modern, 1900–1940 / Thomas C. Hubka.
Minneapolis : University of Minnesota Press, [2020] | Series: Architecture, landscape, and American
    culture series | Includes bibliographical references and index.
Identifiers: LCCN 2019053591 (print) | ISBN 978-0-8166-9300-9 (hc) | ISBN 978-0-8166-9301-6 (pb)
Subjects: LCSH: Cost and standard of living—United States—History. | Working class—Dwellings—
    United States—History. | Domestic space—United States—History. | United States—Social
    conditions.
Classification: LCC HD6983 .H83 2020 (print) | DDC 305.5/62097309041—dc23
LC record available at https://lccn.loc.gov/2019053591

Unheralded Progressives

This book is dedicated to generations of early twentieth-century working-class families who strove continuously to improve the quality of their homes and domestic lives. Although their efforts were largely unnoticed by Progressive Era reformers, these Americans contributed substantially to the domestic reform that has so often been credited to the houses and households of the middle to upper classes. These unheralded progressives from a rising working class, soon to become the American middle class, played a fundamental role in the transformation and modernization of American domestic life.

CONTENTS

PREFACE AND ACKNOWLEDGMENTS

This book tells the story of the transformation and improvement in the housing and domestic conditions of a majority of Americans between 1900 and 1940. In essence, it is a common story of some of the most important first and last experiences in an average family's domestic history. For example, when did working-class families begin eating in dining rooms instead of their kitchens, or use modern bathrooms, or store clothes in closets, or have electric lights or electric appliances such as refrigerators, or fill a shelf with books, or purchase furniture that was intended to be handed down—all for the first time? Simultaneously, when was the last time working-class Americans hand-pumped and hauled water, or used outhouses, or cooked on wood stoves, or washed clothes by hand, or lit kerosene lamps, or lived in two- or three-room houses or apartments, or shared bedrooms with parents and siblings—all for the last time? For many twenty-first-century Americans, these small milestones of daily domestic life are shrouded in a distant past, perhaps conjuring up images of either the comforts of a Victorian mansion or the rigors of pioneer settlement. But for the vast majority of Americans, this story of domestic transformation and improvement is far less exotic, much closer to home, and not so long ago—typically occurring in the late nineteenth and early twentieth centuries, often within the past hundred years. I emphasize the linkage between first and last experiences because they are flip sides of the same quick-succession, working-class domestic improvement story, such as the change from kerosene lamps to electric lights. However, that is not the way American domestic improvement is most often presented in the dominant housing reform literature, which typically concentrates on the initial, earlier stages of housing improvements, often in the dwellings of the upper classes occurring over many centuries. Distinguishing between these contrasting home improvement stories, between upper and working classes, is a major theme of this book.

I first became interested in working-class dwellings through efforts to locate different branches of my own family's housing history in thatched peasant cottages in Poland-Belarus and German log cabins in Central Pennsylvania, and then following their progress through various stages of housing improvement to a middle-class domestic life in America. Once committed to investigating common houses (alternatively called popular, vernacular, folk, everyday, average, working class), I began to conduct detailed case-study documentation of common dwellings in the regions where I lived and taught: Maine, Wisconsin, and Oregon. Along the way, I began fieldwork studies in metropolitan regions throughout the country (cited throughout the book) and became aware of underlying unities in a basic working-class housing and domestic improvement story despite significant differences in buildings, residents, and domestic conditions, and particularly between urban–rural, geographic, and ethnic and racial constituencies. Yet, despite obvious differences in the shape and form of the houses, the process of domestic improvement that went on within those houses, including the improvements working-class families sought and what they obtained, was remarkably consistent nationwide. It is the effort to interpret what I believe is this common story of fundamental unity in the improvement of American working-class domestic conditions that is the dominant theme of this book.

Over the past fifteen years of research, in pursuit of the finest studies illuminative of America's common housing, I have repeatedly consulted the research of scholars such as Joseph Bigott, Richard Harris, Paul Groth, Marta Gutman, Alison Hoagland, Daniel Reiff, and Henry Glassie in order to forge a comprehensive thesis about how American vernacular housing was built and improved in the early twentieth century. Of special note is the outstanding economic analysis of housing development in Robert J. Gordon's *The Rise and Fall of American Growth*, which strongly parallels and supports the more specific findings of this book.[1]

THANK YOU

Many ideas for this book have been planted or vetted by a group of generous scholars and colleagues who influenced this book directly or guided me through their research and writing: Leo Marx, Henry Glassie, Judith Kenny, Howard Davis, Kim Hoagland, Bill Kleinsasser, Richard Longstreth, Chris Wilson, Pam Simpson, Jeff Cohen, Dell Upton, Carl Lounsbury, Peirce Lewis, Kingston Heath, Elizabeth Cromley, Elliot Wolfson, Dianne Harris, Art Goldhammer, Ken Breisch, Todd Gish, Matthew Lasner, Paul Groth, John Archer, and Margo Anderson. The case studies from around the nation were assisted and made possible by the generosity of city and regional historians and local residents. As credited in the notes, I have been enriched by and borrowed from scholars from disciplines both within and outside my architecture and cultural historical studies background: Witold Rybczynski, Gwendolyn Wright, Ruth Schwartz Cowan, Richard Harris, and Lizabeth Cohen. A special thank-you to my editor Abby Van Slyck, more a trusted contributing colleague, who has skillfully and generously guided this project. Pieter Martin at the University of Minnesota Press guided the book's production for more years than should be allowed, with special assistance from Anne Carter. Erik Larson completed most of the drawings, with additions by Scott Mackinson. Family members have also contributed. Thanks to my Portland, Oregon, survey car teammate Kevin Kenny and to Mary Hubka for text support and Terry Hubka for contractor wisdom. A very special thanks to Judith Kenny for her knowledge of housing environments, her tireless support for this project, her inspiring advocacy for the houses and households of the working class, and our sustaining love and partnership.

INTRODUCTION

HOUSING AND DOMESTIC REFORM
FROM A MIDDLE-MAJORITY PERSPECTIVE

During a forty-year period at the beginning of the twentieth century, millions of average Americans experienced accelerated improvement in their housing and domestic conditions. These improvements were intertwined with the acquisition of entirely new mechanical conveniences, new types of rooms and patterns of domestic life, and rising standards of living. Although most of these improvements—such as three-fixture bathrooms, kitchen appliances, public utilities, dining rooms, and bedroom privacy—had largely been obtained by many upper- and upper-middle-class households by 1900, they were increasingly available to American working-class families beginning in the late nineteenth century and at a rapidly increasing rate into the early twentieth century. The speed at which the majority of American working-class households were transformed from a primitive, premodern home life into an industrialized, modern domesticity and the scale of this transformation were without precedent in American history.

This book traces this history of early twentieth-century housing improvement through the lens of material-cultural standards, examining the physical evidence of America's working-class houses. The specific focus is the acquisition of bathrooms, utilities, and other groundbreaking improvements that contributed to what came to be known as "standards of living" and "housing standards."[1] Although these material-cultural standards differ from the traditional measures of class status, such as income, wages, and wealth, they bring exceptional clarity to our understanding of everyday domestic life for average Americans.

That widespread domestic improvement transformed the lives of Americans in the late nineteenth and early twentieth century

Figure I.1. *The model houses of domestic reform.* The early twentieth-century houses of the upper middle class typically shown in the dominant literature and historical studies of the period. (a) Georgian/Federal style, Center-Hall plan, 1920s, Shorewood, Wisconsin. (b) English Cottage style, expanded Cape Cod plan, late 1930s, Portland, Oregon. (c) Prairie style, Four-Square plan, late 1920s, Eugene, Oregon. (d) Colonial Revival/Federal style, Center-Hall plan, 1920s, Portland, Oregon. (e) English Cottage style, expanded Cape Cod plan, circa 1935, Omaha, Nebraska. (f) English Arts and Crafts style, Center-Hall plan, 1920s, Portland, Oregon.

is recognized in most studies of housing and domestic reform and is typically attributed to both Progressive Era social and domestic reform movements and to the industrialized mass production of housing and domestic goods and services. Yet this story of transformation has most often been told from the perspective of a relatively small segment of middle-to-upper-class houses and households typically found throughout the country in suburban residential neighborhoods (Figure I.1). These are the houses that would have been distinguished from smaller common houses by the presence of dining rooms, entrance halls, studies, two or more bedrooms, pantries, a variety of closets, second bathrooms, bay windows, and built-in furniture. For their upper-middle-class residents, those who have been the unacknowledged protagonists of the vast majority of American architectural and housing histories, many of the domestic improvements emphasized in this book had already been obtained before 1900.

In contrast, the domestic life for the traditional working classes during the first forty years of the twentieth century has been less well documented, and their houses mentioned far less frequently in the standard literature of American housing and domestic reform (Figure I.2). Today these dwellings are usually found in older, pre–World War II residential neighborhoods from around the country—often within an inner ring of urban metropolitan, working-class suburbs now averaging about a century old. They are the types of houses many of us may have passed frequently, without giving them much thought. Here, we will be examining them closely, but not because they are necessarily architecturally distinguished or because of their architectural style, their architects, or their role in the history of design development. All the houses in Figure I.2 were selected because they were among the most popular, if not the most popular, types of early twentieth-century houses from such neighborhoods around the country. Throughout this book, we will primarily be focusing on these most popular or numerous forms of housing as a way of locating and interpreting the dominant patterns of improvement to the quality of domestic life.

The houses in Figure I.1, therefore, represent an early twentieth-century national consensus of upper-middle-class houses that has

Figure I.2. *The underdocumented houses of domestic reform.* Typical early twentieth-century houses that brought modern domestic conveniences to a vast middle majority of Americans. (a) Duplex (no standard stylistic name), 1920s, Buffalo, New York. (b) Cape Cod house, Colonial Revival style, center-stair (Cape Cod) plan, late 1930s, Portland, Oregon. (c) Brick row houses, (no standard stylistic name), Side-Hall plan, early twentieth century, Butte, Montana. (d) Classical vernacular style, compact Bungalow plan, early twentieth century, Omaha, Nebraska. (e) Shotgun houses (no standard stylistic name), three-room-deep Shotgun plan, early twentieth century, Macon, Georgia. (f) Four-Square house (no standard stylistic name, neoclassical porch), Four-Square plan, circa 1905, Portland, Oregon.

dominated the national literature of housing reform. Among hundreds of books and articles and thousands of footnotes about American housing and its reform consulted for this study, there is a tendency to focus on these upper-middle-class houses, as if they represented a greater majority. For example, many scholars rarely note the actual percentage or number of American households that are specifically being addressed—especially when assessing or implying "typical" or "average" or "middle class" conditions. This neglect of broad housing demographic analysis opens the door to assertions about what constituted average domestic conditions without supporting data. As Paul Krugman has stressed, we should not ignore the validity or "implication of numbers," as they are a key to determining just how widespread any given idea or practice actually was. In this study, the importance of housing demographics is particularly evident when inquiring, for example, how far and how quickly various domestic improvements extended from the upper classes into the ranks of the middle to working classes.[2]

THE PROBLEM OF "MIDDLE CLASS"

Focusing analysis on the broad central portion of the housing population, however, poses special problems related to historic and ongoing debates about who and what is "middle class."[3] If this book focused on either the upper or lower ends of income distribution, there would be little problem understanding the emphasis of this research. But to focus on the central majority of the population stirs controversy about the complex meaning of "middle class," and this is especially true during the early twentieth century when America's modern middle-class majority began to be formed.

A recurring problem of housing analysis involving the "middle class" is the tendency to use terms such as "average," "common," and especially "middle class" to imply broad, and perhaps even majority social acceptance. For example, in writing about visually complex Victorian houses built in the late nineteenth century, Clifford Clark has argued that "the ideal image of the middle-class house presented by magazine and plan-book writers sometimes suggests that the house itself was an organic system."[4] While his insight into

Figure I.3. *The screening effect of upper-middle-class houses.* The focus of early twentieth-century housing literature on the middle to upper classes has contributed to a deemphasis on and marginalization of the far more numerous houses of the middle to working classes. In the absence of substantive documentation about common houses, the well-documented history of upper-middle-class housing has often been used to interpret the domestic history of most houses.

the way these ornate houses referenced nature is productive, the houses themselves were hardly middle class. Instead, the stylistic complexity that interested Clark would perhaps have applied to under 10 percent of late nineteenth-century houses. As we will see, the standard nineteenth-century usage of "middle class" typically referred to a small economic minority of professionals and merchants and not a numerical majority of the population as it does today. The problem for common housing studies, however, is that this older usage is repeated in housing reform literature into the twentieth century, often giving the impression that a small group of large upper-"middle-class" houses represented a majority of houses (see Figure I.1).

Unfortunately, without really intending it, similar tendencies, repeated many hundreds of times in various literatures of housing, have become the accepted narrative of most houses, leaving little place for the story of common houses. It is as if a focus on larger upper-class houses has screened the presence of smaller average houses (Figure I.3). I will identify this common tendency to expand the numerical significance of "middle class" housing in early twentieth-century literature as "middle-class creep" into the domain of common, everyday houses. To be clear, this tendency to enlarge a frame of reference to include greater housing or population constituencies than is warranted, although a common literary practice, is not a significant debilitating fault in most studies. Yet, the consequence for vernacular housing studies is a tendency to obscure the presence of common houses, especially by concealing their numbers and, therefore, a portion of their significance.[5]

FOCUSING ON A MIDDLE MAJORITY

Up to this point, a variety of terms have been used to define the economic middle of the housing population, with "middle class" being the most common and the most controversial. Scholarly and popular discourse has, of course, added many other terms to the ever-changing interpretation of the middle and all levels of housing and social class (Figure I.4). While acknowledging these unresolved issues of nomenclature usage, the term "middle majority" will be used to describe the book's primary analytical focus: the numerical, central economic portion of the housing population independent of shifting boundaries of social class. "Middle majority" locates this central 60 percent of housing and households that sits between the 20 percent of Americans with the highest incomes and the 20 percent with the lowest incomes (Figure I.5). In economic terminology, it is the central three quintiles (P80–P20, or 80 percent to 20 percent) of income distribution of the population. This 60 percent middle majority is a simple formula but devilishly difficult to constantly maintain within a vast literature with diverse and changing social and economic definitions of class as well as a difficult-to-identify housing stock with changing measures of

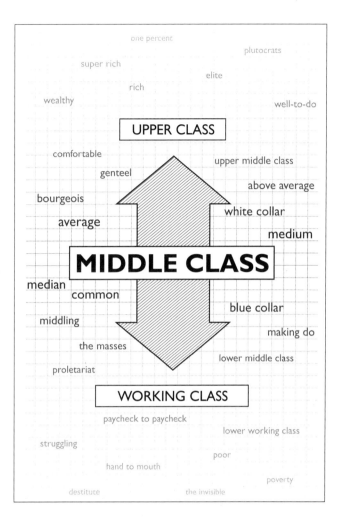

Figure I.4. *Competing terms for evaluating economic and social class.* Evolving terms from various disciplines and popular usage have been used to rank and define a hierarchy of social and economic groups or classes of the population related to housing. An overarching issue for American studies is the problem of who and what is "middle class."

Figure I.5. *Focusing on a "middle majority."* This study documents the central 60 percent of the economic distribution of the housing population without regard to current or historical rankings or terminology. This central portion, usually labeled "middle class," is typically analyzed without reference to the percentage of the population being described.

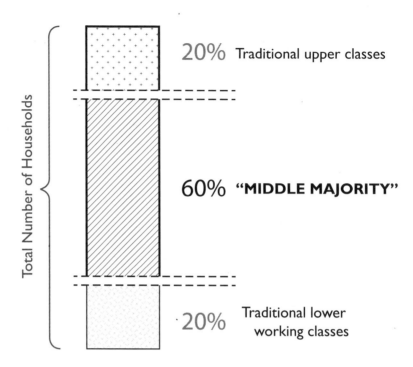

Total Number of Households

20% Traditional upper classes

60% **"MIDDLE MAJORITY"**

20% Traditional lower working classes

economic and cultural worth.[6] Further contributing to these problems, the study of vernacular housing becomes increasingly difficult as one explores less well-documented residential environments and populations of the middle to working classes. But, whatever the difficulties, this study is unequivocal in its pursuit of the history of domestic reform for this economic middle majority—no matter how difficult that constituency is to identify and tabulate in space and time.

HOUSING DEMOGRAPHIC METHODS

Maintaining an analytical focus on the middle majority of America's housing is a challenging task when confronting 80 million houses and 120 million current households. Typically, national-level research would analyze Progressive Era and New Deal housing studies, including U.S. Census statistics for population and housing. However, for the most important factors indicative of home improvement during the 1900–1940 study era—house size, room type and usage, and especially the presence or absence of utilities and mechanical and spatial improvements and the dates of these improvements—there are no accurate, verifiable, national calculations (despite various claims that are addressed in the endnotes). In the absence of reliable national data, this research utilizes an inductive strategy whereby the results of numerous metropolitan and regional housing case studies are extrapolated and projected onto a national scale. In the collection of this information, I have conducted detailed case-study fieldwork investigations for the past fifteen years in twenty metropolitan and rural areas around the country.[7] In this process, hundreds of houses were documented and hundreds of neighborhoods with tens of thousands of individual homes were surveyed in order to understand historical patterns of development for the most numerous local and regional housing types. Without such a broad-based survey, the consistent, localized nature of common house construction and remodeling can be easily overlooked—practices that subtly differentiate local house forms and domestic usage from larger, seemingly uniform national trends.[8]

House Plan Type

In order to interpret patterns of domestic improvement within houses on a national scale, this study primarily assessed dominant, recurring house and floor plan types in successive eras and selected neighborhoods representative of broad metropolitan or rural consensus. Once a region's dominant house types were identified, individual houses were documented to formulate underlying patterns of social usage and housing improvement. This strategy of identifying and analyzing dominant types was intended to maximize the often-undetected underlying unity in the historic patterns of housing, particularly within working-class domestic environments. Such uniformity is not typically found in more diverse and individualistic middle- to upper-class housing environments where such a method would be far less effective.

This focus on the most numerous house types is based on forty years' experience analyzing housing in America's common residential neighborhoods and especially confronting the difficult problem of assessing common housing lacking unified or traditional architectural styles. Alternatively, without such a strategy, common housing documentation (even when conducted within small residential districts) may quickly become a quagmire of an ever-increasing number of architectural styles and housing types that resist synthesis and are frequently lumped into makeshift "vernacular" categories.[9]

For comparative purposes, it is instructive to examine the widely consulted *Field Guide to American Housing,* by Virginia Savage McAlester, which primarily identifies houses according to their exterior styles. In contrast, *How the Working-Class Home Became Modern* primarily examines houses produced in the greatest numbers and focuses specifically on their floor plans. In a book like McAlester's, houses built only a few times are set next to houses built hundreds of thousands of times—that is the nature of a book organized to show the wide variety of stylistic types. In this book, however, the goal is to identify the most dominant house types built in successive eras within neighborhood, district, city, and metropolitan areas. By definition, this strategy focuses on a more limited range of house types. Their significance here is that these dominant houses have demonstrated an underlying unity in America's popular housing and particularly in floor plans—a product of design and construction methods of common house builders as demonstrated throughout this book. This research method of examining selected case studies within dominant house types can, of course, be criticized on many levels, especially because the sheer number of American dwellings challenges the selection of any representative groups of houses to interpret the whole.[10] Yet, all pre-1940s housing improvement scholarship that has attempted a broad, national summary has invariably relied on local and regional studies to address topics not answered because of a lack of national data.[11]

DOMESTIC MODERNITY

The challenge of middle-majority housing analysis has also been compounded by one of the most dominant housing improvement narratives of the early twentieth century—"modernity" or "modernization." In much of the architecture housing literature, modernism is shorthand for the acquisition of mass-produced domestic goods and services and new attitudes about the conduct of domestic life. These terms have their own frequently contested meanings, especially among disciplines and perspectives related to housing and domestic improvement. Indeed, the use of the term "modernity" to describe working-class housing improvement will be surprising to those familiar with its standard usage in reference to avant-garde architecture and lifestyles of the early twentieth century. Yet the term is particularly appropriate for this investigation when describing the acquisition of modern industrial-technological improvements in the early twentieth century. This difference in meaning is diagrammed in Figure I.6, in which a vernacular dwelling in a traditional bungalow style is contrasted with an early modern house in a style of abstract expressionism reflective of machine technology. While both houses employ similar domestic technologies, such as kitchen appliances, public utilities, and mass-produced components, they represent radically different approaches to how twentieth-century improvements were expressed in domestic architecture. The fact that both employed the same basic technologies will in this book render them both examples of modern architecture—despite their quite different appearances.[12] Throughout this study, we will return

Figure I.6. *Modern technological expression.* (a) House in a modern-abstract style, circa 1930. (b) Typical common bungalow, circa 1920–30. Although both houses are stylistically quite different and are typically separated in historic analysis, they shared similar internal domestic technologies and, consequently, many of the same basic patterns of daily domestic life.

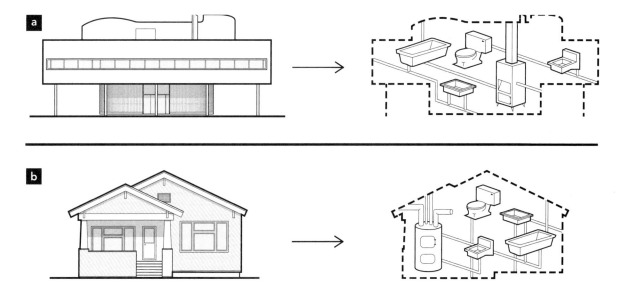

to this issue of the technological expression in common houses where we will be careful to scrutinize the use of both terms, "modernity" and "middle class," to describe the results of domestic improvement for average Americans.

Finally, poverty and the dwellings of those living in poverty, while not the focus of this work, unavoidably influence this analysis. Following other major works documenting early twentieth-century housing for the poor, this study frequently cites the fluid boundaries between the housing and domestic conditions of the middle majority (50–60 percent of the population) and a fluctuating 20–30 percent of those in various conditions of poverty. Although estimates of the percentage of Americans with inadequate housing vary widely, many scholars agree that the percentage of Americans in extremely poor housing conditions was reduced during the forty-year period of this study (1900–1940) from approximately 40 percent to 20 percent of the population with increases during the Depression. These lower-working-class households typically included most Native Americans and African Americans, and America's least well-off urban and rural populations. With regard to the income distribution formula (20–30 percent upper, 50–60 percent middle, and 20–30 percent lower) these benchmark percentages will be constantly scrutinized by era and region and are primarily intended to focus analysis on a middle range of houses and households.[13]

· · ·

The story of how common houses were improved and transformed unfolds in the following chapters.

Chapter 1 presents eleven prevailing theories and assumptions from the literature of American housing and domestic reform that have constrained the exploration of common houses. While these assumptions are not incorrect in themselves, the chapter will emphasize the ways in which each theme has limited or distorted research into vernacular dwellings. Because many of these themes have been so thoroughly accepted, it is important to begin this book by analyzing their constraining effects.

Chapter 2 describes the minimal housing and domestic conditions typical of the vast majority of working-class families at the turn of the twentieth century. These minimal conditions are contrasted with the improved domestic standards achieved by significant numbers of the same working classes over the next forty years. In the process, we will tell the story of how the seemingly impenetrable historical barriers between the upper classes and the traditional working classes were steadily breeched by improved housing standards in the late nineteenth and early twentieth centuries.

Chapter 3 introduces the core themes of housing improvement. Here we analyze the major housing standards and amenities, such as kitchen appliances, public utilities, and dining rooms that constituted substantive domestic improvement for the middle majority of the population. Nine features will be evaluated as the dominant package of improvements that constituted housing reform for the middle majority. The popular, common bungalow will then be highlighted as a summary example of modern domestic reform.

Chapter 4 examines the wide variety of new and remodeled houses that brought significant domestic improvement to vast numbers of working-class families. These houses include seldom-documented and -analyzed dwellings, such as workers' cottages, multi-unit housing, and remodeled houses of all types. Although demonstrating a considerable variety of house forms among geographic regions and urban and rural areas, the basic package of domestic improvements, such as utilities, dining rooms and bathrooms, and technological features, gives these common dwellings a surprising internal domestic unity.

Chapter 5 concludes with a summary analysis of the larger implications of the book's primary research goals—the acquisition of modern housing improvements by the middle majority of the population. Specifically, the chapter addresses a widely held belief that early twentieth-century houses shrank in size as families gave up their large Victorian houses with servants. Similar theories, misinterpreting the production of common, average housing, have restricted our understanding of middle-class housing development.

The Epilogue summarizes the meaning and consequences of

large-scale, early twentieth-century domestic improvement for America's common households. These significant material gains will be evaluated from the perspective of both their new middle-class recipients and by observers from housing literatures and the national press. The goal is to situate the results of twentieth-century common house improvement within a larger cultural context.

CHAPTER 1

HEADWINDS TO RESEARCHING COMMON HOUSES

ELEVEN PREVAILING THEMES

This book explores a subset of a vast literature about American housing history—common, popular houses. Although large in number, these houses have not consistently attracted the attention of many scholars. Consequently, an assortment of unproved assertions, suppositions, and commonsense assumptions have grown up around the subject, forming a brittle shell of received wisdom and making it difficult to approach the topic from new perspectives.

This chapter provides a critical examination of eleven widely accepted theories and assumptions from the dominant architectural and housing literature that have influenced the historical analysis of common houses. Although these themes are substantially correct, many were generated by, and therefore principally apply to, upper-to-middle-class households (representing 20–30 percent of the households by economic distribution). In contrast, the middle majority of American households (variously identified as common, popular, vernacular, average, everyday housing) are often marginalized or missing entirely.[1] When the wide acceptance of these eleven themes is coupled with the absence of substantial common house research, there is a tendency to assign housing interpretation derived from selected unrepresentative examples or from well-documented upper-class examples to less well-documented common houses. Consequently, when common houses are addressed in the dominant housing research, it is often unclear which segment of the housing population is being analyzed, although it may frequently be presented as representative of most, average, "middle class" housing.

The following themes from the literature of American housing contain influential conclusions, suppositions, and assumptions that have limited our understanding of how most Americans first obtained modern domestic improvements during the early twentieth century. Eleven themes are reexamined:

1. The model houses of domestic reform
2. An emphasis on rich and poor
3. The importance of remodeling and repair
4. The distribution of technological development
5. The changing meaning of "middle class"
6. The historic narratives of domestic improvement
7. The importance of "kit houses"
8. The importance of owner-builders
9. The significance of home ownership
10. The effects of the Great Depression
11. Post–World War II technological development

Together, these themes constitute a widely accepted interpretive framework for understanding late nineteenth- and early twentieth-century American housing that, for various reasons, has made it difficult to investigate domestic improvement in common houses and households. It is, therefore, important to identify the ways in which each of these themes has acted to define and delimit the larger story of common house improvement.

1. THE MODEL HOUSES OF DOMESTIC REFORM

Progressive Era reformers and later historians have typically presented large, newly built houses as the primary vehicles of modern domestic improvement and reform in the early twentieth century (see Figure I.1). For almost a century, these iconic images, often labeled the dwellings of "middle class" Americans, have dominated the architectural literature of housing reform.[2] Whenever early twentieth-century housing improvement was supported by reformers in industry and government, their prototypical examples were almost exclusively large upper-middle-class houses. For example, in 1934 the national Better Homes in America campaign, organized to promote housing improvement standards, built a large model house in a conspicuous midtown Manhattan location. Ironically labeled "America's Little House," this Colonial Revival style, 1,800-square-foot house with two-car garage clearly represented an upper .05 percent of houses of its period (Figure 1.1).[3] An earlier, similarly large, two-story Colonial Revival model house was built on the Capitol Mall in Washington, D.C., in 1922. Called "The National Better Home," it was sponsored by the General Federation of Women's Clubs with support from private industry and business and helped launch the national Better Homes movement.[4] Both houses were widely publicized examples of improved domestic standards that were intended to serve as model homes for middle-class domestic reform. Yet many of their features, like large dining rooms and multicar garages, were well beyond possible inclusion in

Figure 1.1. *"America's Little House."* A "Better Homes in America" model house, constructed in Midtown Manhattan in 1934 as an example of modern housing reform. Although built in the Colonial Revival style to demonstrate the benefits of standardized construction and modern technologies for all housing, it reflected concepts of housing reform and domestic usage for an upper middle class. Mattie E. Hewitt and Richard A. Smith Photograph Collection, Department of Prints, Photographs, and Architectural Collections, The New-York Historical Society.

the households of average Americans and well beyond what most could afford. Although they were promoted as solutions for average Americans, houses such as these actually represented a much smaller portion of upper-middle-class housing. While smaller houses are also analyzed within a vast house building and housing reform literature of the early twentieth century, the overwhelming critical mass of dwelling examples display similar larger, finer houses rather than smaller, far more frequently built common houses (compare Figures I.1 and I.2).

This book introduces a range of these modest dwellings that were infrequently included in housing reform literature and do not initially appear to be models of American domestic reform. Yet their role in the story of American housing reform is significant. While not immediately apparent, these older houses once offered new, unparalleled domestic conveniences to a rapidly expanding working class, transitioning to middle class, during the first decades of the twentieth century. Although modest looking today, they were the product of a rapidly expanding, highly industrialized construction industry that brought improved housing standards at affordable prices to a majority of Americans.

As we will see in chapter 4, the more common route to housing improvement and reform was via these smaller, less publicized popular dwellings. This wider assortment of early twentieth-century "improved" houses may be organized nationally into three basic types: (1) newly built, small, single-family houses, both owned and rented; (2) newly built, multi-unit houses, from duplexes to large multi-unit apartment buildings; and (3) remodeled and improved existing houses of all types, including expanded and subdivided houses. Although there is considerable visual variety, they were unified by several popular generic floor plans. However worn and undistinguished they may appear today, these houses were not minimal vernacular creations but the products of a completely industrialized housing construction system that extended modern conveniences and modern patterns of living to the working classes in the form of toilets, kitchen appliances, public utilities, dining rooms, and private bedrooms.

Underdocumented Houses

Accounting for these different kinds of early twentieth-century common houses is difficult because they were not widely documented in their own era and, consequently, have not been well studied and are infrequently included in the historical record.[5] Today their numbers are greatly diminished by remodeling and destruction—although they were once some of the most widely constructed houses of their eras and regions. Readers with a knowledge of housing literature might assume that this claim of common house neglect might apply only to small, isolated segments of the nation's total housing that has somehow escaped analysis. But these modest pre–World War II houses once constituted a much higher proportion of the total housing stock within most periods and regions.[6]

Compounding this problem of historic invisibility is the typical way the histories of American housing have concentrated almost exclusively on stylistically unified, upper-class houses in regional surveys and local histories. Consequently, when asked about the most popular houses from earlier periods, most authorities consistently identify large, upper-middle-class "historic houses," such as colonial mansions, late nineteenth-century Victorian villas, or large "Period Revival" and Colonial Revival houses of the early twentieth century—instead of the far more numerous, smaller vernacular dwellings that characterize American housing in most periods. Figure 1.2 demonstrates this typical contrast between an upper-middle-class Tudor Revival–style house frequently displayed in national literature and historical studies with a more-difficult-to-name, front-gable vernacular dwelling of the same period. Although rarely pictured except in builders' catalogs, this popular house with a wide porch having modest classical details was built in larger numbers throughout the country.

An extension of this practice is documenting and preserving a few of a region's oldest surviving upper-class houses and presenting them as the primary examples of a region's early housing history. This, unfortunately, is a well-established practice throughout the country. For example, in Oregon's Willamette Valley, a distinctive

Figure 1.2. *Elite and common houses.* (a) A stylistically unified, upper-middle-class dwelling: Tudor Revival (late-medieval vernacular) style, Center-Hall plan, circa 1920, Shorewood, Wisconsin. (b) A difficult-to-name and -classify common house: front-gable vernacular house (no standard stylistic term, neoclassical porch), Early Bungalow plan, early twentieth century, Portland, Oregon.

group of large Greek Revival–style farmhouses has dominated the account of the region's late nineteenth-century rural architectural history when, in fact, smaller, one-and-one-half-story Greek Revival houses were far more numerous (Figure 1.3).[7] Usually this practice is justified by the far higher survival rates of a region's largest, finest houses, although this was not the case in Oregon. Whatever the justification, this practice reinforces a common tendency to interpret a region's larger houses as somehow the origin or seed for its other historic houses, when in fact, smaller, more numerous vernacular houses are not typically derived from a region's largest houses. Consequently, the distinctive development of these smaller houses has not been well studied.

This pattern of vernacular interpretation is particularly evident in East Coast colonial settlement areas where old surviving two-story houses are typically analyzed as precursors to the region's entire housing history. For example, Abbott Lowell Cummings's *The Framed Houses of Massachusetts Bay, 1625–1725* gives the impression that large, two-story houses were the dominant houses of the seventeenth-century Massachusetts settlement. In fact, these carefully crafted houses represented the upper 10 percent of the

Figure 1.3. *Early settlement period houses, Portland, Oregon.* (a) Bybee-Howell House, Greek Revival style, Center-Hall plan, 1856, Sauvie Island, Portland, Oregon. (b) Greek Revival vernacular style ("I-House" massing with front-gable entry), two-room plan with additions, circa 1890. Although Greek Revival dwellings such as the Bybee-Howell House are continuously cited in Portland and Oregon architectural histories, they were vastly outnumbered by smaller, modest houses that have not been well documented.

finest houses and were vastly outnumbered by far more numerous, smaller, common houses. To be clear, Cummings's book is one of the finest studies of early period architecture in America, and his purpose was not to place these large surviving structures in their housing demographic context. Yet the effect of this and similar studies has been to narrow the scope of consideration for other types of houses, particularly smaller vernacular houses, and to create the impression, for academic and popular audiences, that these larger houses somehow represented most houses—which they did not. This is far from an obscure issue of early American housing history; few metropolitan areas or rural regions from throughout the country are exempt from narratives in which larger houses represent most houses.[8]

A goal of this book, therefore, is to widen the standard repertoire of houses from the late nineteenth and early twentieth centuries in order to include less familiar dwellings that brought modern housing standards to a middle majority of the population (see Figure I.2). Although today their continually repaired and remodeled exteriors do not reveal it, these houses once had the look of modernity for their new residents. More significantly, on the inside, they introduced a basic package of technological improvements that brought modern domestic conditions to America's middle majority.

2. AN EMPHASIS ON RICH AND POOR

One difficulty associated with investigating middle-majority domestic environments can be attributed to a dominant nineteenth-century literary convention that continued into the Progressive Era: a tendency to focus on either end of the economic and social spectrum—the very rich or the very poor. This binary construct was crystalized in Jacob Riis's now famous muckraking-photojournalistic distinction between the "haves and the have-nots" in his groundbreaking book, *How the Other Half Lives*. His photographs capturing life in New York City's tenements awakened Gilded Age Americans to the squalid, overcrowded domestic conditions of the poor (Figure 1.4). This and similar works also highlighted the problems of inadequate housing and social conditions in cities, industrial re-

Figure 1.4. *Tenement crowding.* Late nineteenth-century tenement housing and working-class domestic conditions, Lower East Side, New York City. (a) Tenements along Hester Street. American News Company / Museum of the City of New York, F2011.33.1383. (b) An immigrant family in a small tenement apartment. From Jacob Riis, *How the Other Half Lives*; Jessie Tarbox Beals for Jacob A. (Jacob August) Riis (1849–1914) / Museum of the City of New York, 90.13.3.125.

gions, and rural areas throughout America. Inspired by similar progressive initiatives, major housing reform legislation was enacted, including early tenement improvement laws that ultimately led to the establishment of building codes and zoning laws that have continued to this day.[9]

Sharing the spotlight of reform were the upper-class "haves," who experienced unaccustomed scrutiny for their responsibility for the newly illuminated conditions of the poor (Figure 1.5). This media spotlight on the lives and domestic conditions of the upper classes was, however, a long-standing component of popular and elite literature of the period.[10] A consequence of this dual emphasis on the very rich and the very poor was the creation of an overall impression that these two populations occupied the majority of housing—which they did not, not even in late nineteenth-century New York City, and not even in lower Manhattan.

Comprehensive inventories and studies of the majority of New

Figure 1.5. *Contrast between "haves and have-nots."* (a) "Sidewalk contrasts" between the extremes of upper and working classes, New York City. *Harper's Weekly,* February 12, 1876, 121; courtesy of the Yale University Library. (b) Stevens House Apartments, built in 1871, providing upper-class accommodations in late nineteenth-century New York City. *Appleton's Journal,* November 18, 1871, 561; courtesy of the Yale University Library.

York's late nineteenth-century housing reveal ranges of middle-majority domestic environments in between the very rich and the very poor (Figure 1.6).[11] These studies make it clear that a vast midrange of small apartments of varying sizes and domestic technologies served a large working class. By contemporary standards, these middling conditions were not significantly better than the poorest conditions that Riis and other reformers revealed, but they were not the same. From the perspective of a middle majority of late nineteenth-century residents, there were crucial differences that will be described in later chapters. The failure to distinguish these differences in subsequent literature—by lumping all houses of the working classes together into the same category of "poor tenements"—misrepresents the foundational story of how the working classes actually began to obtain significant domestic improvement.

Riis's contribution, however, was to succeed in concentrating the public's attention as never before on the housing conditions of the poorest people living in the country's most densely populated cities. In retrospect, however, we can see that Riis's landmark publication contained a seldom analyzed oversimplification in its title, *How the Other Half Lives*. Most analysts of New York's poverty conditions estimate that the destitute portion of the population that Riis recorded was between .05 percent and .10 percent.[12] Although Riis's dialectic exaggeration may have been necessary to raise public consciousness and expose the extreme living conditions of the poor, the uncritical acceptance of this inaccurate two-part construct—by contemporaries and later writers without knowledge of local vernacular housing and social conditions—may have reinforced a misleading and simplistic "half and half" division

Figure 1.6. *Tenement housing for the middle majority.* Apartments for the middle to working classes, late nineteenth-century lower Manhattan. (a) Solomon Jacobs Tenement, 131 Eldridge Street, 1885; Blankenstein and Herter, architects. (b) Weil and Mayer Tenement, 106 Madison Street, 1892; Schneider and Herter, architects. Photographs by Sean Litchfield, from *The Decorated Tenement.*

of a complex, variegated residential landscape with multiple levels of housing (the overall conditions for most residents, however, may appear quite primitive by contemporary standards). In any case, Progressive Era journalism and reform literature, followed by later scholarship, have tended to focus on these extreme upper and lower constituencies along the housing spectrum, and thus have deemphasized a central, middle-to-working-class majority constituency, both in New York and, through similar journalistic-literary influence, throughout the country.[13]

A better way of demographically conceptualizing late nineteenth-century class structure would be to acknowledge a widely recognized division between upper and middle classes and the larger working classes while simultaneously recognizing significant distinctions within these groups, such as the development of improved tenements. Figure 1.7 contrasts these two dominant housing cultures in lower Manhattan at the turn of the twentieth century—a contrast reflective of similar percentages, but far different types of wooden housing from throughout the nation. It is the contrast between a smaller, well-off, combined upper and middle class (20–30 percent) and a much larger, lower-income, combined working and lower working class (70–80 percent). Twentieth-century urban social historians have, of course, emphasized this basic minority "haves" and majority "have-nots" distinction in the quality of life between bourgeoisie-mercantile and laboring-worker classes.[14]

Because New York City has dominated the story of Progressive Era housing reform, it is worth noting that the multistory urban masonry tenements that Riis and others described were a unique type of American housing, largely confined to Manhattan. On a national scale, these urban masonry dwellings were statistically marginal in comparison to the standard types of one- and two-story, and one- and two-family wooden houses characteristic of the vast

Figure 1.7. *Late nineteenth-century cultural divide.* Two economic and social classes dominated the cultural landscape of late nineteenth-century America: a combined upper- and middle-class minority and a working-class majority.

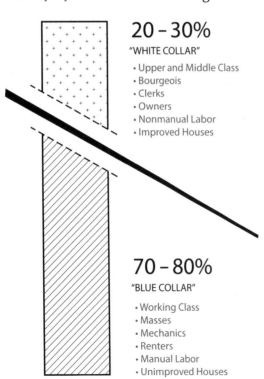

20 – 30%
"WHITE COLLAR"
- Upper and Middle Class
- Bourgeois
- Clerks
- Owners
- Nonmanual Labor
- Improved Houses

70 – 80%
"BLUE COLLAR"
- Working Class
- Masses
- Mechanics
- Renters
- Manual Labor
- Unimproved Houses

majority of residences, whether urban, suburban, or rural, as emphasized by scholars such as Robert G. Barrows.[15]

3. THE IMPORTANCE OF REMODELING AND REPAIR

A major hypothesis of this study, developed in chapter 4, is that house remodeling has played a much larger role in the history of middle-majority domestic reform than is generally recognized. This is primarily because housing scholarship typically concentrates on new-house design and construction or evaluates existing housing conditions. Consequently, Progressive Era reformers, government agencies, and professional organizations generally failed to document, or even to recognize, large-scale internal remodeling of existing housing between 1900 and 1930. These underdocumented internal improvements add to the difficulty of evaluating the extent of significant housing reform, especially to the dwellings of the working classes. Needless to say, if housing authorities and writers from the Progressive Era were either unaware or uninterested in home remodeling improvement, we should not be too surprised when later scholars followed suit.

Lack of interest in the significance of home remodeling and repair to common dwellings did not begin with the Progressive Era but had a long history in the literature of American housing and domestic reform. Beginning in the 1830s, a growing "cult of domesticity" literature criticized existing domestic environments and called for the improvement of America's housing. This reform literature often advocated the development of new, picturesque suburban retreats such as those found in the popular wooden Gothic-style designs of Andrew Jackson Downing. Similar literature of the mid-nineteenth century emphasized rural suburban "cottage residences" in the face of increasing urbanization and industrialization, which acted as a buttress against what many commentators considered to be the physical and moral decline of the American home and family.[16]

Downing's house designs are well-known examples of "model dwellings" frequently found in professional and popular literature that proposed new house designs with little or no regard for traditional vernacular housing solutions. Although similar model-experimental literature is best known for unique perfectionist designs such as circular or octagonal houses and barns, examples of model houses extended to all types of nineteenth- and early twentieth-century popular and professional literature, forming a consensus about the need for new housing solutions. Frequently, this literature also emphasized the inadequacy of existing popular housing, whether rural, small town, or urban, and often recommended removal. Despite occasional articles addressing house and farmhouse remodeling in many types of nineteenth-century and Progressive Era literature, the dominant forms of existing housing and their patterns of usage were almost never pictured or positively analyzed except to be shown in disrepair and dilapidation. Seen from this perspective, the dominant literature presented an unrelenting jeremiad condemning modest existing houses and their domestic environments—including their incremental, seemingly catch-as-catch-can methods of remodeling and repair.[17]

In chapter 4, we will see how the remodeling of common houses contributed to the widespread acquisition of basic housing standards (such as kitchen appliances, bathroom fixtures, and dining rooms) and how the incremental improvement of housing helped to transform a majority of American lives. Several overlapping factors will be evaluated to explain why Progressive Era reformers and later scholars rarely acknowledged continuously remodeled existing houses that brought significant housing improvement to large numbers of middle-to-working-class households. The recent work of geographer Richard Harris has helped identify and record the wide extent of early twentieth-century remodeling practices.[18] This achievement is all the more remarkable in contrast to the massive, well-documented post–World War II development of the home-remodeling industry that was accomplished with overwhelming journalistic, governmental, and institutional support.[19]

4. THE DISTRIBUTION OF TECHNOLOGICAL DEVELOPMENT

Although not the focus of this book, the spread of technological and industrial improvements is central to Progressive Era housing and domestic reform. Of particular significance are the late nineteenth- and early twentieth-century developments of industrialized, mass-produced housing components (such as bathroom fixtures, milled lumber, and windows and doors) and complex mechanical systems (such as central heating, electrification, and plumbing) and their rapid distribution to unprecedented numbers of middle-majority households. In chapter 3, the industrialization of housing construction will be emphasized as the primary source for the spread of domestic improvements to an America middle majority.

Although the history of modern housing industrialization has been extensively documented, it is an exceedingly complex subject with many different types and scales of invention, distribution, and consumption. Unlike industries with less complicated products and with recognized entrepreneurs and inventors such as Henry Ford, the diverse housing industry has few big names and single products. With the exception of Thomas Edison and his electric light, major developments were typically achieved by anonymous inventors in decentralized industries that produced complex, technologically linked products such as furnaces, plumbing fixtures, home appliances, and the components and administration of public utility development.[20]

Consequently, the introduction of new technologies and the inventions into the homes of the middle-to-working classes is often an unevenly documented story. Because most housing technological documentation has concentrated on the dates and circumstances of original invention and initial application, largely within the houses of the upper classes, it is difficult to determine when these technologies and their improvements reached a broader public.[21] Most scholars of housing construction and reform have simply assumed a later, gradual rate of technological acquisition mirroring the upper classes, first by the middle class, and then, more gradually, by "the masses." These assumptions, however, are often contradicted by specific studies about how and when most Americans actually received technological improvements in their homes.

The distribution of housing technology and laborsaving devices to an expanding middle majority was by no means uniform or continuous, nor did it always involve the same improvements already obtained by the upper classes. At the turn of the twentieth century, public utilities, so critical to housing reform, were almost always first supplied to the upper classes and commercial enterprises with widely varying distribution to the general public and usually defined by an individual's or community's ability to pay.[22] As we will see, these are complex stories varying among geographic regions and urban and rural constituencies. Most importantly, they differ fundamentally from standard upper-class documentation. For example, in the case of gas lighting—so prominently featured in the record of late nineteenth-century Victorian dining rooms and parlors—most working-class households nationwide were never lighted by gas in any period. This is probably surprising to those familiar with typical Victorian-era parlor photographs shown in Figure 1.8, where an elaborate gas ceiling fixture (later combining gas and electric lighting) is shown. Yet, middle-majority households nationwide did not typically have gas lighting fixtures and only obtained gas for appliances, such as stoves or furnaces, after World War I, as did most small-town and rural communities.[23] For most of the working classes, the history of domestic lighting was a

Figure 1.8. *Gas lighting in a late nineteenth-century parlor.* Although commonly displayed in studies of late nineteenth-century upper-class housing, gas lighting was infrequently used in a majority of families in average and working-class households, which typically transitioned from candles and kerosene to electric lighting without ever using gas lighting. Photograph by J. S. Lovell; courtesy of the Minnesota Historical Society.

slow, uneven progression from candles, to oil and kerosene lamps and then suddenly to the brilliance of electric light—which is a different history than the one generally told.

Similarly, toilets had a long period of development in upper-class households during the second half of the nineteenth century. This includes a gradual transition from early experimental models to modern plumbed toilets and bathroom fixtures—an uneven transition facilitated, however, by the usually uncredited work of chamber-pot-carrying servants and night-soil men.[24] Alternatively, a much larger portion of the population experienced an abrupt, early twentieth-century transition from the near universal, late-medieval outhouse or privy to modern plumbed toilets in a relatively short period (Figure 1.9). For large numbers of working-class families, early twentieth-century toilets did not arrive in new houses but were inserted into existing, unimproved houses. As Margaret Byington recorded in Homestead, Pennsylvania, "A number of families who owned houses had themselves gone to the expense of putting in baths, while others proposed some day to do the same."[25] Furthermore, in most working-class households, this transformation was accomplished incrementally, involving temporary and shared facilities, and the location of bathroom fixtures in different rooms of the house. For example, a first toilet might be placed in a subdivided bedroom space, or, for ease of installation and lower costs, in a basement. In a housing study in Oakland, California, Paul Groth found that "workers' cottages today all typically have a toilet, a sink, and a bathtub—but all three fixtures are rarely in the same room; if they are, it is part of a new bathroom added after 1960."[26] Similar accounts describing incremental progress are typical of the differences in the distribution of technological improvements between elite and common households and represent two different types of stories in the history of modern domestic technological development.

5. THE CHANGING MEANING OF "MIDDLE CLASS"

Few terms in American social and cultural history evoke more consistent controversy than "middle class." What has often made the

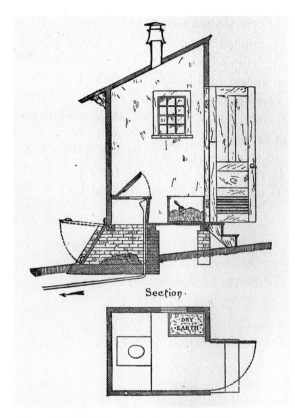

Section.

DRY EARTH

Figure 1.9. *Earth closet (outhouse), 1899.* The contrast between upper-class urban houses with indoor plumbing and average working-class dwellings with outhouses or privies was stark. At the turn of the twentieth century, experts recommended modifying common outhouses or privies with improvements like the earth closet, but these were only minor improvements to the massive problems of public sanitation and were not widely adopted. From *Sanitary Engineering of Buildings,* by William Paul Gerhard (New York: Comstock, 1899), 193; courtesy of the Yale University Library.

term particularly confusing in housing literature is its evolving meaning and expanded application to larger constituencies between the nineteenth and the twentieth century. In this book, we will follow the term "middle class" as it evolved from applying to a much smaller and more exclusive nineteenth-century population, defining an upper 10–30 percent minority, to a broader 50–70 percent majority by the middle of the twentieth century. Figure 1.10 summarizes this transition as the term was gradually widened to accommodate increasing numbers of new arrivals from the traditional working classes. Throughout this book, many of the difficulties related to the interpretation of middle-majority housing can be traced to this basic misunderstanding about the meaning of "middle class" and how this term has shifted from its limited nineteenth- to its expanded twentieth-century usage.

Although different from the contemporary definition, the restricted nineteenth-century meaning of "middle class" reflected the widely accepted, conventional usage of the term describing a smaller social-economic middle of the population, which is different from the numerical-demographic middle of the population, as it generally does in America today. As in so many realms of housing classification and cultural taste, this more exclusive use of "middle class" was a direct continuation of elite British social and literary convention whereby landed aristocracy (the upper class) were differentiated from a new eighteenth- and nineteenth-century mercantile and industrialist bourgeoisie, who were often quite well-to-do or controlled substantial resources.[27] Throughout the nineteenth century, this elite

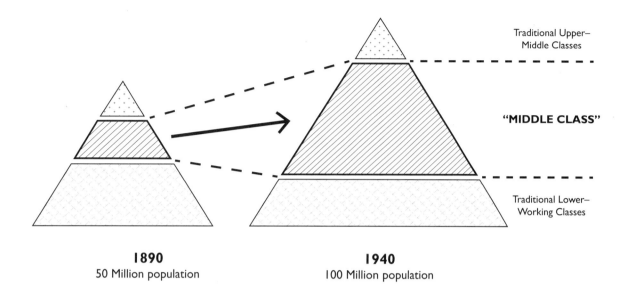

Traditional Upper–
Middle Classes

"MIDDLE CLASS"

Traditional Lower–
Working Classes

1890
50 Million population

1940
100 Million population

English practice was increasingly modified in American usage by more egalitarian attitudes to class integration, but the term never lost its close affiliation with its much more exclusive English interpretation. This lingering elite interpretation helps explain, for example, the standard labeling of large, late nineteenth-century "Victorian" mansions and their domestic environments as "middle class," when, by almost any American economic or social standard in any period, those houses, owned by less than 10 percent of the population, should be classified as upper-class or, at a minimum, upper-middle-class houses (Figure 1.11). This expansion of "middle class" house labeling is particularly evident in late nineteenth- and early twentieth-century building literature of pattern books and builders' catalogs intended for an upper-middle-class market where descriptions such as "low cost cottages" and "inexpensive bungalows" could be applied to both expensive and inexpensive houses of the same period.[28] Of course, we can just attribute this labeling to standard advertising excess, but when it is repeated consistently in the dominant literature and unchecked for accuracy, the tendency has been for readers and scholars alike to assume that larger houses reflected the dwellings of most people.

This transition in the meaning of "middle class" between the

Figure 1.10. *Changing meaning of "middle class."* The historic evolution of the term "middle class" followed the expansion of a late nineteenth-century minority to an increasing, early twentieth-century majority.

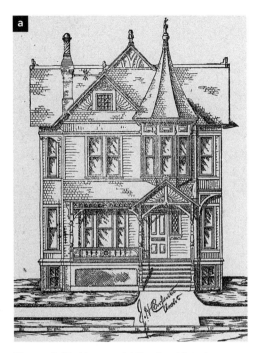

Figure 1.11. *Upper-middle-class Victorian era housing.* In the literature of the late nineteenth and early twentieth century, these large houses are frequently misinterpreted as middle class, average, and popular. Similarly scaled residences represented less than 10 percent of all houses. (a) *The Complete House Builder: With Hints on Building; Containing 88 Plans and Specifications of Dwellings, Barns, Churches, Public Buildings, etc. . . . ,* by Charles W. Quin (Chicago: M. A. Donohue, 1904); courtesy of the Center for Research Libraries. (b) *Specimen Book of One Hundred Architectural Designs, Showing Plans, Elevations and Views of Suburban Houses, Villas, Sea-Side and Camp-Ground Cottages, Homesteads, Churches and Public Buildings,* by the William T. Comstock Company (Bicknell & Comstock, 1880), 14; courtesy of Yale University Library.

nineteenth and the twentieth century may not be a significant issue for many studies, especially ones about the upper classes. In research about common houses, however, it is a significant distortion when the term "middle class" may be assumed to mean the majority of the population when it does not. For example, in an article on early twentieth-century housing, a writer laments the scarcity of immigrants to take domestic service jobs, noting, "The result is that middle-class households increasingly had fewer servants, particularly of the live-in type, which in turn produced a predictable simplification of the American home and its furnishings."[29] Here the plastic term "middle class" is stretched to include the less than 10 percent of the wealthiest households in turn-of-the-century America that employed servants.[30] But even this exaggerated usage would be permissible if the article intended to explore this small, exclusive minority. Like many housing studies from and about the Progressive Era, however, this article goes on to address several different constituencies of the "middle class," implying widespread or majority usage. In hundreds of books and articles reviewed for this research, this type of "middle class creep"—suggesting that trends among an upper-class minority were widespread and commonly accepted by greater portions of the population—is ubiquitous and adds significantly to misunderstanding the role, and even the existence, of common houses and their residents.[31]

6. THE HISTORIC NARRATIVES OF DOMESTIC IMPROVEMENT

The focus on the upper class as proxy for "most households" also has a long tradition in the mainstream architectural scholarship of housing. But rather than a conscious or calculated effort to conceal the history of the common majority, we should consider this influence as an ingrained discourse—a presupposition of long standing where the residential landscape of average households had never really been subject to the same degree of observation, much less documentation and analysis, as the housing of the upper classes. There is, of course, an extensive vernacular architecture scholarship, beginning in the late nineteenth century, that examines common houses, but its major works have primarily focused on preindustrial "folk architecture," and much less frequently on the industrial vernacular housing of America's post–Civil War middle majority.[32] In this respect, this study, along with other vernacular works frequently cited, attempts a modest parallel to E. P. Thompson's reconceptualization of a previously unarticulated class of citizenry in his groundbreaking work, *The Making of the English Working Class*.[33] The anonymous common houses acknowledged in this book have long existed in plain sight, but have often been invisible to earlier writers, historians, and Progressive Era reformers accustomed to interpreting the housing and domestic conditions of the middle to upper classes.

In the case of American architectural and housing history, this more exclusive discourse is reinforced by two dominant, long-standing historical narratives based largely on the record of upper-class housing. In the first, large, excessively ornamented, late nineteenth-century Victorian houses were traded for steadily more efficient, servantless houses, and then later traded for modern, suburban tract houses of the post–World War II era. This theory of declining Victorianism and ascendant modernism typically contrasts the material and societal excesses of the Gilded Age with the new efficiencies and technological improvements of the Modern Age, finally featuring modern housing with smaller "functional" kitchens and open plans as popularly symbolized in the Levittown suburbs (Figure 1.12). Consider the typical way pre- and post-1900 houses are compared in a book on housing technology: "The combination of new technologies, home economists' prescriptions for simpler homes, and rising costs meant that most suburban houses built after 1905 were constructed according to a minimalist aesthetic. Compared to Victorian homes, they had fewer rooms and less total floor space. They eliminated the formal front parlor and merged it into the family room, creating a 'living room' that often opened directly into the dining room."[34] This epic story of the triumph of modern architecture and culture over an antiquated and bloated Victorian world of excess (which we will reexamine in the last chapter) has provided a remarkably durable narrative of middle-class ascendency in housing and has been repeated with surprising consistency in architectural histories and a variety of housing-related disciplines for nearly a century.

The second misleading historical narrative concerns the historical origins of the American domestic traditions, which have been told almost exclusively from the perspective of elite or upper-class European sources (Figure 1.13). Historians of modern domestic development are largely unified in their focus on northern European precedents and have concentrated on a widely accepted three-to-four-century period of modern development beginning

Figure 1.12. *From Victorian mansions to post–World War II suburban ranches.* This narrative of architectural and social transition from an upper-middle-class Victorian housing culture to a middle-class suburban housing culture emphasizes the evolution of modern architectural styles and patterns of domestic life.

Excessive Victorian Mansions and Upper-Class Residences
1870–1900

Reformed Upper-Middle Class Residences (Downsized Mansions)
1900–1930

Modernized Ranches and Suburban Housing
1950–1970

in seventeenth-century England and Holland. For example, Witold Rybczynski's *Home* is an outstanding analysis of the European historical development for the most dominant patterns of American domestic life. While this and similar studies provide the foundation of American domestic history and its colonial development, this narrative was primarily derived from the record of upper-class domestic sources, where the use of dining rooms, private bedrooms, and single-purpose rooms, such as nurseries and libraries, unknown to the vast majority, are typically cited.

Despite many excellent vernacular case studies of early American domestic conditions, the trend in late nineteenth- and early twentieth-century domestic scholarship continues these stories of European domestic roots often based on an upper and "middle class" (10–20 percent) housing history long dominated by wealthy, upper-class English households.[35] Of course, not every architectural study makes these assumptions, but the majority err in this direction. Exceptions to this narrative critique are histories that emphasize the American pioneering settlement and that record early domestic hardships and the lack of household comforts, not domestic finery and European roots.

A simple test of whether a source originates in upper-class European traditions is to inquire whether topics such as dining rooms, private bedrooms, or servants' issues are explored. If they are, it typically means that the sources originate within the upper classes. A recent exception is Judith Flanders's *The Making of Home,* which clearly articulates a more working-class orientation to the historical development of English and American housing paralleling the record of common housing developed here.[36]

Figure 1.13. *From the domestic traditions of the European upper classes to the suburban homes of the American middle class.* This is a narrative of cultural diffusion from elite Old World precedents to spatial usage in twentieth-century American popular culture.

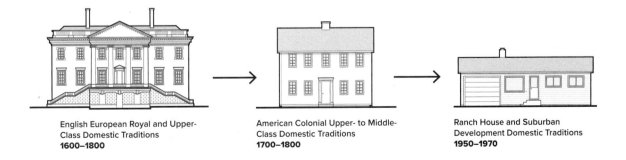

English European Royal and Upper-Class Domestic Traditions
1600–1800

American Colonial Upper- to Middle-Class Domestic Traditions
1700–1800

Ranch House and Suburban Development Domestic Traditions
1950–1970

7. THE IMPORTANCE OF "KIT HOUSES"

In public lectures around the country, I often show an illustration of a Sears, Roebuck catalog house and ask the audience, "What is a kit house?" (Figure 1.14). I have found there are few house-savvy listeners who cannot recount in detail the standard story of the arrival of a railroad boxcar full of the entire components of the manufactured kit house and its subsequent rapid assembly, often by a thrifty owner-builder. It is a compelling, almost mythic story of mass-produced housing and owner initiative that—if broadly true—would make common housing research much easier. Unfortunately, less than .03 percent of the total number of housing units built in any year between 1900 and 1930 were kit houses.[37] As the architectural historian Joseph Bigott observed about kit houses in a detailed study of working-class dwellings in the Chicago region, "Whether manufactured by Sears or anyone else, these structures accounted for a tiny portion of the housing market."[38]

After relaying the minor numerical significance of the kit house, I often ask the audience why the kit house's story would overshadow the story of how the vast majority of houses were actually constructed by small-scale contractor-builders. The answer, I believe, is that the currently accepted account of kit house assembly is an attractive creation story that provides a satisfyingly complete answer to a process that is far more difficult to research and communicate. That process involves the rarely documented account of hundreds of thousands of small-scale builder-contractor-developers who constructed most of America's houses by employing time-tested local-vernacular building practices in combination with a popular housing literature, architectural pattern books, catalogs, and popular journals, supplemented by borrowed architect designs, and all combined with their own local traditions of construction. It is a complex, difficult-to-research history of the standard vernacular construction methods that have produced most of America's common houses.[39]

When considering the difficulties of documenting

Figure 1.14. *Kit houses.* Manufactured or kit houses were largely produced between 1900 and 1940, with the period of greatest construction occurring between 1910 and 1930. *Book of Modern Homes and Building Plans,* by Sears, Roebuck and Co., 1908, cover; courtesy of University of Maryland Library.

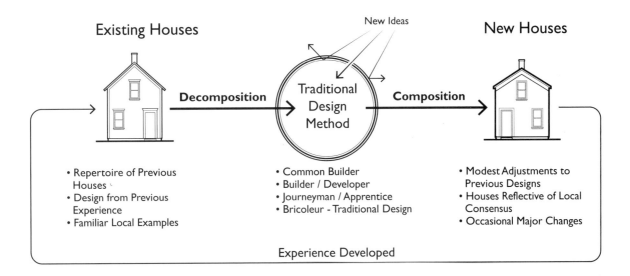

Figure 1.15. *The design methods of common builders.* The traditional method of vernacular builders is to transform design ideas from previous or existing houses into new house construction. Although new ideas are incorporated within these designs, they are typically constrained within a framework of previous designs and local traditions.

these common builder practices, it is not surprising that many scholars and popular writers have concentrated on the story of the kit house. Unfortunately, it is a record that tends to distort the larger history of common house construction, especially by emphasizing a much more hands-on and entrepreneurial account of the role of the owner-buyer in the house construction process. Rather than an owner-initiated process, the design and construction of most American houses have been conducted speculatively, with local builders developing houses for unknown clients (Figure 1.15). Although continually maligned as amateurish and repetitive in professional and popular literature in all periods, these speculative methods of vernacular construction (which I have documented in several publications) represent a modern, industrialized, component-manufactured form of vernacular building practice that has produced the majority of American houses since the Civil War era.[40]

8. THE IMPORTANCE OF OWNER-BUILDERS

Related to the overemphasis on kit houses is the exaggeration of the role of owner-builders in the construction of early twentieth-century housing. In public lectures, I also identify houses built by their owners, but then I go on to emphasize that the number of owner-builders in any era or region is extremely small. During these lectures, I frequently sense a disappointment or skepticism from some in my audience because I have challenged basic assumptions about the American house-building process—both the mythic story of American log cabin building self-sufficiency and a popular do-it-yourself spirit in the obtainment of home ownership. Consequently, the story of the owner-builder is commonly told and assumed to be a major contributor to the totals of American house building—but it is not.

The existing research on American owner-builders is not extensive (although the few sources are extensively cited) and primarily confined to small, unrepresentative areas or eras—such as suburban Toronto, Los Angeles, and various Great Depression environments. These regions and eras are not representative of the dominant demographics of the builder-contractor development in the majority of post–Civil War housing environments nationwide. In the major metropolitan and rural regions surveyed for this study, and in the documentation of early twentieth-century housing construction, the occurrence of owner-builders was extremely rare.[41] To assess these observations of owner-builders, I would like to emphasize several important factors not usually considered.

By the late nineteenth century, previous self-building traditions associated both with pioneer log cabin construction and agrarian vernacular traditions had largely given way to post–Civil War, industrialized methods of speculative builder construction, so that by about 1900, true owner-builders—those people capable of constructing an entire house—had become far less common. Such individuals were, and continued to be, unusually skilled relative to the average population. Furthermore, the overall technical complexity of building increased rapidly in the late nineteenth century, resulting from the introduction of mechanical devices and utility installation that required professional expertise and specialized tools exceeding the capacity of all but the most skilled nonprofessionals. From a modern perspective, there was also nothing equivalent to a Home Depot, tool rental stores, modern building manuals, or Google and YouTube tutorials to support home construction.

Full and Partial Owner-Builders

By far, however, the most severe challenge to documenting owner-builders is differentiating between full and partial contribution to the owner-builder process. The primary exaggeration of the totals of owner-builders, I believe, has much to do with overstating the role of an owner's partial contributions to the building process, a role that is far more extensive than the mastery of the entire construction process. In standard usage and in most definitions, an owner-builder is the primary contributor to the vast expertise, skills, and labor it takes to construct even a modest house in any period. Always difficult to distinguish, however, is the line between an owner's partial contribution and the fundamental role of the frequently uncredited professional builder or technical tradesperson in the overall construction process. The professional builder typically contributes the sophisticated manual techniques and especially the vast technological knowledge and experience of building that average owner-contributors simply cannot provide.[42]

The historical documentation of owner-builder totals is especially fraught with ambiguity often because of simple nomenclature attributions. When owners say they "built a house," it typically means they paid for the construction and perhaps contributed some labor. Many factors such as family pride in an ancestral home or even simply current home ownership frequently contribute to standard overstatements of owner-builder participation. It has been my forty years' experience with interviews of residents and builders that causes me to be alert for such overemphasis on the contributions of previous "owner-builders."

Other exaggerations of owner-builder estimates occur through faulty documentation of the owner's contribution to the building process. For example, the nationwide practice of small-scale builders to establish first ownership of new housing before selling and especially to live temporarily in these houses until final sale has led later researchers to record these houses as owner-built when they were actually small-contractor built.[43] As we will see in later chapters, many of the working-class houses presented in this study were built with the undocumented aid of large numbers of unlicensed, partial, and temporary builders and contractors and especially skilled tradesmen, such as carpenters or plumbers, who were responsible for building houses but would not have been labeled as builders or contractors in municipal records, family documents, or in memory.

The presence of this type of unlicensed partial builder in an "informal housing market" is emphasized by many urban historians such as Olivier Zunz in his study of turn-of-the-century Detroit. For example, while Zunz implies the presence of thrifty ethnic owner-builders, his documented housing examples emerge from a diverse collection of small-scale local builder-constructor-tradesmen, often laborers working in the building trades associated with a particular ethnic community.[44] This is the type of builder documentation that sets a fine line between partial builder and owner-builder interpretations about which there is no exact answer.

Farmer-Builders

One area in which the owner-builder would seem to reign supreme is rural America. Here the mechanical and general building skills of individual farmers have long been recognized. Yet, for the construction of major houses and barns, and even small agricultural buildings, the historic presence of rural master builders, not the typical farmer-owner, is ubiquitous (Figure 1.16). This critical contribution of the expertise of "anonymous" local professional builders to the rural landscape is, however, often concealed from researchers who have not studied rural building practices but have correctly observed that individual farmers typically contributed substantially to the building process. (Although such construction occurred millions of times, the rarity of construction crew photographs from all periods, such as Figure 1.16, may help to explain these misleading interpretations.) Yet frequent owner contributions, no matter how substantial, do not make these farmers complete owner-builders—they typically used a professional for the knowledge and craftsmanship required to build (and often to design) a standard house or barn in any period. This may be surprising to those familiar with the advanced manual-technical skills of most farmers. And yet, they did not, and still generally do not, typically "build" their own houses and barns without the advanced skills of professionals—whatever we choose to call them—although they did, and still do, contribute mightily to the building process.[45]

Figure 1.16. *Professional builders, rural Massachusetts, circa 1900.* Wood framers prepare mortise-and-tenon joints in sawn structural members. The second builder from the right holds the framing square (used to mark and calculate measurements) and is probably the typically anonymous master builder. The two workmen on the left hold hand-powered, mortise-drilling machines. Courtesy of the Ashfield Historical Society, Ashfield, Massachusetts; Howe Brothers Collection. Photograph research by Lindley Wilson.

The major exception to these limited estimates of owner-builders is in housing for the 20–30 percent of lowest-income Americans, where the percentages of owner-builders may be higher. This constituency, however, is outside the boundaries of this study. In environments of very limited wealth and including initial pioneering or homesteading settlement, we do find higher numbers of owner-builders, especially in rural and unincorporated regions and in dense urban environments, where the addition or subdivision of existing housing is more widespread owing to conditions of poverty and minimal code or zoning enforcement. But even for these constituencies, the statistics for full owner-built contribution is confined to unique periods and regions and extremely difficult times such as depressions and natural disasters, for example, the Chicago fire of 1871.[46] Generally, the self-built housing of the least wealthy Americans has not lasted for long periods and has been the most difficult to document.[47]

No current discussion of the role of the owner-builder can be complete without recognizing the groundbreaking scholarship of geographer Richard Harris. I would like to acknowledge the originality and strength of his scholarship, which I cite throughout. My principal critique, however, involves the extension of Harris's research estimates in limited case studies to larger national scales. From the case-study investigations for this research within twenty metropolitan and rural regions, I estimate that the totals of owner-builders were less than .05 percent in any twentieth-century period (except perhaps in areas affected by the Great Depression). Furthermore, depending on how the owner-builder's total contribution is defined (recognizing that owner contribution, no matter how extensive, does not in itself constitute owner-builder status), I estimate that probably only .02–.03 percent of housing nationally was owner built.[48]

To take one example, in Milwaukee, where I have conducted extensive research and housing interviews, working-class Poles were rightly credited with digging under and raising their basic workers' cottages to create small, two-story duplexes, or "Polish Flats" (Figure 1.17). By most standards, owner participation in the foundation excavation and cedar-post-erection process (facilitated by the absence of plumbing, electrical wiring, and foundation connections) would qualify them as owner-builders. But we can also determine that their prodigious efforts were most often overseen and aided by competent Polish builders and tradesmen who are usually anonymous, seldom-recorded participants in the building process. Also contributing to Milwaukee's reputation for owner building are several studies that have exaggerated and misinterpreted accounts of these common building practices as evidence for owner-builder construction. For example, another common practice, building an alley house on the rear of a lot, often before building a later front house, was assumed by researchers to be evidence for owner building in the Polish community.[49] In other instances, simply the presence of inexpensive smaller houses or cottages and their additive construction practices, like irregular building setbacks, were incorrectly assumed to indicate the presence of owner-builders. This is the case in a well-known study of Los Angeles

Figure 1.17. *"Polish Flat."* The common name for a single-story workers' cottage that has been raised above a basement apartment to create a two-story, two-family dwelling. Although associated with the Polish communities in midwestern cities like Milwaukee and Chicago, this house type was built in all working-class communities. Also called a Raised Workers' Cottage with Workers' Cottage plan, early twentieth century, Milwaukee, Wisconsin.

in which varying housing setbacks "strongly suggest the presence of owner-builders in the area."[50]

In all these cases, while some owner participation was common, the bulk of the construction and technical skills necessary to complete even very modest houses (not temporary or shanty houses of the least wealthy) was consistently recorded to be assisted by local construction professionals, often small-scale unlicensed builders (frequently associated with their ethnic communities), but nevertheless, skilled builders and not average owners without professional skills. This type of construction history is infrequently documented but can be gleaned from family histories, interviews, and house inspections, for example, as conducted over a twenty-year period within Milwaukee's Polish community and analyzed at the end of chapter 4.

· · ·

In similar ways, exaggerating the importance of kit houses and owner-builders distorts the story of common house building toward a more owner-centric interpretation. In both accounts, the owner-buyer is interpreted as the primary entrepreneurial initiator in the building process instead of a distant client in a speculative design-and-building process initiated by independent builder-contractor-developers—the way the vast majority of America's houses were (and still are) actually planned and constructed.[51]

9. THE SIGNIFICANCE OF HOME OWNERSHIP

In the story of post-Depression and postwar suburban housing development, home ownership is a sacrosanct component of the "American dream" and one of the defining standards for entrance into the middle class (Figure 1.18).[52] New Deal policies such as the Home Owners' Loan Corporation (HOLC, 1933), and the Federal Housing Administration (FHA, 1934, later supplemented by the Servicemen's Readjustment Act, or GI Bill, 1944) helped to make home ownership as inexpensive as renting and guaranteed the rise of homeownership to record levels of over 60 percent by the 1970s. Consequently, the importance of home ownership to the story of domestic improvement is seldom questioned. Yet, from historic studies of working-class Americans, especially from their ethnic and racial communities, home ownership may have been a widely cherished collective goal, but the limited availability of small affordable housing and limited financing determined that it was not widely obtained until after World War II.[53]

In this study of pre–World War II common vernacular housing, home ownership is still a pillar of domestic ascendency, but the story

Figure 1.18. *The American dream of home ownership.* As this house book from 1950 emphasizes, single-family home ownership has often been portrayed as an ideal of American domestic life. *The Home Idea Book,* Johns-Manville Corporation, 1950, cover; collection of the author.

of housing reform diverges sharply between upper-to-middle-class households with home ownership and middle-to-working-class households both with and without home ownership. The alternative path to domestic improvement without home ownership was, of course, rental housing, which averaged approximately 50–60 percent of all nonfarm housing units between 1900 and 1940 (Figure 1.19).[54] Because the upper classes generally owned their homes during this period, this means that approximately two-thirds of the middle-majority households did not own their homes during the study period. These high percentages of rental housing were especially true for African American and minority households, where even the possibility of home ownership was curtailed or denied, both legally or through real estate development practices.[55] Therefore, in the middle-majority account of how American families received modern housing and domestic improvement, home ownership, despite its widespread desirability, plays a more diminished role.

The issue of home ownership in early twentieth-century common households requires further clarification because it cannot be assumed that ownership was accompanied by modern standards of housing improvement, such as bathrooms, dining rooms, and public utilities, as it almost invariably was for the middle to upper classes. Many housing histories of late nineteenth- and early twentieth-century immigrant communities confirm this assessment by emphasizing the hunger for home ownership by average working-class families, but they also recognize that the sacrifices to obtain these homes often involved severe restrictions in the purchase

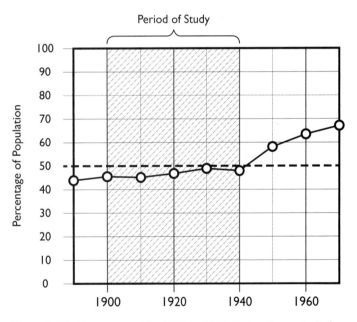

Figure 1.19. *Homeownership, 1890 to 1970.* During the period of study (1900–1940), home ownership averaged 40–45 percent of all dwelling units. Another way of articulating this statistic is to say that 55–60 percent of American families did not own their homes during this same period. Depression Era policies greatly expanded the production and consumption of single-family home ownership opportunities for the middle majority. From Doan, *American Housing Production, 1880–2000,* 186.

of expensive technological improvements such as bathroom fixtures and utility installation.[56]

In chapter 4, we examine many of these typical rental houses and apartments, including smaller versions of popular owner houses, subdivided housing, multifamily housing, and especially remodeled houses of all types.

10. THE EFFECTS OF THE GREAT DEPRESSION

This book celebrates the collective progress of average Americans in achieving significant domestic reform during the first half of the twentieth century. Such praise is typical during this period, but what is unusual is the 1940 end date for this study, just after the Great Depression and at the beginning of World War II. Against the weight of most historical and economic studies, this end date and its progressive conclusions require considerable explanation.

Most historians agree that the cumulative negative effects of the Great Depression and the restrictions and shortages of World War II did indeed terminate or slow most segments of the home-building industry. Less emphasized, however, was a significant late-1930s rebound that made up for many setbacks and delays. Most significantly, and not surprisingly, the worst and most lasting negative effects of the Depression on housing improvement and domestic life were suffered by the least fortunate. By any economic standard, the Depression's harshest setbacks were inflicted unequally upon the least wealthy 20–40 percent of the American population. Consequently, for this group, there was little or no domestic progress during the 1930s, but often only reversals of housing improvements achieved before 1930. Many of these families would receive little overall economic gains or housing improvement until after World War II.[57]

The effects of the Depression on the conditions and improvement in housing for the remaining 60–75 percent of the population are far more contested and infrequently analyzed. While the Depression significantly reduced overall domestic improvement for all classes, the upper 50 percent (and to a lesser degree the next 20 percent) did not generally experience reversals to the major domestic improvements achieved before 1930. Several other factors contributed. By the late 1930s, the rebounding housing construction industry began to approach the levels of the 1920s, assisted by New Deal–era adjustments to lending practices and the development of new products such as plywood, asphalt shingles, and fiberboard. This rebounding production is rarely cited, however, because it was so quickly overshadowed by the greatest expansion in American housing production of all time: the post–World War II suburban development era. In comparison to this massive construction period and in the shadow of the Depression, most historians generally have ignored the considerable construction achievements of this era. For example, the 1930s continued, and even accelerated, public utility production, particularly New Deal electrification, along with sewer, gas, and telephone infrastructure development projects. (The inability of the least well off to pay for these improvements remained, however.) As described in chapter 3, the proliferation of these basic utilities played a critical role in the democratization of domestic improvement throughout the country.[58]

In addition, the 1940 U.S. Census gathered the first extensive assessments of housing and standard household goods and services. In overall review, these data generally support the principal assertions of this study. For example, families with toilets reached 60 percent. Nevertheless, the 1940 census does not provide data for other principal assertions, such as the existence of massive home-remodeling practices, which were especially prevalent during the Depression decade before being curtailed by military production beginning in the early 1940s.[59] The contribution of remodeling practices to early twentieth-century housing reform will be analyzed in chapter 4.

11. POST–WORLD WAR II TECHNOLOGICAL DEVELOPMENT

Postwar suburban housing development, including the application of American industrial technology to the production of housing, is a foundational story of substantive domestic improvement tied to the rise of America's middle class. Without diminishing this story, this research also emphasizes an earlier, "first period" of equally important domestic improvements to the overall quality of domestic life, especially for a middle-majority constituency. These earlier improvements, analyzed in chapter 3, were continued with only minor alterations into the houses of the post–World War II era. Consequently, this book elevates one of the most popular early twentieth-century houses, the common bungalow, alongside the more widely recognized postwar suburban "Ranch" (Ranch house), as an equal if not more important symbol of modern twentieth-century domestic improvement—especially for middle-majority Americans who received these improvements for the first time (Figure 1.20).

Because the story of postwar suburban housing development, especially its technological accomplishments and unprecedented numbers, is so widely accepted, this competing narrative of earlier improvement requires explanation. Consider here the parallel changes in America's automobile industry. For many, the massive development of the car industry in the 1950s and 1960s was a golden era of American automotive and suburban culture. By 1930, however, almost two-thirds of American families owned or had access to a car for the first time. Although the autos of this earlier period appear antiquated today, many of the most fundamental inventions within the industry had been standardized by the 1940s. Of course, during the 1950s and 1960s, radical changes were made to the way automobiles looked, but the basic, most essen-

Figure 1.20. *House symbols of domestic reform.* (a) Early twentieth century, Progressive Era (1900–1930): Bungalow house, 1920s, Portland, Oregon. (b) Post–World War II, Suburban Era (1945–75): Ranch house, 1960s, Madison, Wisconsin. Both dwellings were the dominant houses of their respective eras, representing two of the most productive, sustained periods of American housing development.

tial technological advances in the industry and its assembly-line production had been fully realized by 1940. Therefore, although we celebrate America's love for and culture of the car in the postwar suburban era, the auto industry and its primary inventions, celebrated in the story of Henry Ford, are firmly anchored in technological and industrial development during the first half of the twentieth century.[60]

In strikingly similar ways, America's housing improvements parallel the auto industry's evolution. Despite modernist claims about the revolutionary changes in housing, postwar suburban tract housing development, as symbolized by the Levittowns, incorporated only a limited number of entirely new technologies and materials. Although changes in the speed and scale of construction were substantial, many of the most important industrialized housing components and their systems of construction were fully in place by the late 1930s. Consequently, on the eve of World War II, the basic features of modern housing construction, facilitating modern domestic life, had already been realized. These included public utilities infrastructure, central heating, concrete foundations, modern stud construction systems with plywood, asphalt shingles, major kitchen appliances, and standardized five-to-seven-room plans with attached garages (Figure 1.21). Probably the most important domestic improvement not invented and distributed before the war was air-conditioning. While recognizing the continued development of all construction components and systems during the postwar suburban housing era, this book demonstrates that the most critical building components and construction processes had largely been invented and standardized before World War II.[61]

Beyond these similarities in products and processes, post–World War II housing proponents still emphasize the backlog of dilapidated housing and crowded inner-city conditions that were jettisoned for the new housing prospects of the suburbs—as symbolized by the housing needs of millions of returning GIs. Although a vast number of houses were in need of repair, we should recognize that large numbers of these worn-down dwellings also contained many of the improved facilities, such as bathrooms and basic kitchen appliances, that had signified previous substantial housing

1900–1940

- Stud-and-plywood framing
- Public utilities: water, sewage, electric, gas, telephone
- Concrete foundations
- Central heating
- Major electrical applications
- Asphalt shingles
- Insulation standardization
- Window and door standardization and mass production
- Wall boards, plywood panels

1945–1970

- Air-conditioning
- Laminated structural members
- Aluminum products
- Mass production of all products

Figure 1.21. *Technological and industrial housing innovations before and after World War II*. This chart compares the major innovations in housing construction that became standardized between 1900–1940 and 1945–1970. Although the postwar era initiated the largest period of American housing production, many of the major technological housing inventions belong to an earlier prewar era analyzed in this study. Summarized from sources such as Merritt Ierley, *The Comforts of Home: The American House and the Evolution of Modern Convenience*.

reform. In any case, the importance of the basic domestic improvements in the previous era should not be discounted.

After the war, the basic shape, size, and spatial organization of common housing shifted radically to new horizontal forms with more open plans and attached garages. In ways similar to the evolution of post–World War II automobile culture, the shape and style of housing were substantially transformed, but the basic functions of how the house performed were largely similar to those of previous models. The most radical changes shifted production to single-family, detached, owner-occupied suburban housing and away from multifamily, attached, rental housing.

Furthermore, modernist claims of radical design changes must be dampened considerably in light of the fact that ultramodernist designs with completely open plans, massive plate glass window walls, and exposed, laminated beams were confined to a very small percentage of postwar housing totals. Far more typical, for example, were the Levitt brothers' modern "Capes" of the 1950s and 1960s, which were similar in form to the Colonial Revival–style Cape Cod houses of the 1920s and 1930s with modern detailing and updated technologies. But on the inside, the ways these houses were used by their residents, despite a slightly more open plan and streamlined fixtures and appliances, made them similar to the median middle-class housing of the late 1930s.[62]

Advocates for the importance of suburban housing development may still emphasize the many significant societal and cultural changes resulting from the construction of modern, postwar suburban housing. Yet, whatever the collective impact of the changes middle-class residents experienced as they obtained modern suburban houses after the war, those effects pale in comparison to what the middle majority of a previous generation experienced. These included families who obtained, for the first time, improvements such as three-fixture bathrooms, public utilities, and kitchen appliances. If you really want to experience profound domestic change, imagine stepping across the threshold of a typical working-class house in 1900, as we will attempt to do in chapter 2. Here you will find many domestic conditions that would have been thoroughly familiar to families from a late-medieval household. Then compare that experience with typical domestic environments that emerged over the next forty years—that is the shock and awe of fundamental, transformative domestic change experienced by a vast middle majority of the population between the 1900s and the 1940s. That is the story this book attempts to tell.

For wealthier Americans, these same changes came earlier and less abruptly. In upper-middle-class domestic history, there was no sudden shock of fundamentally new early twentieth-century improvements or conveniences. Rather, there was a far longer period of gradual development stretching back centuries into upper-class European domestic environments. Consequently, middle-majority domestic improvements, such as the first-time acquisition of dining rooms, bathrooms, private bedrooms with closets, and mechanical conveniences of all types—whose arrival after 1900 was so sudden and shocking—were already largely incorporated into upper-middle- and upper-class housing of the late nineteenth and early twentieth century.

. . .

These eleven prevailing themes and assumptions were selected for reinterpretation because their wide acceptance has limited the investigation of early twentieth-century housing reform for a middle majority of Americans. With these constraining influences delineated, housing and domestic reform can now be better considered from a broad middle-majority perspective. Yet it is always easier to outline perceived flaws in current theories and literatures than to propose remedies and alternative explanations. The following chapters will provide more precise answers to the questions and explanations raised in this chapter.

TWO WORLDS APART

DOMESTIC CONDITIONS AT THE TURN OF THE TWENTIETH CENTURY

In 1900 the vast majority of working-class citizenry lived within largely unimproved housing despite the unprecedented development of household improvements during the last decades of the nineteenth century. Their typical housing conditions lacked electrical appliances, plumbing and sanitation infrastructure, and central heating. Although some advances, like simple electrical lighting, were widespread, few observers could have envisioned the material gains of a majority of the population approaching those of the upper classes. Yet, forty years later, at the end of the Depression and the beginning of World War II, this is precisely what had happened.

Although the rise of a dominant American middle class in modern suburban homes may have the look of inevitability today, it did not in 1900. The chasm between improved and unimproved domestic conditions reinforced age-old attitudes concerning the ultimate scarcity of material resources and the achievability of prosperity for only limited numbers—certainly not for a majority of citizens. At the time, no society in history had ever lifted the majority into domestic conditions approaching those of its upper classes. Therefore, at the threshold of the twentieth century, despite the promise of new technologies and the initial gains of Progressive Era reforms, the spread of material abundance and domestic improvement had only limited benefits for the vast majority of Americans.[1]

To understand domestic reform for average Americans in the early twentieth century, it is, therefore, essential to comprehend the gulf that separated an upper- and middle-class minority (20–30 percent) from the "masses" of the traditional working classes (70–80 percent), which combined a mainstream working class (50–60 percent) and a closely linked lower or destitute working class (20–30 percent). Domestic conditions between these upper and working classes were literally and figuratively two worlds apart. Figure 2.1 juxtaposes this contrast of domestic class, which was sharpened in the case of Homestead, Pennsylvania, the site of one of America's most bitter struggles between management and labor. Here the fundamental differences between upper and working classes are revealed in the stark contrast between the town's two major housing constituencies. At the turn of the twentieth century, Homestead's unimproved working-class housing outnumbered improved upper-middle-class housing by a ratio of approximately five or six to one.

This chapter describes this typical housing chasm by analyzing the minimal, but not destitute, domestic environments of the middle majority. When this context is better understood, the depth and breadth of domestic improvement achieved during the first forty years of the twentieth century will become more evident.[2]

NINE COMMON HOUSES, 1900

During the period when Victorian mansions of the upper middle classes dominated late nineteenth-century literature (see Figure 1.11), other types of common vernacular houses were built in far greater numbers. Here we examine some of the most popular or numerous examples of turn-of-the-twentieth-century houses for the middle majority. Compared to the houses of the upper classes, these houses display obvious external differences in size and architectural detail. Of far greater significance, however, was the lack of domestic technologies such as electric conveniences, plumbing facilities, and kitchen appliances that consigned the households of the middle majority to a rudimentary level of domestic life.

Figure 2.1. *Two housing worlds apart, Homestead, Pennsylvania, circa 1910.* (a) Upper-middle-class houses, various early twentieth-century improved house types. (b) Working-class vernacular houses, Two-up and Two-down, unimproved houses. Both types of the Homestead region's houses were built simultaneously in a ratio of approximately one to five or six, upper- to working-class houses. Preceding the building of these houses, Homestead was a center of labor protest and subsequent violence between management and labor in the late nineteenth century.

Although both classes of households were improved in the early twentieth century, we will investigate the more transformational changes to common houses.

In 1900 there were more than sixteen million households in America. The great majority lived in neither the mansions of the wealthy nor the packed tenements of the poor, but modest one- and two-story and one- and two-family, wooden vernacular houses.[3] Although there are no reliable national statistics on house types for this era, from the case-study results of this research, we can identify nine of the most popular common houses—with no commonly accepted names: I-House, Side-Gable, Workers' Cottage, Shotgun, Side-Hall, Four-Box, Parlor-Bypass, Tenement Flat, and Early Bungalow (Figure 2.2). These vernacular houses, built repetitively but not identically, typically contained three to five major rooms (without bathroom and toilet), with a three-to-four-room dwelling being the late nineteenth-century middle-majority average (when all households are compared). The small size and simple plans of these workhorse houses might be surprising to those familiar with the dwellings typically illustrated in histories and the literature of late nineteenth- and early twentieth-century housing, especially the lack of bathroom facilities and most utilities. Yet even these modest houses were larger and better equipped than the typical houses of the lower working class 20–30 percent, which averaged perhaps two to three rooms, especially in multi-unit and subdivided housing, and had few if any domestic improvements.

All nine types of houses were built in great numbers in the last decades of the nineteenth century and first decades of the twentieth century and constitute, I estimate, a synthesis of typical domestic conditions for America's middle majority. Because of the lack of accurate demographics about housing types, this must remain an unproved hypothesis. For example, other common dwellings could have been included, especially popular regional examples such as early forms of the popular Three-Decker of New England. When combined, these nine selected house plans were some of the most popular of their era and probably represented one-third of America's total residential housing units constructed between 1890 and 1920—an extraordinarily high proportion for such a small group of

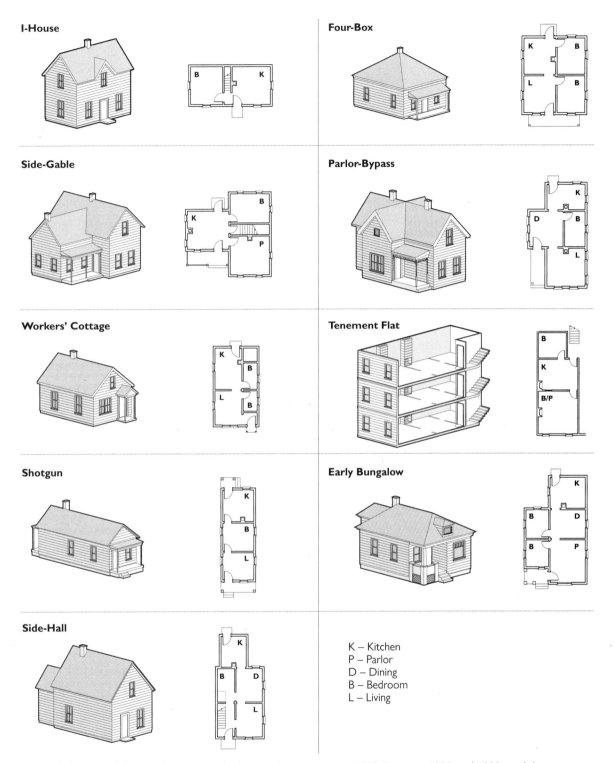

I-House

Four-Box

Side-Gable

Parlor-Bypass

Workers' Cottage

Tenement Flat

Shotgun

Early Bungalow

Side-Hall

K – Kitchen
P – Parlor
D – Dining
B – Bedroom
L – Living

Figure 2.2. *Nine of America's most popular house plan types, circa 1900.* Between 1880 and 1920, each house type was built extensively in most regions of the country (except the southern Shotgun). Although constructed in great numbers, none, except the Shotgun, have commonly accepted names or even names at all. Similar types of three-to-five-room houses (without bathrooms) were typical for working-class families at the turn of the twentieth century.

houses. If these estimates are correct, they would provide a means of expanding the history of American housing to better reflect the development of dwellings for the middle majority.[4]

All nine houses are identified by their basic floor plans. This approach differs from the standard practice of housing authorities and architectural historians of naming and classifying houses by their architectural style and exterior massing. In several publications, I have attempted to demonstrate that the most common forms of vernacular housing, lacking easily classified architectural styles, are better identified by their standard floor plan types. One of the principal reasons why this group of the most popular late nineteenth- and early twentieth-century houses has not typically been identified in architectural books and local histories is that the architectural stylistic classification systems employed by most architectural historians, institutions, and government agencies (such as influential state historic preservation offices, or SHPOs) are inadequate to document or even to identify these basic types of houses.[5] As a group, these small wood-frame houses are often described by social historians as worker housing or workers' cottages. In his book *From Cottage to Bungalow,* the architectural historian Joseph Bigott has labeled these unimproved structures "cottages" to distinguish them from later, similarly scaled but technologically improved "bungalows."[6] In a summary of Oakland, California, worker housing, Paul Groth finds underlying unity in many of the following houses typical of the turn of the century: "Before 1900, workers' cottages were numerically one of the most common house types in American industrial cities, although these houses are only beginning to receive attention in scholarly literature. Millions of workers' cottages survive today. They are almost always wood-frame buildings, typically with an initial size of just two to four rooms."[7]

· · ·

We will explore nine types of these modest houses, occurring nationally, that constituted the typical houses of the middle majority at the turn of the twentieth century.

I-House

The I-House is a common American house with a complex historical development (Figure 2.3). Although its basic two-room, first-floor plan is found in many cultures, it is the English traditions that have shaped its narrow, one-room-deep house plan—hence the confusing name "I" for its thin profile when it is seen from the side. In its earliest American iteration, the functions of its two-room first-floor plan were divided between a kitchen with a fireplace (or, later, a stove) and an all-purpose, multifunctional work–sleep room. Following English precedent, architectural historians have labeled this two-room first-floor plan the Hall-and-Parlor. It is another confusing label because the old English "hall" became the American kitchen, and the "parlor" became an all-purpose bedroom and workroom and, in common usage, not a formal parlor. In the basic arrangement of two rooms over two rooms, the kitchen occupied one of the downstairs rooms, but in its most popular nineteenth-century development a kitchen addition was attached to the rear, forming either a T- or an L-shaped plan (Figure 2.3a). By the middle of the nineteenth century, this kitchen extension became a major room in a middle-class, five-room plan arrangement.[8]

In the extensive literature of colonial housing, considerable attention is given to the development of a major plan alternative—the Central-Hall plan locating a stair hallway extending through the house and separating the two first-floor, hall-and-parlor rooms (Figure 2.3b). The folklorist Henry Glassie is credited with interpreting the development of this hallway (following elite precedent) as a social buffer zone between public and private realms of domestic life and signaling the end of ancient agrarian customs and the rise of a less communal, more isolated modern domestic lifestyle.[9]

Historians of early American housing typically separate one- and two-story forms of this house, but by the end of the nineteenth century one, one-and-one-half, and two-story versions of this house were readily combined and almost always constructed with shed or T-additions to the rear, producing a standard five-room plan. When built before 1850 in the eastern United States, two-story versions of the I-House were distinctly middle-to-upper-middle-class

Figure 2.3. *I-House.* In the eighteenth and nineteenth centuries, this small, originally four-room house was one of the most common dwellings in America. By the late nineteenth century, it continued to be built in expanded forms with rear additions so that it might be labeled an expanded I-House. Despite its long-term production, there are no commonly accepted popular names for this dwelling type. (a) Kitchen addition to rear. (b) Entry types: kitchen entry and center-hall entry.

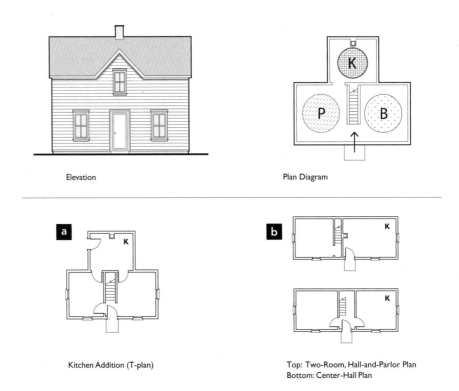

Elevation

Plan Diagram

Kitchen Addition (T-plan)

Top: Two-Room, Hall-and-Parlor Plan
Bottom: Center-Hall Plan

dwellings, but during the second half of the century, they became more commonly built as they spread into the Midwest and western states. Simple one-story-with-attic versions of this house were built into the twentieth century. Called workers' cottages, mining cabins, sharecropper shacks, log cabins, and so on, these small, two-major-rooms-with-attic houses combined temporary and owner-built traditions. These anonymous dwellings, many constructed of logs, existed on an economic and social continuum between middle-majority (60 percent) housing and lower-working-class (20 percent) housing.[10]

Because it was built from the earliest colonial settlements into the twentieth century in so many regions, and because it was such a popular selection of the lower working classes, the I-House is one of the dominant workhorses of American housing in the second half of the nineteenth century. Although there is no accurate documentation, I estimate that in 1900, variations of the two-story I-House, in many expanded versions with rear additions, comprised 10 percent of single-family, middle-majority houses—making it one of the most popular single-family house types in America at the turn of the twentieth century.[11]

Side-Gable House or Temple-and-Wing

The Side-Gable was one of America's most popular nineteenth-century houses in small towns and rural regions of America (Figure 2.4). Yet there is no established or common name. It is sometimes known in the Midwest as a Temple-and-Wing or Upright-and-Wing or more recently, in SHPO designation, as a Side-Gable or (inappropriately) Cross-Gable—all terms that attempt to describe the characteristic massing of two gable structures joined at right angles (Figure 2.4a). Architectural historians recognize this basic form of housing as an (Andrew Jackson) "Downing cottage" or a "Small Bracketed Cottage" when it is adorned in the Gothic Revival style, but it is more widely known nationally in versions of its much more popular Greek Revival style as it spread from a central Atlantic–New York State base into the Midwest during post-1820s settlement. In its functional plan development, it combines different English colonial house forms into a standardized two-part junction

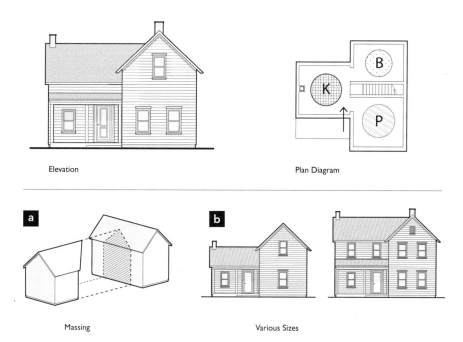

Elevation

Plan Diagram

a

Massing

b

Various Sizes

Figure 2.4. *Side-Gable House.* It is one of the most popular nineteenth-century rural houses nationwide. The Side-Gable form has been interpreted as a variation of an expanded, Hall-and-Parlor plan but with a completely different orientation and historical development. It can be called a Temple-and-Wing or an Upright-and-Wing in the Midwest, but, as with the most popular forms of vernacular architecture, there is no commonly accepted name for this house type. (a) Massing diagram. (b) One- and two-story versions.

of a kitchen–work building with a parlor–bedroom building. If you look at this house from the side, you can appreciate the kitchen gable as an ell addition to the usually larger front-gable structure. Yet in common layout the kitchen in the Side-Gable uncharacteristically faces the front yard or street. There are many explanations for the development of this atypical house plan, including elite architectural sources, but it is probably best to say that it is a product of an early nineteenth-century, multiregional American vernacular builder development with many sources.[12]

Unlike houses that were built in more standardized sizes, the Side-Gable is remarkably flexible and could be built in large, middle, and small sizes with either of its two gabled masses built in one- or two-story versions (Figure 2.4b). Furthermore, it was an ideal starter house because either one of the gabled forms could be built first during early settlement and a second gabled structure added later—as recorded by vernacular housing historian Fred Peterson in the upper Midwest. All ethnic groups adopted the basic house form. It became one of the most popular farmhouses in Wisconsin, and it was similarly adopted in western states, for example, in the small towns of Oregon, where it continued to be built until World War II.[13]

Workers' Cottage

The Workers' Cottage emerged as a popular urban house plan from unrecorded common builders' practices in urban areas following the Civil War (Figure 2.5). Several domestic traditions and house types are combined in a plan that can best be described as a one-story, detached, and condensed version of an urban row house plan (analyzed later in this chapter) without the stair–hall and a major second floor. In the typical room arrangement, it is one-and-one-half rooms wide and two-rooms deep. Like the Hall-and-Parlor house, it has two major rooms: an all-purpose living–bedroom in the front and a kitchen in the back, with a series of small rooms along one side of the plan. Typically, these rooms served support functions of the major rooms such as bedrooms, nurseries, workrooms, and storage.

Elevation

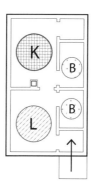

Plan Diagram

Figure 2.5. *Workers' Cottage.* This is primarily an urban house form developed in industrial regions with dense concentrations of single-family houses. It is developmentally a smaller version of the Side-Hall row house dwelling type except that it was built in one-story form and therefore without a stairway and entrance hall passage.

The Workers' Cottage is an appropriately named small, working-class family house found in cities across the country but concentrated in the Midwest and especially in the Chicago, Detroit, and Milwaukee regions, where it may have originated. Because the name is so suited to describing small urban houses, any small, one-story, gable-front urban house with two to four rooms might be called a workers' cottage. But the Midwest Workers' Cottage from Milwaukee and Chicago, with a gable front, a one-and-one-half-room-wide plan, and two major rooms is the dominant standard type (Figure 2.5). In this form, it was built in cities throughout the country, and as Paul Groth concludes, "Before 1900, workers' cottages were numerically one of the most common house types in American industrial cities, although these houses are only beginning to receive attention in scholarly literature."[14] Because of its similarity in outside massing, some observers have assumed that the Workers' Cottage is related to the Shotgun house of the South. But these houses have radically different ethnic and construction origins, as well as substantially different floor plan organizations.

Shotgun House

Most Americans have never seen a Shotgun house. Its name, however, arguably makes it one of the best-known common houses (Figure 2.6). Derived from the domestic patterns of African American and French settlement traditions, the Shotgun is distinctly

Figure 2.6. *Shotgun House.* A regional house of the American South, the Shotgun is well known nationally as a consequence of its memorable name, which captures its line of interior rooms with aligned doorways. It is the only major American house form with non-European, African/French/Creole origins. (a) Camelback. (b) Double House.

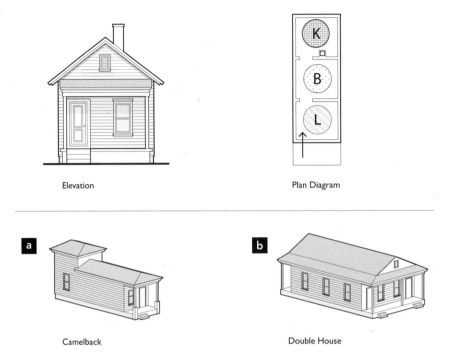

Elevation

Plan Diagram

a

Camelback

b

Double House

different from the dominant patterns of European vernacular housing, particularly English and German, that have shaped the great majority of America's common housing.

The simple plan is one room wide and three rooms deep with the kitchen in the rear. Although the name implies a strict alignment of room-to-room doorways (such that a shot could pass through from the front door to the back), there were variations on this formula. In its three-room form, it has been built in greatest numbers and unlike the other houses in this analysis, it is a distinctly regional house, originating in and confined largely to the South. Two popular adaptations of the standard Shotgun are the unique "camelback" version with a conspicuous second-floor addition to the rear (Figure 2.6a), and the more common Shotgun duplex combining two narrow houses side by side (Figure 2.6b).[15]

Side-Hall or Row House

The Side-Hall house was one of the most popular houses of the eighteenth and nineteenth centuries and, in various row house forms, it is found in cities and towns throughout the world (Figure 2.7). Despite its ubiquity, it has no commonly accepted name (except when it is attached in a "row house" arrangement) and is seldom analyzed in its most familiar American detached form. In elite and upper-class architectural history, it is the type of house that is usually labeled stylistically, such as a Georgian, Greek Revival, or Italianate house and typically identified by the architectural style of its door casing, windows, and front cornice. In its most popular, small-town development, however, this architectural detail is less pronounced, more blended, and difficult to identify—hence it is usually given the all-purpose, homogenizing label "vernacular."

In its early nineteenth-century form, it was often built with two stories and three rooms on each floor and a stair–hall at the front door (Figure 2.7). In its most popular, late nineteenth-century urban row house form, the Side-Hall house was often built with five or six rooms having a narrow, one- or two-story kitchen ell added to

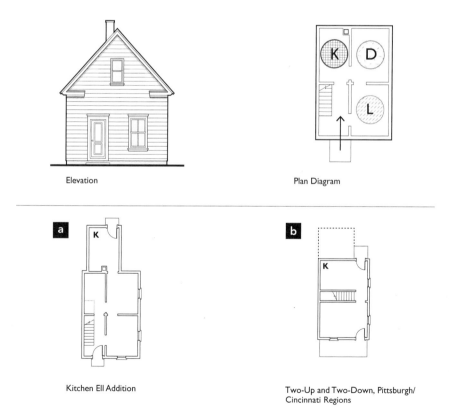

Elevation

Plan Diagram

a   K

Kitchen Ell Addition

b   K

Two-Up and Two-Down, Pittsburgh/
Cincinnati Regions

Figure 2.7. *Side-Hall or Row House.* Although largely unrecognized, the Side-Hall or row house is probably one of the most popular small house plans nationwide, especially because of its construction in both urban and rural environments. Its flexibility to accommodate rear expansions and both single-family and duplex subdivision also made it a popular choice. The Side-Hall plan is a direct continuation of English and European antecedents of the small, urban row house. (a) Kitchen "ell" addition. (b) Two-up and Two-down house, popular in the Pittsburgh and Cincinnati regions.

the rear so that light and air could be provided for the central rooms (Figure 2.7a). In this basic arrangement, it is one of America's most popular urban row house plans, but it was also commonly built nationally in freestanding, detached, front-gabled forms throughout the nineteenth and twentieth centuries. Further adding to the difficulty of identification, it was often subdivided into two, up-and-down, apartments (or flats) or converted to commercial usage on the first floor with an apartment above.[16]

Most European countries have similar row house traditions with a Side-Hall plan, but the American tradition usually continues English precedents. During the colonial era, East Coast cities had high densities of this English row house type in many local variations that were continued into the next two centuries. Throughout this period, Philadelphia and Baltimore and their surrounding regions amassed some of the highest concentrations of these attached row houses outside of England, where the row houses and variations of the Side-Hall plan were and still are the houses of the vast majority.[17]

In its popular row house form, the Side-Hall house was built in several local variations or subtypes. One of the most popular variants eliminated the entrance stair–hall and relocated the stair at the center of the house, parallel to the front facade (Figure 2.7b). It is a small shift in floor plan arrangement, but it allowed significantly different patterns of usage and multifamily subdivision. Sometimes called a "Two-up and Two-down," it was one of the most popular pre–World War II houses in the Pittsburgh and Cincinnati regions and is a direct continuation of the attached urban row houses of the East Coast.[18]

Four-Box

There is no standard name or region of origin for this basic cubic house with a standard four-room plan, various roof forms, and many architectural styles (Figure 2.8). Of the nine popular houses, the Four-Box is probably the newest standardized floor plan without a specific, vernacular line of development (although many regions, such as the upland South, may have produced early forms of this plan). By the 1880s and 1890s, variations of the Four-Box plan appear in builders' catalogs throughout America and seem to suggest a collective abandonment of the long English tradition of one-room-deep houses for small dwellings. As with many of the most popular forms of vernacular housing, there are probably simultaneous, multiple sources for the Four-Box plan that are difficult to identify and are further confused in a literature and cultural climate that tend to emphasize and misinterpret single-source "origins" of complex cultural phenomena. For example, the multicultural development of America's log cabins has frequently been attributed to early colonial Swedish traditions, when in fact the log cabin's construction combines many ethnic and construction histories, particularly German traditions.[19]

By 1900 the rectangular four-room plan, with living room, kitchen, and two bedrooms, was constructed throughout America. Intended for working-class families, it was often built without a bathroom well into the twentieth century, especially in rural areas. For example, the Four-Box "Pyramid" (so labeled because of its conspicuous roof form) was built throughout the Intermountain

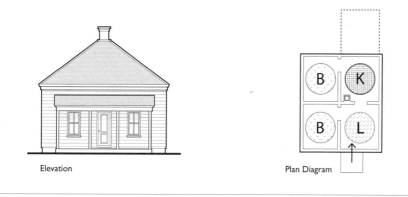

Elevation   Plan Diagram

Figure 2.8. *Four-Box.* Vernacular builders developed this late nineteenth-century house type throughout America. Although most commonly known as a "Pyramid" when constructed with a pointed roof, it was built in multiple local and regional variations of roof shapes, porch additions, and architectural styles. (a) Kitchen ell addition.

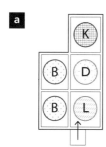

West, where it stands out in early twentieth-century photographs as a seldom recognized symbol of modern industrialized housing, much like the popular bungalow that was to follow.

Like all nine house types discussed in this chapter, the Four-Box was also built with standardized additions. The most common was a kitchen ell addition to the rear. Initially the kitchen was located within the Four-Box plan, but it was later moved into an addition or "ell" when the home was expanded (Figure 2.8a). By the late nineteenth century, the house began to be built with the kitchen addition as a standard part of the basic house form. This type of evolutionary modification generated by local builders nationwide is typical of the way common houses are designed and expanded in modern vernacular development.[20]

Parlor-Bypass House

Among the nine popular houses, the Parlor-Bypass is arguably the least traditional vernacular dwelling, and it is the type most influenced by the houses of the upper classes. At the most basic level of comparison, the Parlor-Bypass house (Figure 2.9) is a small, one-story version of a larger two-story Victorian, Queen Anne house plan. The principal feature of comparison is not the elaborate Queen Anne architectural detail but the unusual organization of

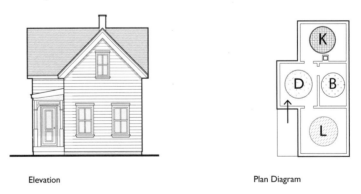

Elevation   Plan Diagram

Figure 2.9. *Parlor-Bypass House.* A late nineteenth-century plan directly related to larger, upper-class Victorian houses with a front door entry that "bypassed" the front parlor in order to enter a second major public room. In its popular construction, it can be understood as a smaller working-class version of a larger late nineteenth-century two-story Victorian house.

the plan wherein the side-porch entry "bypasses" the projected parlor (later called "living room") and enters directly into the second interior room of the plan.

There is little precedent for this Parlor-Bypass plan in vernacular housing (and there are no commonly accepted names for this arrangement of rooms). It is a direct copy of Queen Anne upper-class house plans, and when it is adorned with Queen Anne–style decorative woodwork, it is appropriately labeled a Queen Anne Cottage. In its far more common vernacular variations, with only sparse Queen Anne ornamentation, it was built in four- and five-room arrangements in which the "bypassed" and isolated front parlor could serve in working-class households as an easily converted bedroom and especially as a separated bedroom for rent-paying boarders. In its most modest late nineteenth-century form, the Parlor-Bypass was built without elaborate stylistic ornamentation, no bathroom, and a minimal or unfinished attic second floor.

There are high concentrations of unadorned Parlor-Bypass houses in Cleveland as well as other midwestern cities such as Milwaukee and Detroit. Before 1900 it was one of Cleveland's most popular houses for the working class. While seldom recognized in scholarly literature, it continued to be built into the twentieth century in expanded forms with improved features.[21]

Tenement Flat (Multi-unit Apartment)

A wide variety of modest two-to-four-room "tenement" plans were built across America for multi-unit apartment living (Figure 2.10). In the nineteenth century, the word "tenement" originally referred to most forms of multi-unit rental housing, but the word became most frequently applied pejoratively to a rundown or slum apartment house. Although recorded predominantly in New York City, where they were built in massive numbers of four-to-six-floor masonry tenements, similar floor plans were built in cities throughout the nation, but most often in smaller, two-to-four-story wooden and masonry structures.

In their various exterior forms, tenement apartments are united by similar three- and four-room kitchen-entry plans (there are no

Figure 2.10. *Tenement Flat.* This was one of the most popular floor plan arrangements for both large masonry tenements and small wooden apartment houses in late nineteenth-century America. It was built in urban areas with a two-to-four-room floor plan in many kitchen-entry arrangements. (a) Lower East Side Tenement Museum, typical floor plan.

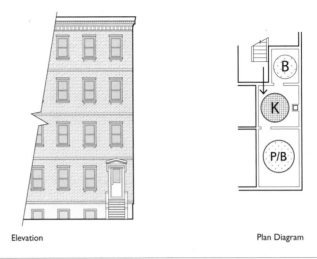

Elevation

Plan Diagram

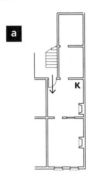

Lower East Side Tenement Museum Plan

standard names). Unlike most single-family dwellings, many small urban apartments (both historically and currently) enter directly into the kitchen or into a small entrance hallway near the kitchen. This kitchen-entry plan is perhaps best known today because it is the floor plan of the apartments preserved in the popular Tenement Museum in New York City (Figure 2.10a). In extraordinarily rare, detailed period exhibits documenting individual tenant families, the museum portrays changing conditions of urban tenement life in various three- and four-room apartments. The museum's exhibits clearly demonstrate the way multifunctioning rooms combined sleeping, eating, child rearing, and income-producing work into a continuous web of domestic activity. Similarly, the primitive technologies and dense patterns of urban tenement life resemble the same patterns of domestic life in all the single-family wooden houses recorded here.

Late nineteenth-century, three-to-four-room urban apartments form a subset of a much larger category of seldom documented urban apartments, both masonry and especially wooden, in cities and small towns throughout the nation. Where they stand out in a critical mass, such as in the Over-the-Rhine district of Cincinnati, such urban apartments are more easily identified (see Figure 4.15b). But as a group, they practically disappear into urban districts, large and small, and dissolve further into many local and regional versions of small tenement apartments, boardinghouses, and near-the-railroad-station or bus-depot transient apartments. These are the types of residences documented in groundbreaking works by Paul Groth and Marta Gutman in San Francisco and Oakland. Although the structures combine several building types and are difficult to assess nationally, I estimate that in 1900, one-third of urban American families lived for a period of their lives in some type of multi-unit tenement apartment or "flat" similar to the three-room, kitchen-entry tenement apartments shown here.[22]

Early Bungalow

The floor plan of the common bungalow became one of the most popular in early twentieth-century America and is the star of the next chapter about the improvement and reform of common housing (Figure 2.11). Yet this floor plan did not suddenly emerge in the early 1900s like its popular Arts and Crafts–derived bungalow style. Like almost all vernacular house plans, it had a long period of incremental development by local and regional builders before reaching national consensus in the late nineteenth century.

Before 1900, the early bungalow plan may have been called a type of Workers' Cottage and was typically built as a one-story, two-room-wide, low-roofed rectangle with four or five rooms, typically without bath. Unlike floor plans such as the Side-Hall, which can

Figure 2.11. *Early Bungalow.* Early or proto-bungalow plans were developed by vernacular builders throughout America in the second half of the nineteenth century. This plan featured a double line of rooms including a living–dining–kitchen sequence along one side of the house and bedrooms along the other side.

Elevation

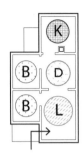

Plan Diagram

be traced directly to English and European precedents, the bungalow's most common plan has no specific ethnic or regional identity but reflects an integrated American, industrial-vernacular housing type—the evolutionary product of local builder consensus on a national scale and supplemented by a growing national literature of architectural pattern books and building supply literature.[23]

By 1900 the basic Bungalow plan was clearly established, but it was not originally called a "bungalow" during its late nineteenth-century developmental period, when it was constructed in a variety of plain, late nineteenth-century vernacular styles. Builders' catalogs beginning in the 1870s show proto-bungalow plans with two rows of parallel rooms, including the soon-to-be dominant living–dining–kitchen arrangement of the most popular type of bungalow.[24] One could say that these Early Bungalow plans lacked a unifying stylistic vocabulary until becoming united with the Arts and Crafts style widely popularized in the literature of Gustav Stickley and the architecture of California architects such as brothers Charles Greene and Henry Greene. In this combination of bungalow aesthetics and vernacular builder floor plan, it became known as the "Bungalow," or "Craftsman," or "Arts and Crafts" house and will be analyzed in the next chapter.

The Early Bungalow plan is included in this section because it was a popular, little-recognized floor plan for many small, single- and multi-unit houses, particularly smaller versions of the common duplex and triplex. In New England, small versions of this floor plan in multi-unit apartment houses evolved into the iconic "Three-Decker" with a bungalow type of plan on three identical floors (see

Figure 4.13a). But before they became standardized Three-Deckers and duplexes, they were developed in smaller, earlier multi-unit apartments. Early Bungalow floor plans also demonstrate the standard developmental process typical of most late nineteenth-century industrial-vernacular (post–Civil War) building types that add to an underclass of small houses and apartments that have not been sufficiently analyzed in the dominant housing literatures.

Although there were once hundreds of thousands of each of these nine common houses spread throughout the country, because they are small houses by late twentieth- and twenty-first-century standards, their numbers have been greatly diminished through destruction and extensive remodeling. There is currently no way to access their previous numbers accurately, but case-study documentation for this research reveals that in many regions and metropolitan areas, they far surpassed any of the standard types of larger, upper-middle-class "Victorian" or Progressive Era reform houses usually documented. Despite their historic densities, these most popular of America's late nineteenth- and early twentieth-century common houses are conspicuously absent from the dominant literature of Progressive Era housing reform, as well as most standard architectural histories and popular literature of American housing.[25]

DOMESTIC CONDITIONS, 1900

Here we move from the exterior to the interior and survey the domestic conditions and daily routines of the most common, late-1800s households. What will make this task difficult are not only the lack of extensive data but also the absence of widely accepted conventions for describing the common domestic environments for most late nineteenth-century Americans. We begin by attempting to understand the kitchen and the kitchen-dominated lifestyle of most families living in this era. The kitchen and its daily cycle of female domestic labor lie at the physical and functional heart of the home. From this vantage point, we will be able to assess more accurately the domestic logic of the various house plans we have just analyzed.

Kitchen-Centered Domestic Life

Placing the kitchen at the center of family life is certainly not a new concept for historians or sociologists of the family. One can argue that it is one of the core principles for organizing the physical environment for historic vernacular households worldwide. But within the domestic literature of the late nineteenth century, with its concentration on servant-facilitated households of the upper classes, a parlor-dining-room-centric interpretation has dominated the domestic literature of the late 1800s. Here we tell a different, kitchen-centered story.

While many cultures have contributed to the development of American domestic traditions, English traditions have dominated the historical literature, especially its kitchen and dining traditions. Most frequently, late-medieval English domestic traditions have been emphasized, often beginning with the evolution of the Great Hall, an all-purpose, multifunctioning kitchen–living room for the nobility. The introduction and development of the fireplace between the twelfth and fifteenth centuries, replacing a central, open hearth, is frequently emphasized. Fireplaces were first incorporated within manor houses but spread to an upper middle class of yeoman houses by the seventeenth century, to finally becoming enshrined within the fireplace dominated kitchens of the American colonial houses for all classes of citizenry.

This historic, fireplace-hearth-dominated kitchen was transformed by the introduction of cast iron stoves between the 1820s and the 1850s. This innovation radically altered and vastly improved the kitchen-centric workplace of female domestic labor. Evidence of this transformation was the presence of a blocked-up fireplace opening and mantel behind a stove that still required a chimney and flue. Although larger "country stoves" are often pictured in Currier and Ives lithographs of late nineteenth-century kitchens, pre-1900 stoves for the middle majority were typically small fireboxes that today are often labeled "Shaker stoves." Increasingly larger stoves were introduced after 1900 although the abandoned fireplace opening and mantel remained in many homes into the twentieth century. Surrounding the kitchen with its stove were subordinate spaces and rooms for multiple domestic functions—a floor plan summary that applies to most of the nine working-class houses we analyzed in the preceding section.

Before 1900, for the vast majority of American families, the repetitive rhythms of kitchen work dominated the daily lives and domestic space of the house. The kitchen, like all rooms in common houses, was organized to accommodate work—either the endless chores of female labors in the kitchen, various income-producing manufactures, or even beds for sleeping often located to facilitate the work or care of family members. This typical mixture of work and family life is shown in a photograph of women sewing in a kitchen-bedroom from turn-of-the-century New York City (Figure 2.12). This rare photograph is consistently used to analyze working-class domestic conditions perhaps because it so clearly summarizes the typical multifunctional rooms combining a space for cooking and eating, working, and sleeping (note the bed behind the women). It is this typical working kitchen of the middle majority that is often omitted from the standard literature of late nineteenth-century

Figure 2.12. *Working at home.* At the turn of the century, many middle-majority households continued to conduct income-producing labor activity in the home. Notice that the work is conducted within a multifunctional kitchen room with stove, major bed, and kitchen cabinetry. The mantel display probably covered an original fireplace opening. A sink and the dining table may have been out of view in the foreground. *Finishing Pants,* circa 1898, Jacob A. Riis Collection, Jacob A. (Jacob Albert) Riis (1849–1914) / Museum of the City of New York. 90.13.3.196.

housing focused on the formal patterns of dining and entertaining in separate rooms, often assisted by servants.[26]

Two major components, one old and one new, facilitated the work of the typical late nineteenth-century kitchen—the stove and the sink with piped water. All activities revolved around these two centers, including the continuous activities of meal preparation, clothes washing, child care, and house cleaning—activities almost always requiring heat and water. Stoves and water delivery are emphasized because they were the most influential and sought-after technological improvements popularly obtained by the middle majority at the turn of the twentieth century (in 1900, electricity for lighting was just beginning to be distributed to the working classes).

Stoves

In 1900 the iron cookstove was, and would continue to be, an indispensable component of domestic life for the middle majority. The stove began to replace the fireplace in American homes after the 1820s, and by 1860 it had become the universal standard for all classes so that only families living in the oldest houses, and the poorest or most isolated rural families, cooked and warmed their homes using a fireplace. Within fifty years, most families had transitioned from the preparation and eating of meals around a fireplace to doing so near a stove. This fundamental change in the overall conduct and quality of kitchen-centered domestic life allows us to rank the common stove as one of the most significant domestic products of the industrial revolution.[27] Interestingly, this critical kitchen transition is mentioned far less frequently in the domestic literature of the upper classes focused on the dining room's architecture and social life and whose continuous servant work typically concealed the introduction of the kitchen stove.

Unlike the houses of the upper classes, which included advanced cooking stoves with hot-water-heating devices and one or more parlor or bedroom stoves, the small kitchen stoves of the middle majority were typically the only heat source in the entire house (see Figure 2.12). Consequently, for many months, depending on the severity of the winter, nearly every major family activity for the middle majority took place near the all-purpose kitchen stove. Beyond the general inconvenience of overcrowding and coordinating multiple work-related activities, single-source heating contributed to the limitation of family gathering opportunities, especially educational opportunities such as reading and schooling. These limitations inhibited the overall development of middle-class patterns of domestic life and, in no small way, the obtainment of the benefits of a middle-class-oriented lifestyle.

It is interesting to note that despite their importance, these kitchens did not stand out architecturally or spatially from other rooms of the house the way they do today. In 1900 kitchens in common houses were architecturally no different from other rooms: they lacked any special wall coverings, built-in counters or cabinetry, or appliances, and only small stoves and the sinks stood out (see Figure 2.16). The rest of the room looked like, and was built like, the other rooms of the small houses.

Water-Sink Work Area

The second most important center of activities was the sink with a cold-water faucet or, in rural areas, a hand pump, or even more minimally, an area for holding hauled water. Next to the stove, the conveyance of water into the home was one of the most sought-after domestic improvements for the middle majority during the late 1800s. Although the upper classes had received various experiments in piped and pumped water-delivery systems beginning in the early nineteenth century, widespread delivery to the middle majority was gradual and erratic following the Civil War. Nevertheless, by the late 1890s approximately two-thirds of America's nonfarm families had some sort of water conveyance into their homes.[28] We should remember, however, that until 1910–20, piped water installation for working-class families was primarily delivered to the kitchen because there was no bathroom or toilet. Not until 1940 did more than two-thirds of nonfarm families have toilets with piped water.[29]

Water delivery marks a major dividing line in domestic improvements between urban and rural communities. Households in cities and towns received piped water inside the home from private and then public municipal systems far ahead of rural households. Rural communities and farms only later received indoor running water from a wide variety of individual household systems, such as hand pumps from rainwater and cistern storage, gravity-fed hydraulic rams and windmills, and into the twentieth century, kerosene and gasoline generators for pumping water. It was not until the 1930s that large-scale electrification, often through New Deal programs such as the Tennessee Valley Authority (TVA), established in 1933, and the Rural Electrification Act (REA) of 1936, revolutionized household and farming life. Only after electrical installation did rural and farm households finally achieve domestic improvements equivalent to those city and town residents had gained half a century earlier. At the same time, however, the proportion of farm families in the United States dropped dramatically from approximately 50 percent in 1900 to only 20 percent by 1940.[30] This great redistribution of the American population toward city and urban majorities significantly contributes to the challenge of calculating housing improvement for the middle majority in the early twentieth century. (These are among the reasons that farmsteads and farm households are often not included in twentieth-century national housing improvement statistical studies.)

Utilities

The delivery of modern utilities (electricity, sewers, gas, and telephones) into the dwellings of the middle majority only began at the turn of the twentieth century (piped water had typically been obtained in urban areas previously.) Utility delivery to significant majorities did not occur until the 1910s and 1920s, when the effects of these utilities initiated a chain of linked improvements that dwarfs all other types of improvement to the quality of domestic life. This package of utilities marks a sea change between a primitive, working-class domesticity and a modern middle-class domesticity and is the critical turning point for this book. In 1900 perhaps half of American families had electricity (for minimal interior lighting only), and less than one-fifth had a fully plumbed bathroom with municipal sewage disposal. At the beginning of the twentieth century, the majority of Americans were on the cusp of modern domestic reform—but still a world apart.

CONSTRAINTS ON DOMESTIC LIFE

In order to understand the quality of common domestic life that was to change so radically over the next half century, we need to focus on typical domestic conditions in which small and minimally furnished spaces with minimal technological facilities enforced tight constraints on their middle-majority users. Seven fundamental constraints dominated the conduct of typical domestic life for the middle majority of American families before 1900. Compared with current twenty-first-century housing standards, you might assume that these constraints primarily defined the domestic life of those in conditions of poverty—but they do not. Outside of a Victorian upper-to-middle-class 20–30 percent, the vast middle-majority 50–60 percent of Americans lived their entire lives constrained by a number of domestic characteristics.

Multifunctional Rooms

One of the defining characteristics of common house interiors at the turn of the century was that many different types of activities occurred in the same room. There were few single-purpose rooms in any of these houses, such as those used exclusively for dining or sleeping. From rare narratives and photographs, we can rehearse the typical overlapping of sleep, work, meal preparation, eating, storage, and every other domestic function in working-class houses of three-to-five small rooms (see Figures 2.12 and 2.16).

In modern American domestic history, most scholarship has assumed the division of the domestic space of home into a standardized formula of single-purpose rooms—living, dining, kitchen, bedroom(s), and bath—providing an underlying spatial typology for describing the basic functions and rhythms of modern domestic life. For the upper classes, this basic spatial structure of architecturally differentiated, single-usage domestic rooms stretches back hundreds of years to become the largely assumed undergirding for the history of housing and domestic life.[31]

Another surprising characteristic of these multifunctioning rooms was their uniformity. Typically, the same architectural details were used in every room without the kind of spatial variety and differentiation we have come to expect of rooms with different functions. This sameness was reinforced by spatial volumes that were similarly sized rectangles with uniform window sizes throughout and little variation, including the absence of bay windows, ceiling light fixtures, and differentiation in architectural millwork and trim, or the presence of built-in cabinetry and ornamental fireplaces or parlor stoves.

Further confusing the assessment of working-class housing was the new late nineteenth- and early twentieth-century practice of using the number of rooms in a house to determine housing quality and improvement. Often in Progressive Era housing reform literature, the number of rooms in lower-working-class and tenement housing was recorded to assess conditions of crowding.[32] Typically, more than one person per room was considered a threshold for crowding and poverty. This ratio was a rough benchmark for evaluating tenement conditions but when used to evaluate standard working-class residences, it has tended to conceal the vast differences among working-, middle-, and upper-class houses with similar numbers of rooms. For example, the smaller size of rooms in working-class housing and larger size in upper- and middle-class housing, plus the addition of modern utilities, built-in furnishings, and subordinate spaces such as entrance ways, hallways, and closets, make a substantial difference in the quality of domestic life (Figure 2.13). Therefore, the differences between a typical five-room Workers' Cottage and a typical five-room, early twentieth-century middle-class house represent an immense gulf between unimproved and improved living conditions in houses with the same number of rooms.

Throughout most of the twentieth century, middle-class Americans have grown accustomed to houses with five to seven rooms

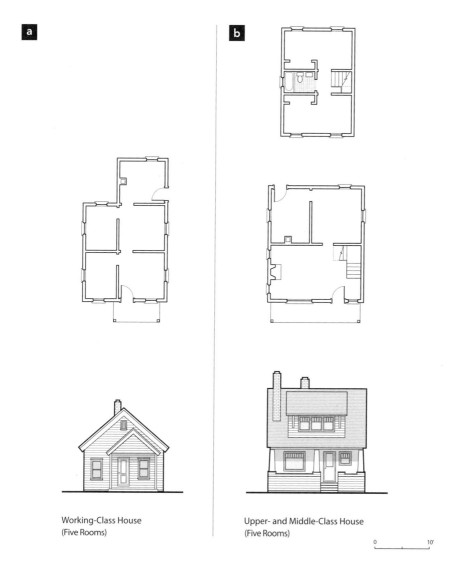

a

b

Figure 2.13. *Number of rooms—a poor gauge of the quality of domestic life.* (a) Working-class, Four-Box house plan with kitchen addition and without bath. (b) Middle-class house with living–dining–kitchen on the ground floor and two bedrooms and bath upstairs. Although both houses had five major rooms, they were vastly different in their size and the quality of domestic life they supported. Both house plans were commonly built during the first decades of the twentieth century.

Working-Class House
(Five Rooms)

Upper- and Middle-Class House
(Five Rooms)

that are differentiated by their single use, typically: living, dining, kitchen, bedroom(s), and bath. It is interesting to note that many of the major housing design changes of the past fifty years have sought to combine or open up rooms to each other (especially between living, dining, and kitchen) and thus reverse the practice of single-usage rooms that was so strongly associated with the rise of middle-class domestic culture in the first fifty years of the twentieth century.

Lack of Privacy

The priority given to individual privacy in our lives today makes it extremely difficult to imagine its typical absence from the domestic experience of most of the middle majority before 1900. Within late nineteenth-century houses averaging four to five persons in a household and containing three to five multifunctioning rooms (but lacking private bedrooms and bathrooms), personal privacy was simply not a typical component of everyday life. Contributing to a more communally oriented family life were endless patterns of female housework, less schooling for children, income-producing work within the home for adults and sometimes children, and the presence of nonfamily members and boarders within the house. These were all patterns that were to diminish or disappear in the improved households of the twentieth century.

Various scholars of European and American domestic history have stressed the fundamental importance of privacy in the evolution of modern attitudes toward the personal and collective development of domestic life. The need for personal privacy is often cited as a cornerstone of psychological development of the self within family life, as reflected architecturally in the creation of private bedrooms (and later bathrooms) for the upper classes since the late medieval period. We should, therefore, understand that the traditional working classes developed their historical attitudes toward self within the traditions of family life up to the twentieth century without a great deal of personal privacy—although personal privacy may still have been highly desired. Here we have focused on these nonprivate domestic spaces of the late nineteenth-century middle majority before they gained the domestic improvements of the twentieth century—including new spaces accommodating more personal privacy.

Minimal Furnishings and Possessions

By contemporary standards, average turn-of-the-century homes of the middle majority were sparsely furnished. Photographic analysis coupled with accounts of the material possessions of average families describes a standard list of minimal essential furniture items: beds and bedding (almost always ranked first and most important), followed by tables and chairs and then a wide assortment of furniture and domestic items primarily related to food preparation and storage, and sleeping and bedroom items.[33] Although many readers are no doubt familiar with a standard criticism of Victorian era domestic material excesses and overwrought decorative motifs, we should recognize that these critiques applied most frequently to the material possessions of the upper classes and to a far lesser extent to the households of the middle majority. In photos of working-class housing from the period, interior rooms may also appear crowded, but this was often owing to the small size of the rooms and the juxtaposition of various activities—such as the frequent appearance of beds in many rooms—not because they were overstuffed with furniture and material objects. There was also the tendency of housing reform advocates to describe and photograph the worst, packed, and disordered interior housing conditions to bring attention to the plight of the poor.[34]

The typical domestic possessions of the vast majority were, of course, considerably less than the standards often pictured in the dominant literature of the late Victorian era. This lack of material possessions in late nineteenth-century common households is confirmed by the minimal opportunities for household storage within bureaus or closets. Trunks, open wall shelves, and small freestanding cupboards appear to be the basic units of storage for the middle majority. Most turn-of-the-century homes had little built-in furniture of any kind, such as cabinetry and continuous kitchen counters for storage, and especially few, if any, closets. In most nonfarm environments, there were only minimal outdoor storage sheds and no barns or garages for bulk storage. By contemporary standards, the material possessions for an entire family amounted to surprisingly little. To take one small example, the limited number of children's toys in most family's possessions is a sobering assessment in comparison to more widely published accounts of elaborately equipped Victorian nurseries attended by servants.[35]

At the turn of the twentieth century, the colossus of American consumer goods production was only beginning to churn out the cornucopia of goods and services that we first associate with widespread material production of the "Roaring Twenties." Characteristically, it was during the 1920s that we first encountered the soon-to-be-standardized critique of the masses and especially the criticism of mass consumerism. Certainly, the iconic symbol of the mass-produced automobile and its assembly-line production were dominant symbols of the increased production of material goods for the majority of the population. It was during this period that we can begin to describe patterns of consumer consumption and the beginning of America's accumulation of standardized, industrially produced, material possession for the home—a topic we will address in the final chapter and epilogue. But in 1900 this was still a distant dream and an unfulfilled potential for the middle majority.[36]

Minimal Domestic Technologies

By the 1880s and 1890s, the wooden construction components for framing and cladding common houses were no longer individually produced by hand but were increasingly the product of highly industrialized, machine-component systems, of which the "balloon frame" and the nail-and-stud systems are the most widely recognized. These machined wood components included most of a dwelling's floors and walls, as well as preassembled doors and windows, which reached modern mass production and technical standards by 1900.[37]

Yet, simultaneously, these same, increasingly well-built wooden shells of common houses typically lacked almost all modern mechanical improvements and labor-saving devices—furnaces, clothes-washing devices, and refrigerators, and especially plumbing and electricity—that were rapidly becoming domestic standards in the houses of the upper classes. Although the exterior wooden construction was now largely modernized, the typical house interior continued to shelter domestic conditions that were primitive in comparison to the homes of the upper classes. Understanding these contrasting characteristics of common houses (that is, the improved exteriors and unimproved interiors) helps us appreciate the transformative impact of interior technological and spatial improvements that fueled middle-majority modern housing improvement in the years after 1900. In chapter 3, we will analyze the acquisition of these modern technological devices that transformed the houses of most Americans.

Rooms Used for Work

Throughout the nineteenth century American domestic reformers advanced the idea of the home as a refuge and retreat from the physical and moral dangers of an increasingly commercial-industrial world. Continuing "cult of domesticity" themes, late nineteenth- and early twentieth-century domestic reform literature called for the elimination of income-producing work in the home and the creation of a sheltered female retreat in suburban homes surrounded by nature (Figure 2.14). As we have seen, this

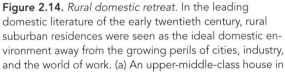

Figure 2.14. *Rural domestic retreat.* In the leading domestic literature of the early twentieth century, rural suburban residences were seen as the ideal domestic environment away from the growing perils of cities, industry, and the world of work. (a) An upper-middle-class house in an idealized rural–suburban environment. *The American Home, Safeguard of American Liberties,* a painting commissioned in 1893 by Judge Seymour Dexter, founder of the United States League of Local Building and Loan Associations. From H. Morton Bodfish, *History of Building and Loan in the United States,* 183; copyright by the United States Building and Loan League, 1931; courtesy of the Yale University Library. (b) Domestic shelter and suburban family life in a female-centered environment. From Robert W. Shoppell, *Modern Houses,* 1887. The Cooperative Building Plan Association, 76; courtesy of the Internet Archive, Canadian Centre for Architecture.

domestic ideal was often worlds apart from the everyday domestic labors experienced by a majority of American families.

Rather than rooms arranged and furnished to facilitate formal social activities or domestic leisure, as they were in the houses of the upper classes (such as guest arrival, dining protocol, and servant control), the multifunctional rooms in common houses primarily accommodated the demands of domestic work, primarily cooking, washing and cleaning, and child care. Typical homes also included the support of the work activities and work schedules of various family members. Following the decline of nineteenth-century home manufacturing, this was a period of growing male salaried labor outside the home. Nevertheless, female labor continued within all rooms of the house. These tasks may have included some income-producing labor, particularly related to clothing maintenance (replacing spinning and weaving of an early generation) as an extension of the standard female work of the home. Although often associated with immigrant working-class history, various forms of income-producing household labor often involving clothes washing or maintenance, were performed by an estimated 20–30 percent of families in the late nineteenth century.[38]

Additional Family Members and Boarders

The presence of relatives and nonfamily members, such as boarders, within the households of the middle majority was a significant constraint for average families. These additional household members included rent-paying boarders or lodgers, but also relatives, orphaned children, aged parents, and young married children, all of whom contributed to a more fluid, nonfamilial, working-class extended family than was typically characteristic for families of the middle to upper classes.

The impact of these additional members for both long- and short-term periods affected the daily routines of families in small houses, but working children and paying boarders were also significant sources of income for families with limited income-producing opportunities. Stanley Lebergott estimates that "in 1900, 1 urban family in every 4 sacrificed its privacy and expanded its income by taking in boarders and lodgers."[39] In a book about boarders, Wendy Gamber observes, "Social historians have estimated that somewhere between a third and a half of nineteenth-century urban residents either took in boarders or were boarders themselves."[40]

The practice of taking in boarders for additional income was a controversial issue. Uniformly condemned in the literature of the Progressive Era, it was nevertheless consistently practiced in families from the lower economic half of the population. The problems associated with boarder accommodation were summarized by a housing reform advocate: "The presence of a lodger in the family, moreover, is attended with great discomfort to the family. He is given the best accommodations the house affords and the family crowds into what is left."[41] Yet, the widespread maintenance of this practice suggests that the economic benefits outweighed the difficult family, social, and female labor costs.[42] In Figure 2.15, we see a rare photo of what was probably a family's living room darkened during the day to accommodate its night-shift-working boarders. Although this may have been an extreme example of lodger accommodation, the once common turn-of-the-century presence of an income-producing boarder or relative within average households,

Figure 2.15. *Boarders' bedroom.* A rare photograph that probably shows the occupants of a parlor–living room converted into a boarders' bedroom. The dark curtains covering the windows might indicate its daytime use by night-shift workers. Ford Motor Company Industrial Archives ACC. AR-84-57033, Photo 308.

perhaps because of its lingering social stigma, has left little detailed documentation or material evidence.

The addition of relatives, orphaned children, and the aged was a common but difficult-to-document occurrence often initiated by sudden changes in employment, but also the result of sudden sickness, accident, and death—factors that reduced middle-class families to working-class status with grim frequency. While families of the upper classes also experienced these changes, the impact was far more severe in families with little income and in rental houses of only three or four rooms.

Residential Impermanence

The need to move and the prospect of short-term residency were constant factors in the domestic lives of the late nineteenth-century middle majority. The vagaries of work—the loss of existing jobs, temporary layoffs, and movement in search of better employment opportunities—were constant components of everyday life, not only for the poor but also for a large percentage of the middle majority. S. J. Kleinberg has estimated that in the last decades of the nineteenth century, approximately 50 percent of households relocated frequently, and it has almost always been the case that the least well off (except the most impoverished families) moved the most.[43] Although celebrated in American frontier mythology and positively interpreted by economists as an engine of national growth, there were also severe negative consequences of residential movement, especially those generated by job loss, sickness, accident, and death, as was so often the case for average Americans at the turn of the century.[44]

With regard to residential longevity, we do not have terms that apply to the common households of the vast majority. Terms such as ancestral home, landed estate, countryseat, hermitage, or even old country home simply do not apply. That is because, except in areas of isolated rural poverty, the traditional working classes rarely stayed permanently in one residence, but almost always moved on. The working classes may have sought and struggled to obtain homeownership, but long-term occupancy was not typically obtained until the twentieth century. Consequently, in local and community history, stories of a working-class family's ancestral home, occupied by many generations, are extremely rare. Along with the inheritance of family possessions in upper-class families that often accompanies these stories, there is almost no parallel tradition in the families and households of the working classes.

Not only were a majority of residents impermanent but so were their small, less well-built houses, which were also subject to more rapid deterioration and removal. As we have seen in the literature of nineteenth-century housing reform, the problems of common house maintenance and repair were continuous, and for families with fewer resources this frequently entailed limited repair and maintenance and deferring or delaying improvements, such as public utility installation.

For these and many other factors, the dwellings of the lowest 30–40 percent of households in most periods and regions experienced a constant grinding down and elimination of the oldest, smallest, or least well-maintained structures. The process of least-desirable-house elimination is important to this study because it is linked to a companion process of affluent recolonization as the least desirable houses of the upper classes are appropriated or re-used (often through subdivision) to become a portion of improved shelter for the lower working classes (a process also described as filtering down). This cycle of decomposition and remodeling of the households of the least wealthy 20–30 percent (and their building owners) is difficult to interpret and almost impossible to assess from official sources.[45] In chapter 4, we will reexamine these complex issues as paths to home improvement through remodeling.

THE TRAJECTORY OF DOMESTIC IMPROVEMENT

The preceding seven limits to working-class existence, summarized by Gwendolyn Wright as "the multiple constraints . . . imposed by society, history, and power," severely curtailed the conduct and possibilities of everyday life for their middle-majority residents.[46] When surveyed together, they provide a baseline from which to measure domestic change and improvements over the next forty years. By understanding the minimal domestic conditions for late nineteenth-century average Americans, we are in a better position to appreciate the magnitude and importance of the domestic improvement changes that were to follow.

To complete this chapter, I was hoping to find a story allowing a Dickensian perspective into the houses and domestic experiences of working-class families on the verge of obtaining an improved home of their own. I have not found that story, but I have found a photograph that I hope will provide an unvarnished glimpse into the lives of a family about to attempt the kind of home improvement we will be following in the next chapters.

Figure 2.16 shows a 1908 photograph of a working-class family inside their small, two-room house in Homestead, Pennsylvania, the location of the Carnegie Steel, Homestead Works, at the time one of the world's largest steel-making facilities. The family was interviewed by Margaret Byington, an extraordinary domestic reformer and social historian of the Pittsburgh region who conducted uncharacteristically thorough interviews with Homestead's working-class families to assess the domestic conditions of mill workers. Because of its rare poignancy, it has justifiably been selected by other researchers seeking to describe the domestic conditions of industrial working classes.

In the photograph, we see the major room of a two-room household, where Byington observes:

> The kitchen, perhaps 15 by 12 feet, was steaming with vapor from a big washtub set on a chair in the middle of the room. . . . On the other side of the room was a huge puffy bed with one feather tick to sleep on and another for covering; near the window stood a sewing machine; in the corner, an organ—all these, beside the inevitable cook stove upon which in the place of honor was simmering the evening's soup. Upstairs in the second room were a boarder and the man of the house asleep. Two more boarders were at work but at night [they] would be home to sleep in the bed from which the others would get up.[47] (The husband returned when the photograph was taken.)

Figure 2.16. *Multipurpose kitchen and living room.* Steel mill worker's dwelling, Homestead, Pennsylvania, 1908. From Margaret F. Byington, *Homestead: The Households of a Milltown* (New York: Russell Sage Foundation, Charities Publication Committee, 1910). Photograph by Lewis Hine. Courtesy of Yale University Library.

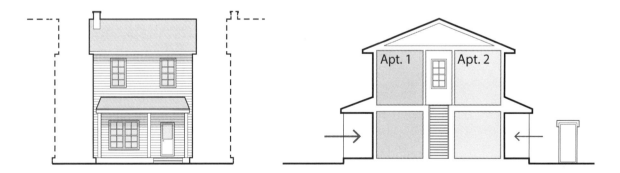

Figure 2.17. *The Pittsburgh region's standard, late nineteenth- and early twentieth-century, "Two-up and Two-down" house.* The drawing shows a typical front elevation for a Two-up and Two-down house, and an interior section diagram depicts the probable subdivision of this house into a two-room dwelling unit as described in the Byington interview. Margaret Byington, *Homestead: The Households of a Mill Town*, 1910.

Byington described a standard, two-room household (with one room on top of the other) that was most probably a subdivided, "Two-up and Two-down house," the Pittsburgh region's most popular working-class house in the late 1800s and early 1900s (Figure 2.17).[48] She focuses on the dwelling's single multipurpose room, shown in Figure 2.16, combining kitchen, bedroom, and workroom functions. This room contains the standard amenities for a majority of Americans at the turn of the twentieth century—an iron cookstove, a sink with a cold running water (both far right), single electric light and kerosene lamps, and a backyard outhouse, through the door on the right. The interview adds critical new information about the dwelling when we learn about the presence of three boarders in the second room upstairs so that, in effect, the room in the photograph becomes an all-purpose family room and boarder dining room, as shown in the plan drawing in Figure 2.18. In addition, the pile of clothes on the floor probably shows the female work of washing the clothes and bedding for the family and the boarders.

We could concentrate on these details of home labor and minimal domestic conditions, but this photograph also contains other, surprising components: a large up-to-date pram, handsome pendulum wall clock, matching bedroom and dining room furniture, well-framed art, and an organ and sewing machine outside the photo's frame (see Figure 2.18). This photograph was selected because I believe it depicts an extraordinarily rare portrait of a working-class family bound for the middle class.[49] If the family were lucky enough to escape a crippling mill accident or death in childbirth, their collection of parlor and household furnishings would likely find its way into one of the modestly improved houses we will soon be describing. Byington also included a photograph of another mill worker's well-decorated parlor, which she found to be a widely shared ideal among many working-class families (Figure 2.19).[50]

But we do not know the fate of this family. As for most working-class families, we have only scattered fragments from which to reconstruct their lives. But make no mistake, the essential components of this scene were replicated millions of undocumented times on the eve of what turned out to be a massive migration

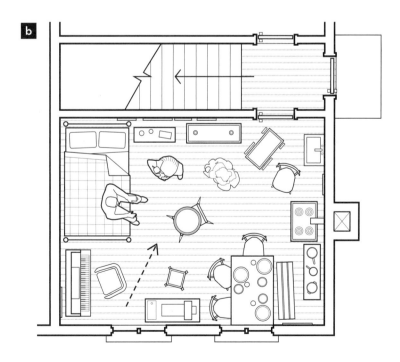

Figure 2.18. *Floor plan drawing showing the location of the interviewed residents and their furniture.* The drawing depicts the mill worker's two-room dwelling containing a first-floor multifunctional kitchen–living room and the second-floor boarders' bedroom. As interpreted from photograph in Figure 2.16 from Byington, *Homestead: The Households of a Mill Town,* 1910. (a) Second floor. (b) First floor.

Figure 2.19. *Where Some of the Surplus Goes.* A Margaret Byington photograph of another mill worker's well-decorated parlor. Presumably, higher wages and savings allowed for the purchase of parlor furniture as well as a larger house with a separate parlor. From Margaret Byington, *Homestead: The Households of a Mill Town*, 1910. Photograph by Lewis Hine. Courtesy of Yale University Library.

toward modern domestic improvement at the beginning of the twentieth century. Even though this family's story does not represent all early twentieth-century domestic environments, this family portrait is far closer to the typical domestic conditions of the middle majority of Americans at the turn of the twentieth century than any of the standard depictions of domestic improvement typically portrayed in the dominant literature.

By carefully examining this photo, we can more fully appreciate some of the terms used earlier to describe typical pre-1900 domestic conditions—terms such as "multifunction rooms," "lack of privacy," "rooms for work," and "the taking-in of boarders." It was a cramped world of work-dominated domestic life, but it was also highlighted by the glow of newly acquired possessions that symbolized the possibilities of middle-class ascendency. In many respects, this photograph is also similar to other early twentieth-century interior photographs of struggling working-class families from across the country. Yet, it is different in several other important respects. First, it is extremely rare to know anything about the family and details about their domestic conditions. We also see them in about as close to unrehearsed domestic spontaneity as we are ever likely to observe in an early twentieth-century photograph.

Of greater rarity is the portrayal of the larger event this photo captures—a working-class family on the cusp of significant domestic improvement. Although such depictions were often staged to show the difficult circumstance of their residents, this photo and interview do not sugarcoat the difficulties of their situation or the work of this particular day. We can almost feel the toil and weariness of the husband's next twelve-hour shift and the relentless grind of labor coiled in the pile of family and boarder laundry on the floor. Yet, if we look closer, we can also observe their steady determination and courage for the prospects of an improved life, which their accumulated possessions staunchly convey. This is a raw, unflinching portrait of a common American story.

We have lingered over this photograph because it encapsulates a world of pre-reform, standard domestic conditions for the middle majority that we have so few ways of entering—conditions that were to change and improve rapidly during the next forty years.

CHAPTER 3

MODERN HOUSES FOR A NEW MIDDLE CLASS

NEW STANDARDS OF LIVING

Historians of American housing generally date the development of modern domestic customs to late medieval northern Europe between the sixteenth and the eighteenth centuries. Subsequently, English customs, such as dining room usage, were brought to America to become the early foundations of our domestic food preparation and eating traditions. Yet, in 1900 the majority of Americans did not even have a separate room for meal consumption and would only begin acquiring their own dining rooms over the next forty years. As reviewed in chapter 2, most family meals would have been prepared and eaten in multiactivity kitchens in small houses and apartments. So, if you have read the dominant literature or have seen pictures of pre-1900 dining rooms, you are almost assuredly viewing the rooms and customs of a small, upper 20–30 percent of the population, not the traditions of the majority of Americans who did not have dining rooms at the turn of the twentieth century.[1]

This chapter places common house improvements, such as the arrival of the dining room (or making a place for eating in a separate room), in a wider context of popular domestic reform, where the previously unbridgeable divide between nineteenth-century upper- and working-class domestic conditions was significantly narrowed beginning in the early twentieth century. Although there were many other contributing factors to this improvement process, including educational, medical, communications, technological, and social-cultural advancements, this study focuses on a specific range of major domestic improvements, labeled an "industrial revolution" by domestic historian Ruth Schwartz Cowan, that were critical to the popular development of modern housing and domestic conditions.[2]

In this chapter, we will discuss nine critically important housing improvements that defined a new "standard of living" for modern middle-class life: bathroom fixtures, kitchen appliances, modern utilities, dining rooms, private bedrooms, larger houses with more rooms, closets, recreational porches, and automobiles. In 1900 few households of a middle majority would have possessed any of these amenities, but I estimate that by 1940 over half of America's households would have most of these improvements while another quarter would have obtained many of them.

As with any overview, it is important to convey that the lowest 20 percent of the population received only partial or minimal domestic improvements during the era of this study. For the poorest families, even the end of the Great Depression did not bring the fruits of modern housing reform.[3] Despite these inequities, early twentieth-century housing and domestic improvements for a middle majority still represented unimaginable, substantive progress relative to typical pre-1900 conditions.

NINE HOUSING STANDARDS OF MODERN DOMESTIC IMPROVEMENT

At the beginning of the twentieth century, journalists and domestic reformers began to employ a new expression to measure improvements to the housing and domestic conditions of average Americans—"standard of living" or "housing standards." The significant new term is "standards," which arose from both Progressive Era reformers and upper-class concerns for assessing the material possessions sufficient for entry into an evolving and expanding "middle class."

Before the 1880s there was no equivalent, comparative discussion of the domestic conditions that separated the traditional upper and middle classes from the laboring and working classes—probably because the chasm between them was so immense. Few nineteenth-century analysts, while beginning to recognize the plight of the poor and the laboring classes, could have anticipated that large numbers of working-class households would actually achieve significant levels of middle-class domestic improvement. After the turn of the twentieth century, however, this once utopian ideal became an increasingly distinct possibility as Progressive Era literature recorded a new kind of dialog about changing social boundaries and generally adopted "standards of living" as a means of measuring and assessing working-class advancement.[4]

The introduction and use of "standards of living" has been cited in most housing reform research. As Marina Moskowitz notes, standards were "one expression of the increasingly shared national culture that stemmed from the proliferation of both material culture and middle-class communities at the turn of the twentieth century. A quality of life to which many Americans aspired, the standard of living was difficult to define or quantify, but it was materialized in the settings of everyday life."[5] The practice of accessing personal and family wealth and social standing according to the amount and quality of housing and material possessions is hardly new, and has been applied continually in most societies and social classes worldwide.[6] Nevertheless, the late nineteenth- and early twentieth-century development of "housing standards" marks a significant new stage of actual working-class entry into a new world of heretofore inaccessible material possession and patterns of consumption.

The widespread obtainment of nine major housing improvements radically transformed the domestic environments of a middle majority of Americans between 1900 and 1940. It is a major thesis of this research that the acquisition of this group of material and technological standards, more than any others, signaled a threshold of middle-class lifestyle for an expanding middle majority of Americans at the beginning of the twentieth century.

Three-Fixture Bathrooms

The combination of toilet, sink, and bathtub into a unified mechanical ensemble offered an unprecedented solution to some of the most interminable problems of domestic civilization related to sanitation, hygiene, health and child care, disease prevention, and personal privacy. It was a package of technological innovations that improved the overall quality of domestic life, probably without equal. For working-class inhabitants who only began acquiring bathroom fixtures and bathrooms after 1900, these technological improvements marked a quantum leap from outhouses, largely unchanged since the late medieval period. For comparison purposes, 73 percent of Chicago's families did not have a toilet in 1893 and Chicago was relatively advanced by American standards.[7] (Perhaps 90 percent of Americans did not have a toilet during this period.) Unlike late nineteenth-century upper-class households that had gradually incorporated these fixtures in a separate room (soon to be called a bathroom), the working classes never had a room dedicated to "bath" functions—only an outhouse and a kitchen sink (or indoor water storage area) for performing all functions now conducted in the bathroom.

The configuration of the three major bathroom fixtures into a minimal standard (five feet by eight feet) floor plan was developed incrementally in broad national consensus between the 1880s and 1900 (Figure 3.1). Rather than the product of an individual inventor, the production of the modern bathroom facilities represents a broad, multistaged industrial process involving inventors, manufacturers, distributors, and local plumber-contractors in clusters of linked development stretching over many decades that facilitated a standardized national development.[8] During the first decade of the twentieth century, this basic plan of newly perfected, porcelain-enamel-coated, cast-iron bathroom fixtures became the standard pattern for almost all new housing, and was especially influential within the tight, efficient confines of small and midsize houses such as the popular bungalow. Along with the three bathroom fixtures, working-class families were introduced to the modern-hygienic touch of ceramic tile, porcelain, and stainless metal—all new materials in households that were made almost entirely of easily worn and difficult to clean wooden or plaster surfaces. In so many ways, the impact of the three-fixture bathroom revolutionized the conduct of early twentieth-century domestic life for the middle majority.[9]

This standardized assemblage of toilet, bathtub, and sink (or lavatory, the early trade name for a bathroom sink) has remained basically unchanged for more than a century and has been adopted in many countries worldwide—a broad consensus for a highly desirable "standard" of modern civilization. Few technological improvements have so greatly affected the overall quality of domestic life. Although more recognized items, such as railroads, skyscrapers, and computers vied for their era's most significant technological improvement spotlight, the modest three-fixture bath deserves a prominent place.

Figure 3.1. *Three bathroom fixtures—sink, toilet, and bathtub—in a standard bathroom plan.* This drawing was adjusted to stand outside the normal viewing distance from within a five-by-eight-foot (minimum) bathroom. Consequently, the room appears larger than normal. By 1900 this arrangement became standardized and by 1940, more than 60 percent of households had the equivalent of a three-fixture bathroom. Courtesy of the Library of Congress, Prints and Photographs Division, LC-USZ62-77716.

• • •

Perhaps more determinative of one's status and comfort than the presence of a bathroom was its absence. For the middle majority in the early decades of the twentieth century, the lack of domestic conveniences provided by the typical three-fixture bath would have significantly compromised their claim to middle-class status, regardless of income, job status, education, or cultural background—so fundamental were the combined benefits of the modern bathroom. The widespread distribution of the three-fixture bathroom, therefore, signaled a gateway for middle-class ascendency and modern domesticity in the early 1900s. For example, an economist writing in the early 1920s emphasized that "a housing standard which is to provide health and decency must include a complete bathroom," defined as containing a toilet, sink, and bathtub, and perhaps shower.[10] In atypical ways, there simply were, and still are, no good alternatives or better ways of delivering the bathroom's package of services essential to the conduct of modern domestic life.

These unusually strong claims are verified, I believe, by the unprecedented longevity of the three-fixture bathroom's design despite unimaginable constant progress in many other parallel realms of domestic and societal development. In other words, the bathroom, substantially perfected by 1900 and obtained by most Americans over the next half century, solved some of society's most complex multiple public health problems in such a complete way that it could have only been invented once. This singularity of the most important technological inventions is a central thesis of the economic historian Robert Gordon's *The Rise and Fall of American Growth*. As applied to the three-fixture bath, this was a one-time cluster of unique technological solutions for which there have been few significant alternatives.[11] This remarkable singularity of design invention will be paralleled (if not so fundamentally) by the eight other domestic improvements discussed in this chapter.

This long-term success of the three-fixture bath is all the more striking in the fluid field of housing design and construction where continuous change in house plans, styles, materials, and technologies has been (and continues to be) the norm. Yet until very recently, there have been few competing alternatives to this now century-old formula, as there are, for example, in the selection of heating systems and types of windows and doors. Even more remarkably, there were no significant numbers of rejections to this basic bathroom formula; no major groups of architects, builders, or homeowners that chose other bathroom systems or simply chose not to participate. That is why the bathroom can be used as a standard benchmark for twentieth-century domestic improvement and a significant marker of entry into the middle class.[12]

Kitchen and Housework Improvements

A wide range of new kitchen- and housework-related technological improvements greatly reduced the everyday, primarily female, domestic labor required of middle-majority families during the early twentieth century. By 1940 major improvements included new devices or processes in three principal areas: food preparation and storage, clothes washing, and housecleaning. Figure 3.2 shows some of the improvements linked to the widespread delivery of first private, then public, utilities: electricity, gas, and sewage (including piped water, obtained in the late nineteenth century). The list of individual inventions and appliances that brought improved services includes mass-produced washers, refrigerators, and hot water storage as well as vacuum cleaners and central heating furnaces that serviced the entire house.

ARMSTRONG'S LINOLEUM FOR THE KITCHEN

Figure 3.2. *Kitchen and housework improvements.* By 1940 domestic improvements had transformed the traditional work areas of the kitchen: (1) food preparation and storage, (2) clothes washing, and (3) housecleaning. Most of these improvements are shown in this advertisement for linoleum flooring. By 1918 these standards included (from left to right): hot water heater, gas stove, storage cabinets with counter, sink with hot and cold running water, and sinks for washing clothes. The linoleum floor greatly facilitated housecleaning. *Helpful Hints for Linoleum Salesmen,* Armstrong Cork Company, 1918, 35. Courtesy of The Winterthur Library: Printed Book and Periodical Collection.

The major technological improvements to the three principal areas of housework were addressed by three leading inventions: washing machines, refrigerators, and vacuum cleaners. Together these improvements both reduced labor and facilitated some of the most difficult maintenance problems of domestic life. Of the three main appliances, the washing machine stands out as one of the most important, sought-after improvements to the female work of the home. Washers have a history of development from late nineteenth-century hand-powered washing-and-wringing machines to more advanced mechanical devices to electrical appliances that were beginning to be mass-produced and obtained by 50 percent of households on the eve of World War II.[13] From their earliest development, washing machines appear to be the first and most popular of all modern appliances, whether in urban or rural households, such was the overwhelming desire expressed by women to reduce the drudgery and even dangers of clothes washing, including water heating and rinsing and wringing.[14]

The refrigerator has two distinct phases of technological development, the icebox and the modern electrical refrigerator. The simple icebox was dependent on delivered ice, and this demand was met by surprisingly extensive ice delivery facilities by the middle of the nineteenth century in most regions outside the Deep South and the desert West. Modern electrical refrigerators begin to be massed-produced in the 1930s, so that by World War II, 40 percent of American families had some sort of electrical refrigeration device. Cooling and refrigeration appliances solved age-old problems of food spoilage and storage and contributed to an increase in the types and quality of foods available to average working-class households.[15]

Electrical vacuum cleaners began to be commonly acquired in the 1920s, so that by the 1940s, two-thirds of households had acquired them—a high percentage for an electrical device that was developed and mass-produced over a period of only twenty years.[16] For the upper classes, the vacuum cleaner replaced a range of nineteenth-century mechanical sweepers, but it is a less noted improvement in upper-class-dominated domestic literature because servant labor eased the transition without substantial improvement. In common domestic history, the vacuum cleaner is usually emphasized, however, because it replaced laborious broom sweeping and rug beating. Although not as significant as the washer or refrigerator, the electric vacuum cleaner still contributed to a vastly cleaner and more sanitary domestic environment than had previously been possible. Although it is difficult to gauge, most turn-of-the-century common households would have contained a substantial amount of unremovable dirt that was simply accepted. The vacuum cleaner, along with other improvements, such as linoleum and better carpets, contributed immensely to a far healthier domestic life than had previously been possible. This new standard of household cleanliness came to be associated with, and was a conspicuous sign of, middle-class ascendency. We will examine the unintended consequences of modern, post–World War II standards of housekeeping in the epilogue, including the criticism that these technological improvements actually created "more work for mother."

Like the three-fixture bath, the refrigerator, washer, and vacuum cleaner were singular breakthrough inventions that happened only once. Although aspects of their performances have been improved, the leap between before and after their popular dissemination crosses a true chasm of near primitive-to-modern proportions that was achieved by the middle majority during the first half of the twentieth century. Simultaneously, these same transformations were not experienced by the upper classes, who obtained these improvements earlier and for whom the impact was shielded by the labor of others.

Perhaps the most significant overall improvement to the work of the kitchen was the application of electricity to the various tasks of food preparation, laundering, and cleaning. It is not an exaggeration to say that electricity changed almost everything about domestic work, and most significantly, kitchen work. While electricity for lighting began to be installed in houses of the middle majority during the late nineteenth century, the harnessing of electricity to solve the work of the home did not generally begin for the middle majority until the 1910s, increasing in the 1920s during an era of mass-produced electrical and gas appliances. Gradually electrical appliances began to replace nonelectric versions of the same items, as washing machines replaced hand agitators and hand wringers, hot water heaters replaced stove-fired water tanks, vacuum cleaners replaced brooms and carpet beaters, and refrigerators replaced iceboxes. Social and technological analysts of American domesticity are nearly unanimous in emphasizing the critical importance of these new electrical appliances for decreasing the labor of the household and improving the overall quality of domestic life for growing numbers of Americans.

Because domestic work involves so many tasks and the story of improvement is so diverse, no single advancement or moment of invention defines the many different types of housework reduction. In the extensive literature of kitchen and housework improvements, many other inventions and laborsaving devices, such as central heating and hot water systems, could have been emphasized. Hence, the importance of their collective total has often been diffused in historical analysis. Yet the cumulative effect on the overall quality of life for their primarily female users was incalculable. Ranking alongside the quality-of-life benefits of the three-fixture bathroom were the combined benefits of these labor-saving devices that transformed the immense labor of housework for average Americans during the early twentieth century.

Utilities and Public Services

In the 1890s the only utility consistently distributed to the majority of the population in most cities and larger towns was piped, cold running water. This lack of sewage, gas, and electrical service to average citizens is surprising if you have surveyed late nineteenth-century Victorian era domestic literature in which the arrival of these utilities had already revolutionized the houses of the middle and upper classes.

Although the distribution of major utilities to the middle majority was uneven, the overall results of this process were remarkably straightforward. The upper 20–30 percent generally received major utilities before 1900; the middle majority 50–60 percent generally received utilities between 1900 and 1930; and the bottom

20–30 percent of the population, including most people in rural areas, did not receive major utilities until after the Great Depression and sometimes much later. New Deal electrification is a well-documented example of utility distribution to the least-served rural segment of the population.[17]

Public utilities are an important component in the creation of all modern residential environments but are of vital importance in denser urban environments. This has been true since the Roman development of sophisticated water and sewage systems. In the majority of American cities and towns, the initial instillation phases of the earliest, most critical utilities were usually privately owned and financed by subscriptions from individual homeowners or commercial enterprises. Consequently, the first families serviced were almost always the wealthiest homeowners in proximity to largest industries. Before progressive public reforms beginning in the late 1880s, the major available utilities were rarely delivered to a middle majority of the population, and when they were delivered, it was usually the result of atypical circumstances. For example, when a large portion of the residents of Homestead, Pennsylvania, including working-class households, received gas during the late nineteenth century, it was primarily because they lived next to the Carnegie Steel Works, a major gas producer.[18] Only after 1900, however, do we begin to see public utilities being delivered to larger portions of the population. For example, the electrification of households nationally improved from approximately 3 percent in 1900 to 80 percent in 1940, and the 1910s and 1920s are considered the decades of mass electrification for nonrural Americans.[19]

Installation and unit consumption costs were always major factors in the distribution of utilities, but many other factors influenced the uneven delivery of services to the majority of users. For example, sewage or garbage disposal, so critical to the conduct and success of urban life, typically had a much lower priority in rural areas. Margaret Garb documents late nineteenth-century Chicago with an uneven distribution of utilities primarily through private companies and subscriptions beyond the reach of average citizens.[20]

Meanwhile, electrical service was equally transformational in both urban and rural settings. Regional distribution factors, such as local industry consumption, progressive initiatives, and geographic irregularities all influenced the rate and extent of utility acquisition. Therefore, great discrepancies in the rate and extent of utility distribution and related domestic improvement exist even within cities and regions.[21] A further complicating factor is cited by historian S. J. Kleinberg, who cautions that the distribution of major utilities from urban centers to expanding middle-class (white-collar) suburbs actually diminished the prospects of utility installation in the public sector. She finds that for many metropolitan areas, improvement funding was actually drained away from the inner city and urban industrial suburbs to more affluent suburbs during the late nineteenth century and early twentieth century and thus accelerated a working-class versus middle-class utility installation gap that was not healed until the adoption of Progressive Era and New Deal reforms of the 1920s and 1930s.[22]

One of the most significant accomplishments of Progressive Era domestic reform was the overall success in advocating for and obtaining the establishment of public utilities and community services for the middle and working classes. These utilities included water, sewage, electricity, gas, and the telephone as well as municipal services—garbage collection, street lighting, road and street maintenance and sweeping, police and fire protection, tree planting, and building and public safety inspection.[23] Unlike most improvement products, such as washing machines and vacuum cleaners that had considerable variations according to their quality, utility networks delivered a product of nearly universal equality. As Robert Gordon observes, "Everyone rich and poor, is plugged into the same electric, water, sewer, gas, and telephone network. The poor may only be able to afford to hook up years after the rich, but eventually they receive the same access."[24] While recognizing that access to utilities was rarely equally distributed, once households were connected, the quality of the delivered service, for example, electricity, was generally the same for all. This type of equality in product consumption had never occurred previously on such a large scale.

· · ·

Of the nine domestic improvements emphasized in this chapter, the first three—bathrooms, kitchen technologies, and utilities— are by far the most important. In various combinations and particularly after the application of electricity, this interconnected group of three critical domestic advancements radically reduced the toil and drudgery of some of society's most difficult, intractable domestic problems and thus increased the overall quality of domestic life. In a book largely detailing the nineteenth-century development of technological and mechanical improvements for the home, Merritt Ierley summarizes the distribution of domestic technologies and utilities in twentieth-century America:

> Most houses built before 1900 contained little if anything of twentieth-century technology. Well into the twentieth century many of these houses relied on kitchen and parlor stoves for heat, kerosene lamps for light, portable tubs for bathing and laundering, and outdoor privies for use as bathrooms. For the vast majority of homes at the turn of the century modernization came gradually as technology developed; as electricity, water, and sewerage became available; and particularly as people could afford to install these sometimes-expensive creature comforts.[25]

Another way of describing the impact of these major technological improvements is to focus on a specific, representative example. One well-documented case study was the David and Ida Eisenhower house, in Abilene, Kansas, the boyhood home of President Dwight Eisenhower. Figure 3.3 shows the order in which many of the bathroom, kitchen, and utility improvements were added to the Eisenhower household in the early twentieth century.[26] While the Eisenhowers' improvements were not added in the same sequence as in lower-working-class environments, each geographic region and socioeconomic stratum had varying needs and constraints that facilitated or denied the order of housing improvements. For example, in rural areas, toilet installation followed many other improvements, notably clothes-washing aids and appliances while in urban areas toilet and plumbing installation was always one of the highest priorities.

Therefore, although we track the larger movement in domestic reform, the final distribution and sequence of improvements to individual families, communities, and regions varied significantly. The Lynds haltingly describe this typical "crazy quilt" pattern in the order of distribution for all types of improvements in their widely publicized 1920s economic study of Muncie, Indiana, *Middletown*: "A single home may be operated in the twentieth century when it comes to ownership of automobile and vacuum cleaner, while its lack of a bathtub may throw it back into another era and its lack of sewer connection and custom of pumping drinking-water from a well in the same back yard with the family 'privy' put it on a par with life in the Middle Ages."[27]

If we place the improvements to the Eisenhower house and the Muncie houses in a wider context, we can discern the outlines of a popular transformation of the American residential landscape for the middle majority. Unlike the typical story of major utilities

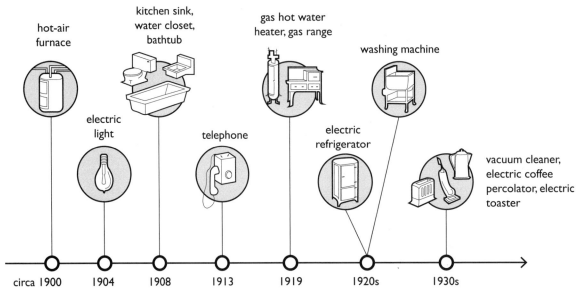

Figure 3.3. *The acquisition of major laborsaving conveniences in the Eisenhower household, Abilene, Kansas, 1900–40.* This graph shows the record of major domestic improvements for the David and Ida Eisenhower family, reflecting some of the standard acquisitions for middle-majority households across the nation. The only unusual addition relative to national trends was the early acquisition of the hot-air furnace before other improvements. National Archives and Records Administration. Drawing adapted from Merritt Ierley, *The Comforts of Home*, 176.

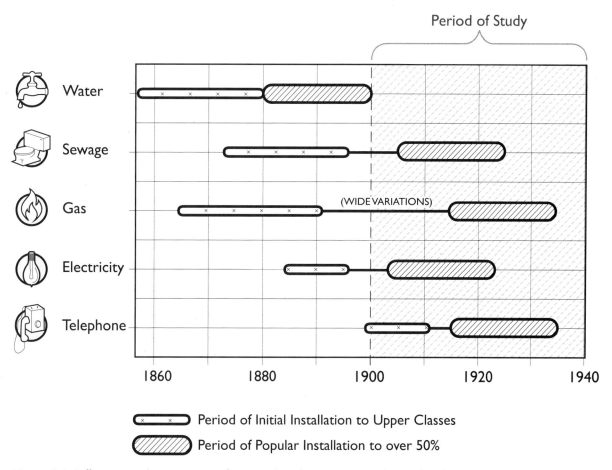

Figure 3.4. *Differences in the acquisition of major utilities between upper-class and working-class households.* The upper-class acquisition of major improvements is estimated to occur when approximately 10 percent of the population obtained improvement. Middle-majority acquisition is estimated to occur when more than 50 percent of the population obtained improvement. Graphs adapted from Robert J. Gordon, *The Rise and Fall of American Growth,* 114–15, 120.

distribution to the middle to upper classes, Figure 3.4 also emphasizes the attainment of groundbreaking domestic utilities at a central tipping point—the period during which a middle 40–60 percent of the population obtained these basic improvements.[28] Although this is a generalized chart of utility distribution blending many sources, it clearly demonstrates a twentieth-century period of massive middle-majority improvement concentrated in the 1920s and 1930s.

· · ·

Improvements in the remaining six areas are not as essential as the function of the bathroom or kitchen, yet they were still critically important to the attainment of early twentieth-century, middle-class standards of living for middle-majority families. Although it is difficult to track the arrival of these amenities in new and remodeled houses, it is important to emphasize that before 1900 these features were not found in common houses. By 1940, however, they would become standard amenities within the houses of a vast majority.

The Dining Room

Throughout the nineteenth and early twentieth century, housing analysts placed great emphasis on the dining room as a center of family and domestic cultural traditions in direct continuation of European and particularly English cultural practices. For a rising middle majority, this upper-class perspective often contained a mixed message. It was both a genteel summons to domestic improvement and a sharp critique of long-standing working-class domestic traditions, including dining etiquette and domestic lifestyle. Central to this critique was the implicit and explicit criticism of the custom of meal preparation and consumption in the same kitchen room—a tradition probably as old and universal as the preparation of meals inside dwellings. This consistent pattern of working-class food consumption is shown in Figure 3.5a—a rare photograph of an immigrant family having dinner in a tenement kitchen. Notice the kitchen stove in the right foreground that stands in front of a covered fireplace opening with a decorated mantel. In the center, behind the seated family, is a large interior window intended to allow light and air passage from the adjacent room, probably a parlor–bedroom—a common late nineteenth-century tenement practice. This typical scene is contrasted with the image of an upper-middle-class family seated in a dining room separated from the kitchen (Figure 3.5b). It is interesting to note that current twenty-first-century domestic practices have returned the kitchen to its dominant central role in the development of American family life as well as a proper place for dining.

Figure 3.5. *Dining in the kitchen or dining room.* (a) An Italian immigrant working-class family eats dinner in the kitchen of their East Side New York City tenement apartment, 1915. The kitchen stove at the right stands in front of a covered fireplace opening with decorated mantel. From photo-study by Lewis W. Hine. Courtesy of the Milstein Division, The New York Public Library, 464293. (b) An upper-middle-class family from Moorestown, New Jersey, prepares to eat a meal in a dining room, possibly with the assistance of servants. Courtesy of the Moorestown Library and Moorestown Historical Society, Moorestown, New Jersey.

From a working-class perspective, the practice of food consumption in the same room as food was prepared was not only a historic tradition but one also shaped by the small size of common houses. In late nineteenth-century working-class houses, which averaged three-to-four multipurpose rooms, the creation of a separate, single-purpose dining room was not a practical option. Although there is little statistical documentation about specific dining practices for the working classes (or data on specific room usage), I estimate that in 1900, perhaps 20 percent of all families would have had a separate room primarily for dining, so that at least 80 percent would have eaten their meals in the same kitchen that the food was prepared.[29] This practice would have been reinforced for seasons when temperatures dropped and the only heat source would have been a kitchen stove. Although there are also no accurate estimates for the number of stoves in housing, I estimate that more than 80 percent of all households in 1900 would have only one heat source—typically a kitchen stove—and, therefore, kitchen dining, whatever the size of the house or room arrangements, would have been practiced for a significant portion of the year. Counter this interpretation with the image of a Victorian parlor with a "parlor stove" (or fireplace), including second-floor bedroom stoves, that accompanied the portrayal of "middle class" families typically analyzed in early twentieth-century domestic literature.

Although not as influential to the quality of domestic life as the installation of modern bathrooms or kitchens, the dining room held great symbolic importance for new arrivals from the working class and was consistently incorporated into the new homes of the middle majority to become a crowning achievement of middle-class ascendency.[30] This important status is captured by Margaret Byington in an observation about the use of dining rooms in the working-class dwellings of Homestead, Pennsylvania:

> In the four-room house, the family eat in the kitchen. In five-room houses we find an anomaly known as the "dining room." Though a full set of dining room furniture, sideboard, table and dining chairs, are usually in evidence, they are rarely used at meals. The family sewing is fre-

quently done there, the machine standing in the corner by the window; and sometimes, too, the ironing, to escape the heat of the kitchen; but rarely is the room used for breakfast, dinner, or supper. . . . The kitchen is the important room of the house.[31]

Byington also observed working class families in more crowded apartments and their attempts to provide dining room and parlor like settings:

It has often been said that the first evidence of the growth of social instinct in any family is the desire to have a parlor. In Homestead this ambition has in many cases been attained. Not every family, it is true, can afford one, yet among my English-speaking acquaintances even the six families each of whom lived in three rooms attempted to have at least the semblance of a room devoted to sociability.[32]

As we will see in chapter 4, the rising popularity of the dining room for the middle majority can be seen in the production of new four-to-five-room houses and even smaller apartments. The popularity and surprising presence of the dining room in small houses and apartments of the 1920s and 1930s were often accomplished by combining dining with other room functions. Most popular were pullout or concealed Murphy beds, or simply moving furniture to temporarily create a dining room (Figure 3.6). This type of conversion might have been used only occasionally for formal dining, but it does not distract from its fundamental purpose as the obtainment of an important symbol of domestic progress and entry into a new middle class. The new dining room for the middle majority also appears to have served as an important place for new cultural-educational activities, such as a place for reading and homework, activities that for many reasons had found little place in the late nineteenth-century kitchen-stove-centric homes of the middle majority.[33]

. . .

Figure 3.6. *Hideaways or Murphy beds (folding beds).* New types of small, early twentieth-century efficiency apartments with modern technological improvements sometimes included hideaway beds. These new multi-unit apartments also included space-saving built-in bookcases and storage units, foldout ironing boards, and compact kitchens. Hideaway beds were typically located in dining rooms and living rooms to add sleeping space in small houses and apartments. Murphy beds by A. H. Andrews & Co., in *Decorator and Furnisher,* October 1885, 31; courtesy of Yale University Library.

Closely associated with the incorporation of the dining room into the dwellings of the middle majority was a new emphasis on interior architectural style and historic symbolism. This was reflected most prominently in the architectural embellishment of the new dining room, typically including modest interpretations of beamed ceilings, wooden wainscoting, and perhaps a window seat and built-in cupboards and shelves referencing late medieval English and European traditions.

This symbolic reference of architectural detail to historical periods was an entirely new phenomenon for working-class residents of modest houses and was a practice borrowed directly from the interior styles of the upper classes. Although many historic vocabularies were employed, the English and German Arts and Crafts movements, associated with the craftsman ideals of William Morris, reached their apogee during the first great wave of modern house construction and remodeling for the working classes. The Colonial Revival style, also popular for interiors during the same period, may have been selected less frequently because of its greater expense and because of its more direct association with the houses and lifestyles of the upper classes. Consequently, modest versions of the Arts and Crafts style appear to be the dominant vocabulary for the interiors of middle-majority homes during the early twentieth century.

This new practice of historic architectural referencing requires clarification because common house builders in all periods constructed houses that incorporated historic molding and details, even in the most modest vernacular dwellings. Typically, however, this symbolism did not invoke a particular historic era, such as the English medieval or Colonial Revival periods, but was derivative of broader historical traditions of long duration. In any case, the incorporation of any historical vocabulary, such as the English Arts and Crafts style related to English medievalism, was a new phenomenon of selected historic borrowing and symbolism for working-class entrants to the middle class.[34]

After 1900 it is surprising how quickly and thoroughly these new stylistic and aesthetic vocabularies were adopted into middle-majority homes. For almost all working-class American immigrants, the process of becoming American had already entailed the jettisoning of Old World folk or domestic building traditions, both for architectural exteriors and interior decoration and furnishings. Despite an extensive scholarship that focuses on the many ways immigrant cultures maintained their Old World traditions, the overwhelming majority of immigrant households were associated with construction and remodeling practices that did not incorporate ideas or patterns from their ethnic material cultures into the exterior or interior architecture and furnishings of their new houses.[35]

Yet, simultaneously we can also observe the stripping down of these borrowed historic styles in their application both outside and inside common houses in a process of vernacular minimalization.

It is an approach that has typically been disparaged in elite analysis as a folk misunderstanding of aesthetic principles, but from an immigrant, working-class perspective, it involved the extraction and reinterpretation of borrowed styles in a vernacular, "functional" expression. Another way to understand this typical pattern of minimalization of architectural styles in common housing is to interpret it as an expression of an American industrial vernacular—a folk aesthetic practiced with the machines of production and defined by its simplicity and functionality.[36]

The Private Bedroom

As we have seen in rare photographs depicting turn-of-the-century working-class domestic conditions, beds are frequently shown in most rooms, especially kitchens and parlor–living rooms (see Figure 2.12). Before 1900, within common houses averaging three to four rooms, each room may have been used, at one time or another, for all the various functions of family living, including sleeping, child care, domestic work, eating, and storage.[37]

After about 1900, however, the families of the middle majority began to obtain larger houses with four or more rooms. This allowed a greater separation of domestic activities, particularly the establishment of single-function bedrooms. Although rarely analyzed from a working-class perspective, this transition significantly expanded the opportunity to experience personal privacy. Little information is available about the experiential impact of increased bedroom privacy on the conduct of family life, but it occurred during an era of decline in the historic communal traditions of working-class family life previously enforced by small, crowded houses with multifunctional rooms. Although bedroom privacy was rare, the desire for a good and comfortable bed appears to be a consistent theme among average families with minimal possessions so that a substantial bed was often one of the most expensive and most prized pieces of furniture.[38]

One sought-after improvement for the middle majority in larger houses was the separation of parents and children in separate rooms, and later, the separation of children by gender, ultimately leading to the provision of individual rooms for each family member within post–World War II houses.

Bedroom privacy was first obtained for great numbers of Americans within a new type of popular five-to-six-room house with bathroom—the common bungalow. The early twentieth-century obtainment of the bedroom, along with bathroom privacy, may not rank as highly as kitchen and bathroom improvements, but accompanying bedroom privacy came new possibilities and approaches to child care, interpersonal relationships, hygiene, and individual well-being—opportunities summarized in chapter 5. The important acquisition of bedroom privacy, at least between parents and children, is, however, usually unmentioned in the dominant housing literature because upper-class households had long been accustomed to larger houses with bedroom privacy as a standard component of everyday domestic life.[39]

Larger Houses with More Rooms

As a general rule, houses for the middle majority have consistently increased in size and number of rooms, from the period of post–Civil War industrialization in the 1870s to the 1970s.[40] This is another instance where the development of middle-majority houses in larger numbers veers sharply away from the development of a smaller number of upper-class houses where there is a surprising overall consistency in house size and number of rooms during the same period. The reasons average houses gradually expanded after the Civil War can be attributed to economic progress of the middle majority aided by the increasing industrialization of the housing construction industry and the development of modern speculative construction methods by common house builders. America's vast material resources—especially a seemingly limitless supply of wood—combined with advancements in woodworking machinery also led to an increasing volume of milled lumber and construction components, such as fully assembled windows and doors, that fueled the production of slightly larger, increasingly better-built common houses (Figure 3.7).[41] By the beginning of the twentieth century, this expansion facilitated the popular construction of

Figure 3.7. *Larger and better-built houses.* Following the Civil War, the industrialized production of wooden components reached a structural and technical quality that far surpassed all previous house building, even of the finest handcrafted dwellings from previous eras. Large-scale manufacturing of doors, windows, siding, and structural members greatly facilitated the expansion of house sizes in the late nineteenth century. From "Ready Made Houses," in *Carpentry and Building Journal,* April 1889, 67; courtesy of Yale University Library.

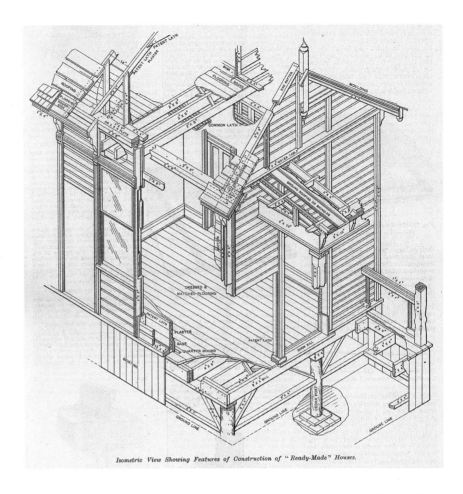

Isometric View Showing Features of Construction of " Ready-Made " Houses.

larger, new types of five-to-six-room houses, such as the bungalow, for the middle majority.

By the 1890s, even very modest houses for the working classes, such as Workers' Cottages and Four-Box Pyramids (see Figures 2.5 and 2.8), were built with very high standards of mass-produced wood-frame construction that, still today, with the addition of new mechanical systems, can be readily converted to modern habitation. In fact, these small, late nineteenth-century structures were some of the first houses constructed entirely of mass-produced industrial components. In contrast, builders of larger, upper-class houses of the same period continued to employ older, handcrafted traditions for elegant detailed work, while also incorporating the latest technological, mass-produced amenities inside the houses.

Storage Closets

Although not actually a room, the closet was an entirely new type of space for middle-majority residents at the turn of the century. Previously, closets were rarely found in common houses. The few items that did require storage were placed on open shelves or stored within modest pieces of furniture like cupboards and trunks. Photographs of common house interiors help us understand both the limited range of goods requiring storage and the minimal places to store them.[42]

Within the larger story of middle-majority domestic improvement, the closet is a small but significant indicator of a larger cultural transformation. Like the ripple of ocean waves predictive of a mammoth whale below, the new incorporation of specialized storage spaces in middle-majority homes of the early twentieth century accurately signaled the arrival of an unprecedented volume of popularly available, mass-produced, personal and domestic goods. The closet, although a modest entrant into middle-majority houses, represented a significant reconfiguration of the nature of working-class domesticity, one previously dominated by scarcity and a very limited palette of material possessions.[43]

The sudden appearance of built-in closets within average houses between 1900 and 1920 is, therefore, an accurate barometer to gauge the arrival of mass-produced industrial goods into common houses. Soon, the proliferation of different types of closets indicated the widening availability of specific types of goods for individual rooms with specialized functions. For example, the bedroom clothes closet within the new private bedroom accurately reflects the unprecedented worldwide production of cotton cloth and manufactured clothing beginning in the late 1800s and increasing at the turn of the twentieth century.

Other types of closets gradually appeared in early twentieth-century houses, such as the bungalow, within or near the new types of rooms they served. A closet near the front or back door signaled a new, greater availability of coats and outerwear and new traditions of in-home entertaining requiring the storage of guests' coats. A closet in or near the kitchen contained new items for food preparation akin to an upper-class pantry. A new kind of "broom closet," perhaps containing a vacuum cleaner, reflected new ideas and standards of middle-class cleanliness. A linen closet outside bedrooms indicated a new availability of multiple bed covers and linens. These were all entirely new domestic concepts for arrivals from the traditional working classes.

Other storage opportunities are well documented in the domestic literature of the early 1900s, including popular "built-ins," which were consistent aesthetic-functional features of the early twentieth-century, Arts and Crafts–influenced homes. Other new closet-related containers included medicine cabinets in the bathroom, built-in cupboards in living and dining rooms, and all manner of built-in cabinets and under-the-counter storage in the kitchen. While many of these storage areas had a long period of development in upper- and upper-middle-class houses of the late nineteenth century, they were almost totally without precedent for average families.

In retrospect, the products of this era serve as markers of a pivotal change in the relationship between average people and material culture. Previously, and throughout history, the relationship between average consumers and most material possessions was based almost entirely on principles of scarcity and the basic limitations on the quality and quantity of housing and domestic possessions. The Industrial Revolution fundamentally changed this seemingly eternal equation and made available mass-produced items of lower cost, increasing quality, and unprecedented quantities. For average American consumers, this marked a sea change in their domestic possessions from locally produced and handmade items to mass-produced goods often manufactured elsewhere. Coupled with steady increases in the quality and quantity of housing, mass-produced domestic goods and services greatly facilitated the expansion of middle-class standards of living.

The Front Porch

On the inside of the house, the new dining room was a dominant symbol of middle-class domestic life for the new middle majority.

On the outside, a new type of front porch became a popular symbol of newly acquired internal domestic improvement and external leisure opportunities for the middle majority (see Figure 5.1). In bungalows and various two-to-six-unit apartment houses, the residential front porch had begun to symbolize a middle-class lifestyle made possible, in part, by workplace and domestic reforms, including, for example, the standardization of the eight-hour workday. Over time the bungalow's picturesque, Arts and Crafts–style front porch came to represent the new possibilities of comfortable living, including the public enjoyment of leisure activities in a new lifestyle not totally consumed by the unending demands of domestic and industrial work.

Throughout the 1800s, there were no equivalent spaces or places constructed for leisure activities either inside or outside typical middle-to-working-class homes. As noted by labor reformers at the turn of the nineteenth century, the ten-to-twelve-hour workday did not leave time for the kind of leisure symbolized by the front porch. More than any other architectural feature, the front porch accommodated a new type of domestic activity intended primarily for leisure and social gathering as well as the function of entrance shelter. Porches, of course, have a long history both for formal-symbolic entry into the houses of the upper classes and for entry shelter and work activities on modest houses, especially on farms and rural environments. But new to most of the emerging middle majority was the presence of a porch not primarily intended for either protecting from foul weather or sheltering work activities.

In the late nineteenth century, instead of merely an attached roof of minimal functional proportions, front porches for new middle-majority houses became far more integrated with the architectural styles of those houses. This trend culminated in typical bungalow porches that are often fully integrated with the massing and architectural style of the main body of the house. In fact, many scholars would argue that bungalows large and small are not truly bungalows without prominent and fully integrated front porches.[44]

Considering the significance that bungalow builders and residents gave to the front porch, it is surprising how rapidly the porch would go out of fashion beginning in the 1920s, when Colonial Revival and European "Period Revival" houses either formalized or eliminated the porch without providing a place for leisure activities. Later, during the modern suburban ranch house era, the porch was almost completely banished from the front facade of the ranch house as the private backyard absorbed most of the leisure activities associated with the original bungalow porch. Today, as in the bungalow era, the urban revival and New Urbanism movements have reintroduced the front porch and reenergized its importance as a place and symbol of human activity and community cohesion on the public facade of the house.[45]

Car and Garage

The automobile was a late addition to working-class households, first arriving in large numbers in the 1920s, often as the popular, universally acclaimed Model T. As recognized by almost all interpreters of American culture, the popular use of the automobile significantly contributed to the transformation of the American home and lifestyle in the early twentieth century. For the middle majority, this transformation occurred with tremendous speed and impact, so that by the beginning of the Great Depression in 1930, 60 percent of American families had automobiles. (For comparison, 44 percent owned homes at the same time.)[46]

Since all early cars needed substantial protection from weather, some form of shelter or garage almost always accompanied the introduction of the car. The early transition from a detached horse stable near the house to a detached garage in a similar location was an architectural transition from the sheltering of the horse and carriage to the sheltering of the automobile in the same or a similar type of building. While this transition has been well documented in the history of housing, this was not the way the middle majority of Americans experienced the acquisition and sheltering of their first automobile. For the overwhelming majority of non-farm households, there was no horse and carriage and stable because walking was the primary and only means of transportation

(Figure 3.8). Since less than 10–15 percent of nonfarm households owned a horse, and especially a carriage, most nonfarm Americans never transitioned from a stable to a garage but rather found new types of shelter for their first automobiles.[47] The surprise to most contemporary observers is that before the car, most of the population walked or took some form of urban transportation, such as

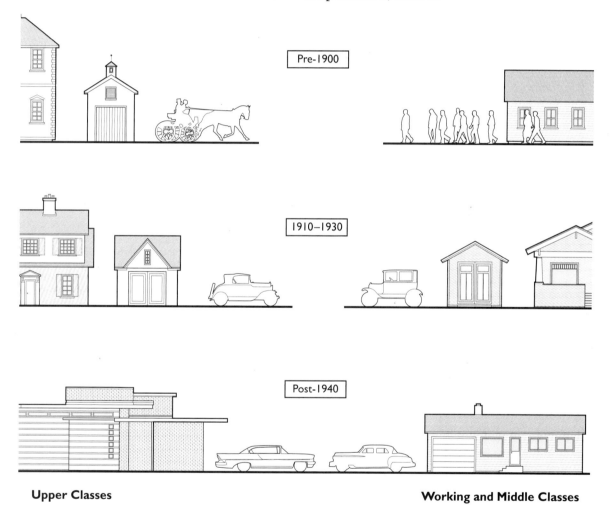

Upper Classes   **Working and Middle Classes**

Figure 3.8. *Evolution of the garage in twentieth-century housing.* In standard housing histories, the stable is the direct precedent and prototype for the garage. In working-class domestic history, however, there were typically no stables (or horses or carriages) for the vast majority of the nonfarm population. In an overview of car storage beginning in 1900, the separate garage was gradually moved closer to the house until it was commonly attached during the 1920s and 1930s. The complete unification of the house and garage in popular culture is associated with the development of the ranch house during the post–World War II suburban era.

horse carriages or electric streetcars. Even for average farmers, a separate stable was a rare farm building as horses and wagons (and perhaps carriages) were commonly stored in traditional barns in most regions of the country.

As a result, Henry Ford's Model T was frequently the first means of privately owned transportation for a nonfarm majority of the population, and that is why it became such a defining symbol of middle-class ascendency for the traditional working classes. Between 1915 and 1930, the car was typically accommodated in small, detached, "Model T" garages often located at the back of a property and thus requiring a driveway to bypass the side of the house (in neighborhoods without back alleys). More typical of car storage in small towns and urban areas were new forms of multicar, row garages and larger one- and two-story parking structures that have seldom survived into the late twentieth century. Before 1940, in cities and towns, these multicar garages were at least as popular for middle-majority car storage as individual garages.[48]

Gradually, between 1925 and 1950, individual garages were built and placed closer to and often attached to the house (see Figure 3.8). The writings and design ideas of Frank Lloyd Wright are often credited with anticipating the influential role of the car in American domestic life and especially the integration of the garage and carport within the modern house. The introduction of the car, however, did not typically transform the physical shape and plan of improved common houses until after World War II, when the car's garage was fully integrated into the standard ranch house and other common houses.

Cultural historians have appropriately emphasized the automobile's importance in the postwar era when the suburban house and car become fused together. Yet, by 1930, at the beginning of the Depression, the fundamental conditions for this popular revolution were firmly established for the middle majority of the population. Unlike other major domestic improvements, the car with garage had only a minor impact on the way most houses were built before 1940. Yet the automobile had a profound effect on every aspect of American domestic culture, and that is why it is included as a one-time improvement that fundamentally altered and improved the quality of domestic life for the middle majority.

To complete the working-class story of transportation, we should also mention the changes brought about by public transportation, such as the electric streetcar, changes that occurred during the period of transition from walking to automobile. Streetcar usage was extended from the 1890s to vast metropolitan networks at the dawn of the automotive era and was gradually displaced by the automobile and the more flexible motorbus in the 1920s and 1930s. Although we could emphasize the streetcar as a transitional mode of transportation linking walking and the automobile, recent scholarship has scaled back this connection by emphasizing the streetcar's prohibitive expense for average working-class riders and by demonstrating that streetcar routes were often developed primarily to enhance upper-middle-class suburban expansion and not to directly facilitate transportation to preexisting working-class communities.[49]

The preceding nine housing standards were key post-1900 improvements to new and remodeled housing for a new middle majority of American households. Without these domestic advances, the obtainment of a middle-class lifestyle (however it is defined) would have been greatly inhibited or nearly impossible. In pursuit of this thesis, it has been a consistent theme of this book that the differences between when the middle majority (50–60 percent) received these improvements (1900–1940) and when the middle to upper classes (20–30 percent) received them (1860–1900) have not been sufficiently emphasized in the literature of American housing reform. Figure 3.9 depicts this two-stage process by highlighting the different periods when the upper classes and the middle majority first obtained a particular improvement, such as a washing machine or a flush toilet. The differences between when these constituencies first received modern conveniences summarize the focus of this chapter and the major themes of this book. Next, we will see how these working-class improvements were actually implemented and installed within new and remodeled houses of the middle majority.

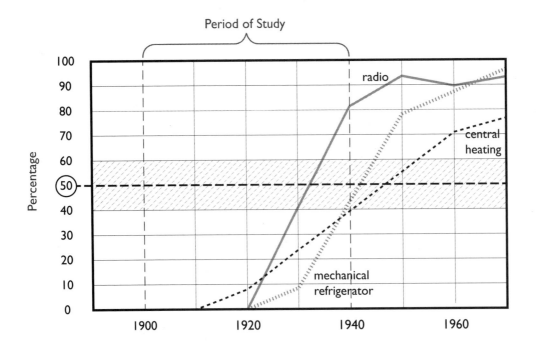

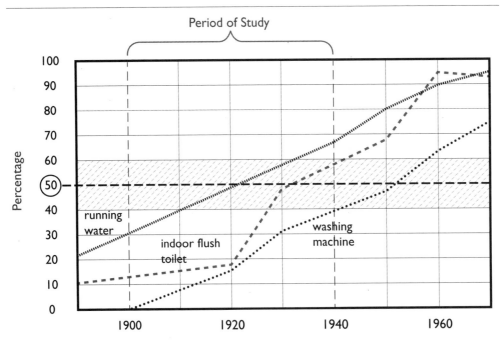

Figure 3.9. *Diffusion of modern appliances and conveniences for the middle majority, 1890–1970.* These graphs depict the rate of household acquisition for major domestic improvements. The central horizontal bar in each graph represents the point at which a middle 40–60 percent of American households obtained a particular improvement. Adapted from Robert J. Gordon, *The Rise and Fall of American Growth*, 114–15, 120, 357.

A NEW TYPE OF HOUSE FOR A NEW MIDDLE CLASS

Between 1900 and 1940, American housing for the middle majority was fundamentally transformed by the acquisition of the modern domestic improvements we have examined. As might be expected, the shape and form of the houses themselves were altered, producing a wide variety of houses that we will be examining in the next chapter (see Figure I.2). Because there was considerable exterior variety in these houses, it might seem difficult to summarize any fundamental underlying unity. Fortunately, amidst this exterior variety, these improved houses were highly unified in their basic patterns of spatial usage as reflected in their floor plans. And the most popular was the floor plan of the common bungalow.

The Progressive Era or Bungalow Plan

The standard floor plan of the common one-story bungalow was one of the most popular plans developed before World War II and represents millions of similarly scaled houses throughout the country.[50] Figure 3.10 shows the "Stanhope," a modest bungalow from the 1917 Aladdin Houses catalog as a typical example of this floor plan. Although there are no accurate national surveys of house plan types, because of its consistent popularity in many of the case-study investigations for this book, coupled with the analysis of local authorities, I estimate that among the approximately seven million single-family, owner-occupied housing units produced between 1900 and 1930 (the years when this house plan was most widely constructed), approximately a half million (or more than .05%) were various forms of the Stanhope's Bungalow floor plan—a large share of the national housing totals for a single house type.[51]

Some readers might recognize the "Stanhope" bungalow as a manufactured "kit house," although the largest percentages of common houses and bungalows were neither architect designed nor kit houses but were obtained from a vast national literature of house and plan books and magazines, all speculatively interpreted by local and regional builders and developers. The Stanhope is pictured

Figure 3.10. *The Stanhope Bungalow.* This classic one-story bungalow was built by speculative contractors, as well as kit house builders, throughout the country. (a) Floor plan. (b) Aerial cutaway plan. Aladdin Homes, *Built in a Day,* The Aladdin Company, 1917, 76–78; courtesy of Yale University Library.

The Stanhope

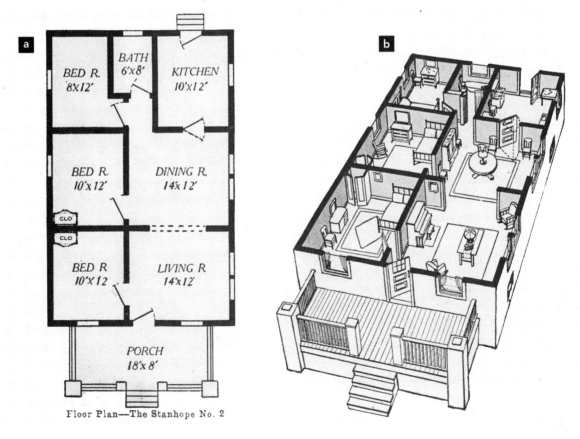

a

BED R.
8'x12'

BATH
6'x8'

KITCHEN
10'x12'

BED R.
10'x12'

DINING R.
14'x12'

CLO

CLO

BED R
10'x12'

LIVING R
14'x12'

PORCH
18'x8'

Floor Plan—The Stanhope No. 2

b

here because it was a widely selected basic type of bungalow and because kit house construction companies were typically not design innovators but often emphasized the most well-tested national designs in their publications.[52]

Both architectural historians and popular writers have long recognized the popularity of similar modest bungalows. Most analysts, however, have emphasized the exterior architectural style of the common bungalow, especially its picturesque, Arts and Crafts–influenced aesthetic with wide projecting roof overhangs, wide barge boards at the roof's edge, and structural brackets. This popular "Craftsman style" for the bungalow was derived from the English Arts and Crafts movement of William Morris and influenced in America by writers such as Gustav Stickley and architects like Greene and Greene and Bernard Maybeck—all combined in vernacular development by local builder-developers. In many studies, the bungalow's architectural style or aesthetics typically guides analysis and discussion.

This book shifts analysis from aesthetics to domestic function and the deployment of technological improvements within these common houses—of which the bungalow is a prime example. Witold Rybczynski addresses this focus on the importance of the functional and technological aspects of common houses rather than on their external appearances as emphasized by architects and architectural historians: "It is not the absence of wallpaper and ogee trim that made a house 'modern,' it was the presence of central heating and convenient bathrooms, electric irons and washing machines."[53] In order to understand the bungalow's improvements and its popularity for its middle-majority residents, we examine the organization of the bungalow floor plan and the functional arrangement of its domestic technologies.

The architectural floor plan has a long record of use as an analytical tool in material cultural studies for charting the complex rhythms of daily domestic life that are otherwise difficult to observe and analyze. This is especially true when studying classes of people and civilizations that have provided little or insufficient literary record of their domestic activities.[54] We have just used plan analysis to interpret several minimally documented working-class houses in chapter 2. But in the case of the bungalow's Progressive Era plan, however, we have a room arrangement of extraordinary popularity and widespread documentation that allows a careful assessment of the way the era's leading improvements were most commonly set out and arranged. This will allow us to see how this chapter's nine foundational "standards of living" were incorporated into one of the most popular floor plans of the early twentieth century.

The standard bungalow plan was typically organized in a rectangle with its long axis aligned perpendicular to the street (Figure 3.11). The major rooms were then arranged in two parallel rows divided down the middle between public and private realms. The bungalow is usually entered from a generous front porch directly into the living room without a filtering entrance hall or vestibule. The living room is the first of three public rooms linked in a standard sequence from the front to the back of the house—living, dining, and kitchen. Along the opposite side of the house, the bungalow's private zone links bedrooms and bathroom in a typical arrangement placing the bathroom between two bedrooms—all connected by a small hallway off the dining room. This private zone of the bungalow may also include a third bedroom or study near the front or the back of the house. Porches are then added front and rear in an additive or subtractive process to the basic rectangular plan. This volumetric flexibility of the bungalow's porches allows considerable picturesque variety in the look of the common bungalow that would otherwise be a repetitive, rectangular, gable-fronted house (see Figure 5.1).

Although the greatest period of bungalow plan construction was between 1900 and 1930, earlier forms were developed in the late nineteenth century, and the basic floor plan, without the bungalow style, continued to be built until World War II.[55] As described in chapter 2, the early development of the common bungalow plan was the product of local and regional builders' experimentation reaching national uniformity by about 1900 (see Figure 2.11). When placed into a wider historical context of American housing, we can see that the bungalow's development culminated a nineteenth-to-twentieth-century transition in the basic floor plan arrangement for a middle majority of American households. This transformation can be distilled in three analytical diagrams:

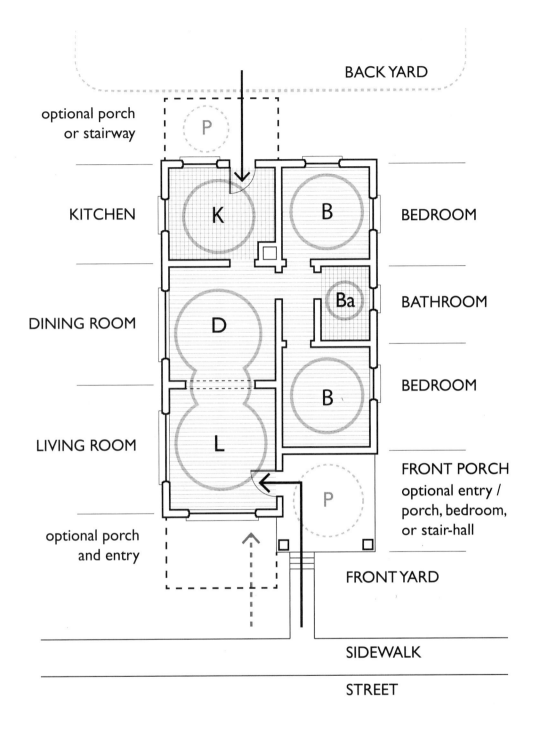

BACK YARD

optional porch
or stairway

P

KITCHEN

K

B

BEDROOM

Ba

BATHROOM

DINING ROOM

D

LIVING ROOM

L

B

BEDROOM

FRONT PORCH
optional entry /
porch, bedroom,
or stair-hall

P

optional porch
and entry

FRONT YARD

SIDEWALK

STREET

Figure 3.11. *Bungalow or Progressive Era plan.* This diagram shows the typical room organization and patterns of spatial usage. It is one of America's most popular house plans before post–World War II suburban development.

(a) kitchen-centered to multicentered domestic space, (b) increased differentiation of rooms by separate usage, and (c) increased acquisition of technologies and utilities (Figures 3.12, 3.13, and 3.14). These three sets of diagrams help to explain the modernization of American domestic life for the middle majority by focusing on the technological and industrialized methods of housing production in the late nineteenth and early twentieth centuries that dramatically transformed both the making of common houses and the domestic conditions and lifestyle of their inhabitants.

Consequently, the historical development of America's common houses can roughly be divided into three overlapping stages reflective of the great divide between a late nineteenth-century, rural, pre-improvement period (1870–1900) and an early twentieth-century, industrialized, improvement period (1920–40). In between these major periods, an overlapping, transitional period (1900–1920) marks the slow, incremental progress in the application of new technological improvements to the households of the middle majority. This domestic transformation also marks the gradual emergence of a new, widening middle-class majority housing culture and a fundamental change from a two-tiered nineteenth-century system of upper classes and traditional working classes.

Kitchen-Centered to Multicentered Living

Most analysts of domestic history have emphasized some variant of kitchen-centered households as representative of typical premodern and working-class domestic conditions worldwide. As the central focus for working-class domestic life, the kitchen area was common to all agrarian-based European immigrant peasant cultures that arrived in America as well as most African, Asian, and Native American domestic traditions. Several fundamental differences consistently separated these vernacular traditions from elite, upper-class domestic conditions, which included the spatial separation of food preparation and eating areas and the separation of sleeping from other activities.

Figure 3.12 depicts the evolution of typical working-class housing as it transitioned from a single-room-centered, kitchen-dominated

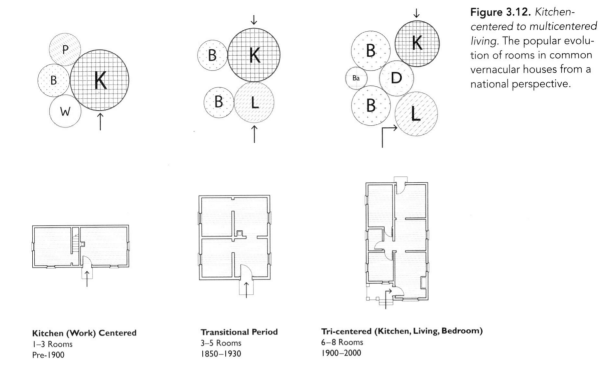

Figure 3.12. *Kitchen-centered to multicentered living.* The popular evolution of rooms in common vernacular houses from a national perspective.

Kitchen (Work) Centered
1–3 Rooms
Pre-1900

Transitional Period
3–5 Rooms
1850–1930

Tri-centered (Kitchen, Living, Bedroom)
6–8 Rooms
1900–2000

lifestyle to households with more space for separate rooms and toward patterns of modern domesticity with multiple centers of domestic functions. In the final diagram, we see the tricentered spatial organization of the modern bungalow's Progressive Era plan with kitchen, living, and bedroom spatial separation.

Multiple Rooms with Separate Functions

In chapter 2, we traced the development and transformation of small working-class residences with multifunctioning rooms, such as the kitchen–workroom into larger houses with multiple rooms and single functions beginning in the early 1900s. This house expansion and room differentiation also mark the arrival of new conceptions of domestic comfort within the home. The gradual expansion of the size of American common houses allowed for greater differentiation of rooms by task and away from multifunctional rooms enforced by the limitations of common houses with two to four rooms (Figure 3.13).

Figure 3.13. *Increasing differentiation in room usage and number of rooms. The popular evolution of room usage in common vernacular houses from a national perspective.*

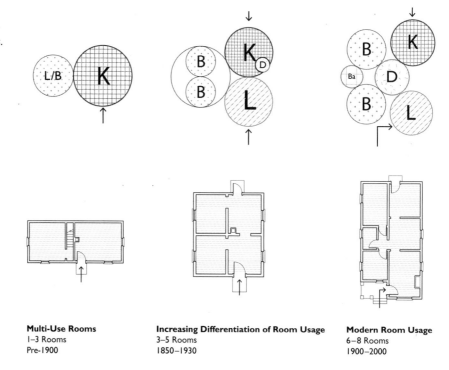

Multi-Use Rooms
1–3 Rooms
Pre-1900

Increasing Differentiation of Room Usage
3–5 Rooms
1850–1930

Modern Room Usage
6–8 Rooms
1900–2000

Technological Improvement

As we have seen in this chapter, the increase in technological improvements and laborsaving devices for the home underlies the domestic progress for the middle majority during the late nineteenth to early twentieth century. Certainly, the clusters of new technological inventions in the kitchen and bathroom accelerated the differentiation of rooms by usage in twentieth-century housing for the middle majority. Figure 3.14 emphasizes the improvements attributable to the instillation of utilities in common houses, although as we have seen, the actual delivery of these improvements to the houses of the middle majority was marked by wide discrepancies in the quality and rates of distribution.

Figures 3.12, 3.13, and 3.14 summarize the way common American houses have developed in the nineteenth and twentieth centuries. The common bungalow typifies this model house with average floor plans of 800–1,500 square feet and a 5-to-6-room-with-bath floor plan arrangement. This unified assemblage of domestic im-

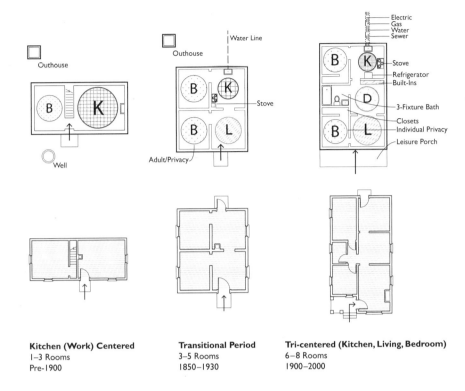

Figure 3.14. *Increasing acquisition of utilities and amenities.* The popular acquisition of utilities in common vernacular houses from a national perspective.

Kitchen (Work) Centered
1–3 Rooms
Pre-1900

Transitional Period
3–5 Rooms
1850–1930

Tri-centered (Kitchen, Living, Bedroom)
6–8 Rooms
1900–2000

provements and utilities, popularly established and nationally rec-ognized by the 1920s, still provides a viable platform of domestic spaces and services even for twenty-first-century users. Only the bungalow's small and separated kitchen has required adjustment to recent twenty-first-century trends to allow for more open patterns of residential living. This limitation, however, is typically remedied by enlarging and opening the kitchen both to the dining room and to the outside of the house.

A Modern Expression of Domestic Life

On the inside, the bungalow's groundbreaking package of tech-nological improvements was typically expressed in two very dif-ferent architectural vocabularies (or decors) reflective of different attitudes toward the appropriate setting for modern domestic life. This contrast is crystallized in the abrupt difference between the bungalow's two most important sets of rooms: living–dining versus kitchen–bath. Essential to the fully developed American bungalow style was a juxtaposition between the traditional historical themes of the living–dining rooms derived from English medieval and Arts and Crafts historicism and the more modern, functional expression of the kitchen–bathroom (Figure 3.15). Although contemporary readers are hardly surprised by this change in room furnishings, for working-class families transitioning from houses where all rooms looked practically the same, this was a stunningly new domestic experience.

Figure 3.15. *Contrasting interior styles in the bungalow.* (a) The bungalow's historically themed Arts and Crafts living room and (b) the bungalow's modern technological expression of the efficient kitchen. Gustav Stickley, *The Craftsman,* October 1905 and September 1905; courtesy of Yale University Library.

The historic traditions of the bungalow were embedded in the living room's iconic fireplace, symbolic of America's pioneering past, and the dining room's paneled wainscoting, beamed ceiling, and small-paned windows, symbolic of a late medieval English and colonial domestic heritage. From a working-class perspective, the reemergence of the bungalow's fireplace within the modern bungalow should be seen as surprising, especially because the toil associated with its upkeep had only been eliminated from many laborers' homes less than half a century previously. Yet the consistency with which the fireplace was reconstructed within the popular, Progressive Era bungalow plan (even within very modest houses at considerable expense) also demonstrates the new strength of the fireplace-hearth tradition for its working-toward-middle-class constituency.[56] In very modest bungalows, these historically symbolic features were, of course, minimalized but were almost always included in some form. For example, in common Milwaukee duplexes, authentic-looking, nonworking fireplaces completed many living room interiors.

Although these historic elements were often applied within common bungalows in modest, simplified vernacular fashion, they followed the same English medieval sources that guided widely publicized elite precedents of the Progressive Era. This type of historical referencing to distant cultural traditions had long been practiced in the parlors and dining rooms of the upper classes, but these practices were almost completely unknown to middle-majority residents whose preindustrial, vernacular traditions did not typically include this type of selective, imported historical referencing in the dominant vocabularies of carpentry and the interior woodwork.[57]

Also new to first-time residents of the bungalow was a new type of spatial relationship uniting its two principal public rooms—an "open plan" connection. This joining of living room and dining room by a wide opening was borrowed from earlier English and Victorian patterns of interconnecting parlors and dining rooms, often through the use of paired sliding doors. In the common bungalow, however, this same type of opening was typically framed by flanking Arts and Crafts–style columns often with attached bookcases (Figure 3.16). This "open plan" relationship of living and dining

Figure 3.16. *The bunga-low's open living room to dining room connection.* A popular application of the open plan within an Arts and Crafts bunga-low interior. (a) *Aladdin Homes, "Built in a Day,"* 1915, 67; courtesy of Yale University Library. (b) Dia-gram of the living room to dining room connection.

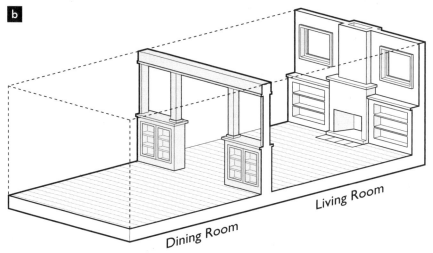

rooms was one of the first examples of a nontraditional spatial rela-tionship in common housing that broke from the standard pattern of linked rectangular rooms with doorway connections.

In contrast to the strong historical associations of the living and dining rooms, the bungalow's kitchen and bath both reflected mod-ern ideas about domestic efficiency, functionality, and hygienic con-siderations (see Figure 3.15b). Even within a small bungalow, this contrast is experienced in the passage between the dining room into the kitchen as English medieval themes abruptly switch to a new modernist vocabulary of efficiency and cleanliness without historical stylistic references. These new ideas were expressed in new types of ceramic floor and wall surfaces for kitchen and bathroom, new metallic kitchen appliances and porcelain bathroom fixtures. New wall and floor surfaces included ceramic tiles for walls and bathroom floors, such as popular white ceramic "subway tiles" and many new types of linoleum products for kitchen floors and entry spaces. Together, these sanitary and aesthetic improvements communicated the clean, hygienic symbolism of a modern kitchen and domestic improvement.

For average families of the middle majority, these contrasts were, of course, never as unified or spectacular as those pictured in publications intended for the middle to upper classes. Nevertheless, even the addition of a single sheet of easily cleaned linoleum on a worn wooden farmhouse kitchen floor or the installation of floor and wall tiles around a newly installed toilet were significant transformative improvements to the overall quality of domestic life for the middle majority. While typical bungalow kitchens and bathrooms may look small and technologically quaint by today's standards, they were actually showplaces for both the latest technological inventions, domestic labor-saving devices, and modern materials, such as ceramic tile, linoleum, and porcelain.

DIFFERENT HOUSES WITH BUNGALOW PLANS

Figure 3.17 shows six different types of houses from around the country that were built between 1900 and 1930. They include different types of single-family and multi-unit houses in a variety of building materials and architectural styles. Far from an exotic assortment of structures, most were either the most popular or among the most popular house types produced in their cities or regions during this period. They are shown together not to demonstrate their significant exterior diversity but to emphasize their underlying internal unity. They all share similar versions of the same plan, what we call the Bungalow or Progressive Era floor plan, in the absence of a single accepted term (see Figure 3.11). Consequently, each house functioned in similar ways to shape and organize the basic routines of domestic life for their middle-majority residents.

Figure 3.17. *Different houses with similar Bungalow/Progressive Era floor plans.* The bungalow's basic one-story floor plan was duplicated in a variety of bungalow and nonbungalow-looking houses, including some of the most popular houses in the early twentieth century. (a) Brick, Arts and Crafts Bungalow style, Bungalow/Progressive Era plan, circa 1915, Shorewood, Wisconsin. (b) Early Bungalow with hipped roof, Bungalow/Progressive Era plan, circa 1905, Portland, Oregon. (c) Three-Deckers, Italianate and Neoclassical style, early twentieth century, Boston, Massachusetts. (d) Duplexes (one-over-one type), Arts and Crafts/Bungalow style heavily remodeled, Bungalow/Progressive Era plan, 1920s, Buffalo, New York. (e) Bungalow vernacular style, Bungalow/Progressive Era plan, early twentieth century, Baton Rouge, Louisiana. (f) Masonry duplexes (one-over-one type) placed back-to-back to create a fourplex, builder vernacular styles, Bungalow/Progressive Era plan, circa 1900, Chicago, Illinois.

In some cases, these houses have wide regional recognition, such as the Three-Decker of Boston and New England and the duplex of Milwaukee and other midwestern cities. But most houses sharing these plans are not so widely recognized, and their numbers have been reduced through destruction and marginalized in comparison to post–World War II suburban residential construction. Consequently, their former densities and significance are, today, often difficult to discern. What may also be surprising about these houses is the amount of multi-unit housing among the primarily single-unit housing we have been examining. As we will soon see, the production of multi-unit housing in the early twentieth century added significantly to the totals of new and improved houses for the middle majority.

This grouping of some of America's most popular houses of the first decades of the twentieth century highlights an important insight not typically emphasized—namely, that there is an underlying unity in the plan and functions of domestic improvement obtained by a middle majority of Americans during the early twentieth century. (Such unity was far less evident in the houses of the upper classes during the same period.) Here we highlight one of the most popular architectural plans expressive of this unity—the Bungalow or Progressive Era plan as it was developed within many types of different looking dwellings. Historians such as Joseph Bigott have also recognized this basic unity of plan by emphasizing the dominance of bungalows and "two-flats" (the midwestern term for a one-over-one duplex), which share a basic, one-floor, bungalow type of plan.[58] Most architectural historians would agree that this unity is concisely expressed in the era's most popular, one-story common bungalow and its basic floor plan. At the beginning of this chapter, we emphasized the Stanhope bungalow not because of its architectural style (or that it was a kit house), but because its widely popular floor plan contained a standardized package of middle-class-defining domestic improvements.[59]

In this chapter, we elevated the bungalow's plan because it was a well-tested, masterful synthesis of the most popular domestic reforms of its era. Although floor plans for common houses are seldom given much attention, the bungalow plan deserves historic recognition and is one of the stars of this book (see Figure 3.11). What made this single-story, five-to-six-room-with-bath arrangement so unusually popular was that it could be reproduced in such a wide variety of the era's most sought-after, different-looking types of houses, as we can observe in Figure 3.17. For example, the "two-flat" types of duplex in Figures 3.17d, 4.8a, and 4.8d, which occurred throughout the nation, have very similar floor plans but various exteriors defined by local and regional traditions combining different architectural styles, entrances and porches, and construction techniques. This standard duplex with a Bungalow plan changes slightly when two duplexes are placed back-to-back as in the Chicago fourplex (with basement apartments) in Figure 3.17f.

In single-family houses, one of the most popular national forms of the bungalow plan are, of course, classic Craftsman Bungalows with picturesque porches and Arts and Crafts details, as we have seen earlier in the Stanhope model (see Figure 3.10). But probably ranking in equal numbers nationally are simple front-gable "vernacular" forms of the bungalow plan (no commonly recognized name) with only minimal Craftsman or any stylistic details (see Figure 1.2b). To further complicate identification, there are bungalow plans hidden behind facades of almost every type of early twentieth-century architectural style. This practice of facade and plan interchangeability is frustrating to architectural historians and disliked by architectural designers, but it is a standard practice of vernacular builders and builder-contractors in all periods since the middle of the nineteenth century.[60]

The New England Three-Deckers may stand out among the other wooden bungalow plan examples in Figure 3.17c, but they share similar plans. In various two-to-four-story forms, in wood and masonry, these stacked bungalow plan apartments constituted a major early twentieth-century building type in urban areas throughout the nation. But this standardization of the bungalow plan did not constrain their contractor-builder-developers from producing substantially different-looking apartments by adapting them to different regions and local markets.

Collectively these similar dwellings established the Bungalow/ Progressive Era plan throughout the country as one of the most popular modern plans of the early twentieth century. In its various forms, I estimate that among the sixteen million total housing units (both single and multi-family) produced between 1900 and 1930, versions of this Bungalow plan probably accounted for 20–30 percent of America's new housing—making it one of the most popular, if not the most popular, floor plan in the United States before the housing expansion of the post–World War II suburban ranch house era.[61]

• • •

In the next chapter we examine a wider range of improved houses with floor plans that differed from this Bungalow or Progressive Era plan, but which also brought the same package of modern domestic improvements to middle-majority Americans.

CHAPTER 4

THE DWELLINGS OF MODERN DOMESTIC REFORM

COTTAGES, DUPLEXES, MULTI-UNITS, AND REMODELED HOUSES

In chapter 3, we highlighted the bungalow's floor plan as the popular summation of modern domestic reform, and we have just seen many different-looking houses that were built using this same basic floor plan. Now we widen this analysis to include other types of houses with different floor plans but all containing the same early twentieth-century housing improvements that brought domestic reform to the middle majority. Today many of these once popular houses remain unobserved in older neighborhoods and working-class industrial districts and towns bypassed and outnumbered by the suburban expansion of the past seventy years. Contributing to their anonymity, these houses were largely developed outside the design channels documented in upper middle-class architectural and domestic reform literature, following instead little-publicized vernacular builder-contractor construction and development practices. Researching these houses has, therefore, required attention to less well-recorded patterns of building and domestic life, considering renters as well as owners; single and multifamily occupancy; subdivision and remodeling transformations; nontraditional patterns of family usage; and varying local, regional, and national expressions of all these factors.

Figure 4.1. *Common housing variety in pre-1940 neighborhoods.* Modern common housing developments are frequently portrayed as endlessly uniform, but the persistence of a subtle variety of forms and different model types is the norm. In pre-1940 housing construction, there is generally more variety of basic house types than in later periods. Late nineteenth- and early twentieth-century housing: (a) Portland, Maine. (b) Homestead, Pennsylvania.

VARIOUS PATHS TO MODERN HOUSING AND DOMESTIC IMPROVEMENT

In the vast majority of America's neighborhoods, a subtle but persistent variety of closely related but not identical housing types is the norm, and this is particularly true in the pre-1940 neighborhoods analyzed for this study (Figure 4.1). This variety of forms is due to many factors, including a tendency on the part of regional builders to develop local variations on national patterns of housing construction. While local-regional variation has been recognized as one of the hallmarks of preindustrial American folk housing, local variety in house types persists in the post–Civil War era of industrial-vernacular housing production. Although largely unobserved, this local-regional variety of housing continues today, despite increasing levels of modern technological and design standardization and large uniform housing projects.[1] To take one well-known example, the "Chicago Bungalow" is actually a unique regional variation on the bungalow's most popularly recognized forms (Figure 4.2). When compared to the Stanhope discussed in chapter 3 (see Figure 3.10), it does not look like a bungalow. After all, it typically includes a large projecting living room bay, a floor plan with an entry that bypasses the living room, full brick-wall construction, a low hip roof, and a raised basement plan—all features uncharacteristic of most bungalows in national comparison.[2] For Craftsman bungalow aficionados, the absence of a large porch

Figure 4.2. *Chicago Bungalow, Chicago, Illinois, circa 1920.* The Chicago region is known for its large number of bungalows of all types. One of the most widely recognized and admired is the Chicago Bungalow, but this is a rare type of bungalow in comparison to more popular forms from throughout the nation. Photograph by Joseph Bigott.

at the front of the house, a front door that does not enter the living room, walls not made of wood, and a high basement are uncharacteristic of the most common types of bungalows. Although widely photographed and admired for the high quality of its Arts and Crafts interiors and the overall quality of its construction, the Chicago Bungalow is geographically and statistically a minor bungalow in comparison to America's typical wooden bungalows, even within its "Chicagoland" region.

To cite a similar example of unanticipated vernacular housing diversity, Portland, Oregon, has a well-deserved reputation for dense wooden bungalow neighborhoods. Various estimates of its 1900–1930 bungalow house production range between 30 and 40 percent of all single-family dwellings—perhaps the highest percentages for a major American city.[3] Therefore, as I assessed its bungalows over the past ten years (through conducting surveys, courses, and neighborhood tours), I expected to encounter America's most popular types of common bungalows. While these standard bungalows such as the Stanhope do exist in great numbers, surprisingly, Portland's most popular bungalow is what is called a "Colonial Bungalow" in builders' catalogs of the era (Figure 4.3).[4] (There is no commonly accepted name.) When compared to Portland's more recognizable bungalows (e.g., the Stanhope type), the Colonial Bungalow does not seem to be a proper bungalow because it is typically symmetrical (not picturesque) with a small, neoclassical-style, Colonial Revival front porch. However, most of its architectural vocabulary, both inside and outside, is solidly expressive of the bungalow Arts and Crafts style and, therefore, properly associated with the major era of bungalow construction. What makes this house type so difficult to interpret is its maintenance of bungalow characteristics while simultaneously integrating new aesthetic features from an increasingly popular Colonial Revival vocabulary/style of the 1910s and 1920s. Furthermore, many Colonial Bungalows were built during the 1920s, a period of stylistic transition in common house construction from Bungalow to traditional, "Period Revival," historical styles such as Colonial Revival. The 1920s were also Portland's greatest period of single-family housing construction until the 1950s.

Why this variation on the bungalow became the most popular in a city thick with standard bungalows is a complex story that

Figure 4.3. *Colonial Bungalow.* Modified bungalow plan, circa 1925, Portland, Oregon. Portland has some of the highest concentrations of bungalow houses of any large city in America. The most popular form of the city's bungalows is a stylistic hybrid called a Colonial Bungalow in builders' catalogs. It was constructed in large numbers in the 1920s, and its exterior style combines Arts and Crafts and American Colonial Revival architectural features. Such stylistic hybridization is the product of regional speculative builders following local client preferences.

touches on the dynamics of speculator-builder and anticipated-resident design development in popular culture.[5] At its core, however, we should understand that the Colonial Bungalow was the house most desired by early twentieth-century Portland residents and consequently the house most often built by Portland's speculative builders.[6]

The local prominence of Portland's hybrid Colonial Bungalow and the limited geographic region of the Chicago Bungalow are surprising to residents of both cities who typically do not consider the demographics of housing types in local and national comparison. Rather than unique occurrences, similar patterns of vernacular unity and diversity are a consistent, although difficult-to-detect, characteristic of common housing in all eras and regions, and in urban and rural housing environments nationwide. Such recognition, however, requires both close analysis of local housing types and broad comparisons to national trends. Through analyses at both scales, we can recognize both the underlying unity and unexpected diversity in the many types of America's most common houses—especially in the types of housing we will be presenting next.

To approach this complex issue of similarity and variety, we organize America's common dwellings into three categories: (1) single-family houses, both owned and rented; (2) multifamily housing, from common duplexes to larger apartments; and (3) remodeled houses, including all forms of previously existing housing improved and modernized during the early twentieth century.

Single-Family Houses

In the early twentieth century, many members of the middle majority lived in single-family houses, although they often rented their dwellings. Some of these homes were small, modified versions of middle-to-upper-class houses. Others were local-regional vernacular structures that combined local traditions with borrowed architectural styles to produce local hybrid building types. Most of them contained at least some of the domestic improvements found in larger middle-to-upper-class houses that signaled the attainment of middle-class domestic standards.

Small Versions of Popular Houses

For most types of popular middle-class houses, there were smaller, locally produced, less expensive models, usually containing many of the same domestic improvements in smaller or partially completed versions. Some of the most numerous examples of scaled-down houses for the middle majority are smaller versions of the common bungalow. In the first decades of the twentieth century, when middle-class bungalow houses ranged from 800 to 1,400 square feet, these smaller versions of the bungalow might range from 500 to 800 square feet. For those familiar with the bungalow style, these houses may not look like classic, Arts and Crafts–inspired bungalows, yet they functioned like modern bungalows by providing their working-class residents with a basic package of modern domestic improvements. For example, Figure 4.4 shows three of Portland, Oregon's most popular types of small, working-class bungalows from the Westmoreland neighborhood. Constructed between 1910 and 1925, many were originally speculative rental units built for workers from the nearby Southern Pacific rail yards. With their sparse bungalow-Craftsman architectural details inside and out, their small plans were slightly larger, more varied versions of the working-class Four-Box (four-room) plan that included a living room, kitchen, two bedrooms, and a small bathroom. In most cases, these houses received rear additions for expanded kitchen areas and bedrooms. Reflecting some of the amenities of their Arts and Crafts era, many might contain a small fireplace with decorative tile, a bedroom closet, and perhaps a built-in kitchen breakfast nook or an art-glass window at the entrance way.[7]

These condensed bungalows, typically located in early twentieth-century working-class neighborhoods, do not attract the attention of tourists or admirers, like their Arts and Crafts–inspired, Craftsman bungalow neighbors, but they account for approximately one-sixth of the city's total bungalows.[8] Because of their small size and modest construction, they are frequent candidates for extensive remodeling and expansion, or demolition, so that their previous densities are difficult to discern.[9] In every city and region surveyed, there are consistently smaller unadorned versions of the most popular types

Figure 4.4. *Small types of the popular bungalow.* Similar to other cities where bungalows are found in high concentrations, Portland, Oregon, has several distinct types of small, working-class bungalows. They are modest, stripped-down versions of popular Arts and Crafts–styled bungalows with floor plans that follow small vernacular house plans. Three common types are (a) small version of a Colonial Bungalow with a five-room-with-bath plan; (b) Four-Box plan with bath; (c) Early Bungalow with a five-room-and-bath plan.

of middle-majority houses. For example, in the small towns of rural southern Maine, the most popular early twentieth-century dwelling was a one-and-one-half-to-two-story, Side-Hall plan house in classical styles and often built in a pattern of connected farm buildings with an attached stable (Figure 4.5). In many towns almost 50 percent of new, late nineteenth- and early twentieth-century dwellings were built in this pattern if we include many smaller, unadorned one-story versions of the same house, often constructed for "mechanics" and laborers for the small-town industries of their rural region. Throughout the country, smaller, modest versions of the most popular forms of housing, with both similar and different floor plans, were, and still are, produced in substantial numbers.

Figure 4.5. *Small versions of popular houses.* In the towns of late nineteenth- and early twentieth-century northern New England, a classically styled Side-Hall house built in the connected-farm building arrangement was a dominant popular selection. The same house form was often constructed at two different scales: one larger type for a merchant middle class and a smaller version for the working classes. (a) Two-story Side-Hall house with connecting buildings and stable, circa 1900, Portland, Maine. (b) One-and-one-half-story Side-Hall house with connecting buildings, circa 1910, Portland, Maine.

Local and Regional Vernacular Houses

In contrast to new construction that drew on national trends and referenced architect-designed buildings, housing contractors also relied on local and regional vernacular prototypes, often communicated in builders' catalogs and manuals. These types of dwellings were not smaller versions of standard middle- and upper-class housing but were earlier and evolving vernacular houses that were often built in simplified, stripped-down versions of the dominant architectural styles but following traditional house plans. These houses include the nine dominant pre-1900 vernacular houses analyzed in chapter 2, such as the popular I-House, Side-Gable, and Side-Hall houses (see Figures 2.3, 2.4, and 2.7). Other early twentieth-century vernacular houses combined vernacular housing traditions with new plans and industrialized construction systems, such as the Four-Box Pyramid, Parlor-Bypass, and Early Bungalow plans (see Figures 2.8, 2.9, and 2.11). For working-class constituencies, these hybrid industrial-vernacular houses were often built with only a partial or minimal package of state-of-the-art improvements as those found in fully improved bungalow plan houses typically containing a three-fixture bathroom.[10]

These types of earlier vernacular houses are readily evidenced in a review of early twentieth-century builders' publications. Toward the end of many catalogs, one can usually find an odd assortment of dwellings—often best sellers from earlier periods that "went out of style" in architectural publications and catalogs of new houses but were still quietly in demand. Often these houses can be recognized because they conspicuously lack a bathroom, most closets, and almost all architectural detail. (Some catalogs, however, would upgrade the presentation of these older houses and include improvements such as bathrooms.) Figure 4.6 shows a house from a 1908 Radford Architectural Company catalog that shows a type of dwelling that was popular in the 1880s and 1890s but was still constructed into the 1920s.

When newly constructed, these older-looking houses frequently received the spatial and mechanical upgrades that were not included in earlier versions of the same house. Therefore, a house that was built before 1900 without a bathroom would typically have received one when built anew in the 1920s. This type of common house improvement is difficult to identify from field study or documentation alone and adds complexity to the story of silently improved modest housing. These catalogs, however, record only the tip of the iceberg of small, partially improved early twentieth-century houses that were built nationally and designed and built by local contractors following traditional patterns of construction without formal house plans or the assistance of architectural literature.

These examples make clear that a portion of new houses in any period or locale consist of improved versions of older traditional house types. Because housing literature typically focuses on new and recent styles and plans, we frequently do not receive a complete picture of all houses in national or regional surveys. This practice of using older successful house styles or plans in later periods is far more common than popularly realized or recorded and continues, often unrecognized, especially

Figure 4.6. *Improved versions of older popular houses.* Older house types, originally built without modern facilities such as bathrooms and electricity, were often built in a later period with modern conveniences and are frequently pictured in manufacturers' and builders' catalogs. *Radford's Artistic Bungalows,* No. 5068, Radford Architectural Co., 1908, 212. Courtesy of Yale University Library.

Figure 4.7. *Houses from different periods, built at the same time.* Both sets of three houses were constructed, side by side, in 1904, by the Portland, Oregon, firm of Stokes and Zeller. (a) Three Porch-Gable, Arts and Crafts–style houses with Four-Square, first-floor plans. (b) Three Queen Anne–style houses with Parlor-Bypass plans. Although the floor plans and architectural styles were from different periods, both sets of houses contained the same utilities and technological improvements.

in working-class housing neighborhoods. In this respect, popular builders' catalogs differ from elite architectural and mainstream literature that typically emphasize the newest, latest house models. These catalogs more properly represent collections of the most popular houses during twenty-to-thirty-year periods. After construction, these new houses with older designs are easily mistaken for houses from earlier eras, and in any case, are seldom recognized or documented in the standard building literature.[11]

A vivid example of this type of retro construction is demonstrated in the comparison of two side-by-side 1903 building projects in the Buckman neighborhood of Portland, Oregon (Figure 4.7). Here the architect-builder firm of Stokes and Zeller constructed six houses along Ash Street in two completely different styles. Three houses displayed a new Arts and Crafts and Shingle-Style, Porch-Gable form (no standard name) with a first floor arranged in a new Four-Square plan. Built simultaneously next door were three houses in a late nineteenth-century version of the Queen Anne cottage style with an older, Parlor-Bypass floor plan. Although the Queen Anne cottages reproduce an earlier style and plan, they were built with spatial and mechanical upgrades that were not included in earlier versions of the same house. With their six-room plans, three-fixture bathrooms, and modern utilities, the older-looking houses offered their residents the same domestic comforts as their more up-to-date, Porch-Gable neighbors.

Multifamily Housing

Multi-unit or multifamily housing is a category of dwellings often minimized in domestic reform studies focusing on single-family, owner-occupied residential environments. There is, of course, an extensive scholarship on the many forms of multi-unit housing, such as tenements, apartments, condominiums, and especially public housing, but this literature is not well integrated into the leading studies of housing reform emphasizing single-family dwellings.

Multi-unit housing provided dwellings for more than one-third of middle-majority households during the forty-year period of this study, 1900–1940. During the 1920s, the decade with more housing construction than any two previous decades, more than 40 percent of new dwellings were within multi-unit structures. In many metropolitan regions, multi-unit housing accounted for almost half the new housing units produced between 1900 and 1930. Even in Los Angeles, a city known for its developments of single-family houses, multifamily housing represented almost half the housing units built between 1925 and 1930.[12] As historian Matthew Lasner notes, the 1920s can be considered "the apartment decade."[13] Furthermore, although early twentieth-century single-family housing was built in both improved and unimproved versions, almost all multi-housing units built after 1900 contained the complete package of modern domestic improvements outlined in chapter 3. Thanks to these facilities, pre–World War II apartment buildings were widely perceived as examples of modern contemporary housing.

In contrast to large apartment buildings, smaller multifamily rental structures have not received a great deal of study. Indeed, such structures were assiduously ignored by New Deal housing experts, who supported single-family housing initiatives and whose policies helped ensure that single-family housing dominated the postwar housing boom. Yet, small, nontenement, multifamily rental structures played a pivotal role in the introduction of middle-class housing standards and domestic conveniences for a middle majority. Although statistics are difficult to establish because of short-term rental occupancy, I estimate that before 1940, almost half of working-class families first experienced modern, middle-class domestic improvements in modest multifamily rental units, such as duplexes and small, multi-unit apartments, rather than in an owned, detached, single-family house.[14] For example, before moving in 1954 to a new four-room Cape Cod type of house in Levittown, Long Island, Eddie and Etta Jacobs and their two daughters had lived in an attached multi-unit apartment house in the Brownsville section of Brooklyn. (Similar to many of their neighbors, the Jacobs had left unimproved smaller apartments in either Brooklyn or Manhattan before 1940.) Although slightly smaller and not as stylish as their new Levittown home, their four-room, first-floor apartment in a mid-1920s brick fourplex contained most of the same modern conveniences, utilities, and room usages. In their move to iconic Levittown, the Jacobs became owners of a new single-family, detached house and gained the advantages of modern suburban living, but they did not fundamentally add to or change their basic package of modern domestic improvements.

Multi-unit housing brought improved domestic conditions to the middle majority in a range of common apartment houses repeated across the country. Three groups define the dominant arrangement of housing units: two-unit duplexes in many variations, small, multi-unit houses with three to eight units, and larger multi-unit apartments with eight or more units.

The Duplex: Two-Family Housing

The unassuming American duplex has been called by several names—two-flat, flat, up-and-down, side-by-side, and double house—although generally, since the late nineteenth century, duplex is the most common. Figure 4.8 shows many of the most popular forms of the duplex, some of which look like typical stand-alone dwellings. Often designed to disguise their multifamily character, these duplexes have made it more difficult to appreciate the role of the two-family house in providing modern domestic facilities for large numbers of the middle majority.

Duplexes can be organized into several basic unit-types (Figure 4.9). From the documentation of this study, the most popular national arrangement of the duplex's apartment units is the "one-over-one" (or "two-flat") (Figure 4.9a). The second most popular form is the side-by-side—a type of duplex that can be created by joining any standard house type in a side-by-side arrangement (Figure 4.9b), as we have seen in the popular Shotgun duplex (see Figure 2.6b). The side-by-side type has been built since the colonial period nationwide and continues to be constructed today in working-class neighborhoods. In the Philadelphia region and the small towns of central Pennsylvania in the late nineteenth and early twentieth centuries, high percentages of side-by-side duplexes line the principal streets in structures that most observers may mistake for single-family housing except for the central side-by-side front doors.

Other less popular versions of the duplex are the "front-and-back" arrangement (Figure 4.9c) and the first-floor-above-basement type (Figure 4.9d), such as Milwaukee's and Chicago's popular "Polish Flat" (see Figure 1.17). Although its two units are not connected, the detached, front-house and back-house (or alley house) arrangement is a popular national solution for locating two detached units on the same site (Figure 4.9e).[15] The categories

Figure 4.8. *Duplexes.* The two-family house was a silent workhorse of middle-majority household improvement. Situated between single-family, owner-occupied houses and larger multi-unit housing, rental units in duplexes played a major role in the introduction of twentieth-century housing improvements to the middle majority. (a) One-over-one duplexes (two-flats) (no standard stylistic name), Bungalow/Progressive Era plan, circa 1910, Milwaukee, Wisconsin. (b) Side-by-side shotgun duplex, three-room Shotgun plan, early twentieth century, Macon, Georgia. (c) Polish Flat, first-floor-over-basement duplex (Raised Workers' Cottage), remodeled exterior, Workers' Cottage plan, early twentieth century, Milwaukee, Wisconsin. (d) One-over-one duplex, Arts and Crafts style, Bungalow/Progressive Era plan, circa 1910, Milwaukee, Wisconsin. (e) Side-by-side, working-class duplex, four-room plan with bath, circa 1920, Portland, Oregon. (f) Side-by-side duplex, row house type with kitchen addition, eclectic styles, circa 1915, Philadelphia, Pennsylvania.

and total number of duplexes can be extended significantly by adding single-family houses that have been subdivided into two units. The number of such conversions is extensive but difficult to estimate nationally and will be further addressed in the next section on remodeling.

Examples of America's most popular type of the early twentieth-century duplex, the two-flat, one-over-one duplex apartment, can be found in significant numbers in midwestern cities such as Milwaukee, Detroit, Cleveland, Chicago, and St. Louis, in eastern cities such as Boston and New York, and in hundreds of other metropolitan regions around the country. Milwaukee probably has the highest percentage of "two-flat" duplexes of any major city in the nation; there, despite significant removals, it is still the most popular house in the city's history (see Figure 4.8a). Prior to 1940, duplexes comprised over one-quarter of the city's total housing units.[16] Although they appear more uniform today under aluminum siding and similar patterns of exterior remodeling, three distinct subtypes of the duplex (large, medium, and small) provided residents with a range of housing choices, helping to explain its extraordinary popularity during nearly a half-century of building. Most of Milwaukee's duplexes were of a medium size, with two identical up-and-down flats whose unit entries were grouped to one side with either two doors or one door leading to units top and bottom. A larger version of the duplex typically separated the two front doors left and right with the upstairs apartment entry leading to a stairway. These larger, separate-door duplexes often had slightly different first- and second-floor plans reflecting more customization of the building plan. A third type of the duplex is typically unrecognizable from the street, but it is generally smaller in overall

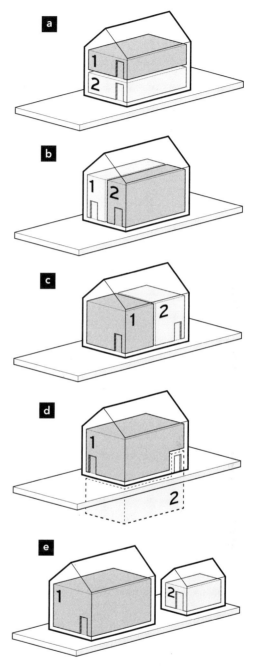

Figure 4.9. *Different types of duplexes.* The diagram shows the most popular arrangements of units in the duplex. (a) One-over-one duplex (two-flat). (b) Side-by-side duplex. (c) Front-and-back duplex. (d) Basement-unit duplex. (e) Detached unit (alley house).

dimension. It is different from most duplexes because the second-floor unit does not have a front entry, only a back entry leading to the kitchen. Here the second-floor apartment was clearly designed as a secondary rental unit, usually for the larger downstairs owner's apartment. Several long-term residents have told me that this type of duplex was an ideal solution for a live-in son or daughter.

Although the duplexes' two units are primarily rental apartments today, neighborhood surveys make clear that Milwaukee's duplexes were more typically owner-occupied in the early twentieth century, with the second upstairs unit commonly providing a source of rental income. Such duplexes stand on a middle ground between homeowner and rental occupancy, a liminal space that has helped disguise their importance in the American architectural and cultural landscape.[17] (Today, this pattern of owner occupancy has dramatically reversed so that many more duplexes have become two-family rental units with an absentee owner. Another reversal is that when owners are occupants, their apartments are more frequently second-floor units.)

As a building type long developed in many cultures, the American up-and-down duplex does not have a single regional or ethnic hearth, much less an original architect or inventor. As we have seen with other popular late nineteenth-century vernacular examples, its early twentieth-century popular forms appear to have been developed simultaneously in many locations over a quarter century period from the 1870s to 1900. Although this house type was typically associated with urban or dense suburban environments, the modest duplex also achieved late nineteenth- and early twentieth-century popularity in small-town America where versions were constructed in middle- and working-class neighborhoods and especially along Main Street, often mixed with commercial establishments on the ground floor.[18] In midwestern cities such as Milwaukee, duplexes were commonly built of brick for neighborhood stores or corner taverns. Milwaukee's well-known taverns were frequently large, well-crafted substantial structures that incorporated several apartments, often including a first-floor rear apartment for the tavern owner (Figure 4.10).

Within America's residential neighborhoods, duplexes of all types

Figure 4.10. *Living over the store.* Before the 1930s, the one-over-one duplex that combined commercial use on the ground floor and residential units above was extremely popular in both large cities and small towns throughout America. Milwaukee, Wisconsin, tavern, Arts and Crafts commercial style, circa 1910, with residential units above and behind the tavern.

both stand out from and integrate themselves within their housing context. In some cases, duplexes were literally designed to blend into neighborhoods of single-family, detached houses by disguising their scale and two-family architectural features. For example, in the Atwater School neighborhood area of Shorewood, Wisconsin, more than twenty duplexes were designed so as not to be obviously recognizable as duplexes. (These houses differ from standard Milwaukee area duplexes that do not disguise their twin identity, often with two prominent front doors and especially identical and aligned windows on the first and second floors.) Figure 4.11 shows two of these duplexes where, except for double mailboxes and street numbers, these houses would be mistaken by most observers for substantial single-family residences. These disguised multi-unit houses built on a national scale were clearly designed by their builders to address the single-family detached housing aspirations of their residents in dwellings with lower prices and greater densities.

Another standard approach to disguising the duplex was to construct two-family housing on corner lots or simply to arrange the entrances so that the two doorways could not be seen together, thus disguising the most identifiable characteristic of the

Figure 4.11. *Disguised duplexes.* Duplexes and small, multi-unit houses were frequently built in suburban residential neighborhoods before their construction was prohibited by post-1930 zoning laws. Their numbers are often difficult to assess because many were designed to look like single-family houses within single-family residential neighborhoods, as were these two duplexes in Shorewood, Wisconsin. (a) English/German country house style, circa 1920. (b) Brick gable, Dutch Colonial style with side entry, circa 1925.

two-family residence. In towns and cities throughout the country, many residents are unaware of large numbers of duplexes that have been successfully designed to fit into the dominant pattern of single-family housing. Furthering its acceptance in single-family neighborhoods, the basic duplex and other small, multi-unit apartments of the early twentieth century were far more socially acceptable middle-class residential alternatives than they are today. As a result, there was a wider range of middle-class "starter home" options in these neighborhoods than generally exist today. After World War II, duplexes and other multi-unit housing arrangements were increasingly prohibited by single-family zoning restrictions in suburban residential environments. Consequently, middle-class duplexes and small, multi-unit apartments are still most plentiful today in the inner-ring suburban neighborhoods of cities that expanded during the early twentieth century.[19]

Without much recognition from housing reformers, the duplex has played a key role in helping to introduce domestic improvements to a rising working class across the country. In this role, it was a workhorse of modern domestic reform in the Progressive Era, ranking alongside the widely acknowledged common bungalow as the provider and symbol of modern improved housing. Significantly, the common duplex in its most popular bungalow floor plan was usually constructed with the domestic improvements we have emphasized in chapter 3. Until the Depression curtailed its production, the standard duplex was built in record numbers nationally, averaging almost 20 percent of all housing units during the 1920s. Surprisingly, the percentages of new single-family houses actually decreased during the 1920s from nearly 60 percent to 40 percent. Were it not for the Depression and the resultant New Deal housing policies favoring single-family houses, the duplex and other multi-unit rental apartments, totaling nearly 60 percent of dwelling units during the 1920s, were on track to rival new owner-occupied, single-family houses as a distinct variation on the American dream. Although the percentages of new multi-family houses like the duplex declined rapidly after 1930, duplexes have continued to be built and still account for almost .05 percent of the total housing unit production in most periods up to the present.[20]

Midsized, Multifamily Apartments (Three to Six Units)

Three-to-six-unit apartment houses are housing hybrids that straddle the line between popular two-unit duplexes and larger, multi-unit apartment houses (Figure 4.12). Although occurring nationally, they are rarely the subject of housing analysis. There is one

Figure 4.12. *Multi-unit houses, three to six units.* Situated between duplexes and larger, more conspicuous apartment houses, these were built in large numbers during the 1920s within inner-ring, industrial suburbs of metropolitan areas throughout the country. (a) Fourplex, Craftsman-Bungalow style, Bungalow/Progressive Era plan adapted to side-by-side arrangement, 1920s, Portland, Oregon. (b) Three-Decker, eclectic styles, Bungalow/Progressive Era plan, circa 1910, New Bedford, Massachusetts. (c) Brick fourplexes, front-and-back unit arrangement with two basement apartments, late 1890s, Chicago, Illinois. (d) Threeplex, Arts and Crafts details, circa 1920, Los Angeles, California.

significant exception, however—Boston and New England's iconic Three-Decker. It is urban New England's popular early twentieth-century multi-unit, working-class house and a well-known example of the type of improved housing emphasized in this book. As analyzed by Kingston Heath, the Three-Decker typically consists of three identical plans stacked one on top of the other with stairways and porches, front and back.[21] For example, Figure 4.13 shows a typical Three-Decker from New Bedford, Massachusetts. Averaging approximately 1,000 to 1,200 square feet per unit, these were large, working-to-middle-class apartments that facilitated various patterns of room usage for multigenerational immigrant and extended families, including the accommodation of boarders in the front rooms. As we have seen at the end of chapter 3, the Three-Decker's typical floor plan is an expanded type of Progressive Era or Bungalow plan with two parallel rows of rooms; living–dining–kitchen on one side and bedrooms on the other. More importantly, in its most popular forms after the mid-1890s, it contained all the major housing standards addressed in this study. In other words, the Three-Decker is a shining example of a fully equipped, modern, early twentieth-century house for the middle majority.

Figure 4.13. *Three-Decker apartment, New Bedford, Massachusetts, 1912.* (a) Street view. (b) Typical floor plan. The Three-Decker typically stacks three identical apartments with Bungalow/Progressive Era floor plans, one on top of the other, with porches and stairways front and back. In many of New England's cities and towns, the Three-Decker competes with the usually more popular duplex as the most numerous multi-unit residence. Photograph by Kingston Heath from *The Patina of Place.*

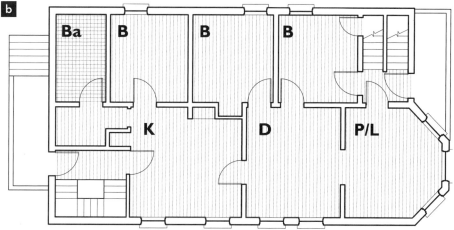

Given the recognized influence of New England's architecture throughout the United States, one might expect the popular Three-Decker to have been exported in great numbers to other parts of the country. They were not. In fact, Three-Deckers, in their three-story, all-wooden form with porches front and back, are not found in significant concentrations outside New England. What this confirms is that local forms of vernacular housing strongly reflect regional building cultures, often rejecting nationalizing influences toward design homogeneity.[22] This surprising dominance of regional vernacular house types is a consistent but difficult-to-document characteristic of local housing throughout the country.[23]

In two-to-three-story multi-unit housing, four-to-six-unit apartments are more popular than three- and five-unit arrangements throughout the country (except in New England). This is probably because the four- and six-unit combinations can be symmetrically subdivided and balanced into repetitive arrangements. For example, Figure 4.14 shows a popular type of 1920s Portland, Oregon, apartment with four separate doors for four units. (The two center doors lead to the upstairs apartments, left and right. The outer doors lead to first-floor apartments, left and right.) Despite a variety of arrangements, many related apartment buildings are unified by a type of side-by-side bungalow floor plan and similar technological and spatial amenities. Adding to the complexity of these midsized, multi-unit apartments are a wide variety of row house and courtyard apartments, from simple bungalow courts to larger courtyard apartments (many with irregular massing and different unit sizes) that greatly increase the standard categories and amounts of small-apartment, multi-family housing.[24]

Large, Multi-Unit Apartments

An extensive literature describes the growth and development of larger, multi-unit urban apartments of more than twenty units for upper and upper middle classes during the late nineteenth and the early twentieth century.[25] Less well documented is a parallel story of more modest, early twentieth-century apartment houses for the middle majority. These apartments of approximately six-to-twenty

Figure 4.14. *Four-unit apartment.* A popular example from Portland, Oregon, aligns its four-unit doors in a row. Fourplex, Arts and Crafts/Bungalow style, Bungalow/Progressive Era floor plan adapted to a side-by-side plan arrangement, circa 1925.

units began to be constructed in the late 1800s and the early 1900s, often accompanying the development of streetcar lines and inner-ring suburban communities on the edge of major metropolitan centers and larger towns (Figure 4.15). Along with the other types of multi-unit housing we have just reviewed, these apartments served a new type of expanding white-collar, urban clientele of starter families and new single occupants, especially women, in the expanding urban districts of America.[26]

Although there are many different plan arrangements, often dictated by lot size and street entry conditions, the two- and three-story rectangular block apartment building with a central corridor and stairways front and back was ubiquitous during the 1920s. This simple rectangular plan (sometimes called a double-loaded corridor plan) allowed various-sized apartment units (one- and two-bedroom units, and studio apartments) to be strung along either side of a central hallway with a stairway at either end. For example, Figure 4.16 shows a three-story, center-corridor apartment house from Shorewood, Wisconsin, commonly built between 1910 and 1930. This mid-1920s apartment house was a compact version of the center-hall plan with four units per floor for a total of twelve

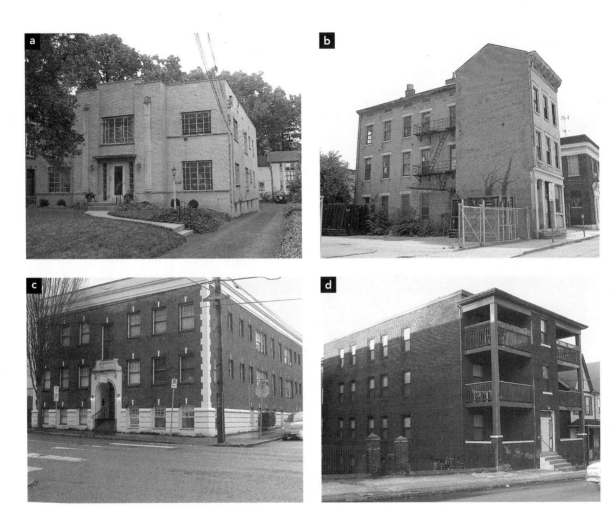

Figure 4.15. *Large, multi-unit apartment houses.* Like all multi-unit housing, their numbers rose during the 1920s and fell during the Great Depression. (a) Center-corridor plan, early modern, Art Deco style, late 1930s, Cincinnati, Ohio. (b) Center core-and-ell unit plan, late Italianate and Classical commercial style, late 1890s, Cincinnati, Ohio. (c) Center-corridor unit plan, Beaux-Arts Classical style, Portland, Oregon. (d) Sixplex with basement units, stairways front and back, (porches and facade remodeled), early twentieth century, Homestead, Pennsylvania.

units plus two small basement apartments. The basic apartment floor plan aligned two rows of rooms along the central hall with major (sunlit) rooms along the exterior walls and windowless minor rooms (baths, closets, and passageways) along the inner corridor wall. (This building, unlike many others, had a small light-well to illuminate each bathroom.) Although built without a parking garage (six garages were added later), many similar 1920s urban apartments were built with detached garages, often to shelter a first automobile for their new middle-class residents. A popular pattern was to string a line of attached garages across the apartment's back/rear or side lot line.

This popular type of apartment for 1920s middle-class housing was built in a dense cluster of differently styled but similarly arranged apartment houses along Oakland Avenue, a major suburban artery leading to downtown Milwaukee. Similarly scaled buildings with eight to thirty units were built nationally in urban areas throughout the country.[27] (In cities with large, deep blocks, such as Salt Lake City, this type of apartment produced longer versions of the central-corridor plan.) Based on the frequency of this type of residence encountered in fieldwork for this book, I estimate that apartment buildings like the ones in Figure 4.15 played a significant role in the great surge in multi-unit dwellings between 1925 and 1930—perhaps accounting for as much as 25 percent of the 1.5 million, more than three-unit apartment buildings constructed during this period.[28]

The growth in these types of multi-unit residences can be attributed to a dramatic increase in new types of urban employment for office employees, especially for single female clerical workers. As summarized by Roger Roper, "It was only after the turn of the century that multi-story 'urban' apartment buildings were constructed in Salt Lake City, Utah. Women looking for independent housing before then would have had far fewer options. Apartments quickly replaced boardinghouses and hotels as the most common and popular form of multi-unit housing" (Figure 4.17).[29]

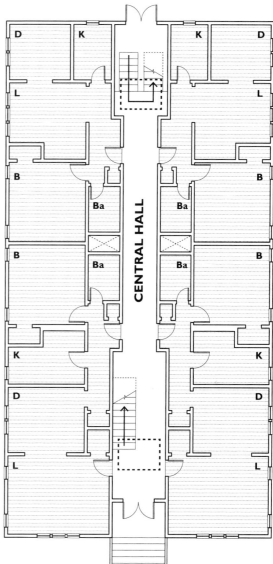

Figure 4.16. *Center-corridor apartment house plan.* Throughout America during the 1920s, the center-corridor housing block was an extremely popular arrangement for organizing various-sized apartments in large apartment blocks. The drawing shows a center-corridor plan with four apartments on each of its three floors. Second-floor plan, circa 1925, Shorewood, Wisconsin.

Figure 4.17. *Urban living for a new middle class.* Apartments served an expanding population of office and clerical workers. Central corridor plan, Classical and Arts and Crafts style, 1920s, Salt Lake City, Utah. Photograph by Roger Roper.

Less well-documented forms of large multi-unit dwellings are minimal rooming and lodging houses and inexpensive residential hotels that served a wide range of clients but are best known for accommodating single, low-income residents. In *Living Downtown*, Paul Groth has carefully analyzed the range and unexpected densities of these types of accommodations in San Francisco and throughout the nation. For example, in 1910, San Francisco's hotel rooms of all types totaled sixty-five thousand, or one hotel room for every ten people in the population—an extraordinary total of the city's housing.[30] Yet during the nineteenth and early twentieth century, small urban hotels, rooming houses, and boardinghouses (or private multi-unit housing) were a ubiquitous component of housing throughout America. In medium and small towns, these residential hotels were typically converted and subdivided previous larger houses. Figure 4.18 shows a converted rooming or boardinghouse from the eastside of Portland, Oregon, where second-story windows located the single rooms that sat atop a commercial establish-

Figure 4.18. *Lodging or boardinghouse.* Early twentieth-century, Buckman neighborhood, 1874, Portland, Oregon. Boardinghouses were often converted and subdivided larger houses. The arrangement of first-floor commercial usage and second-floor small rental rooms was also common. In this photograph, note the row of apartment unit windows on the second floor. The structure was moved to its current location in 1909.

ment. This structure was moved to its present location from an area of East Portland that once contained hundreds of residential hotels and rooming houses in a two-hundred-block waterfront area near the Willamette River now completely industrialized without residential buildings.[31]

Remodeled Houses

Between 1900 and 1940, the remodeling of existing houses was a major source of domestic reform for the middle majority, especially for the 50 percent of those with the lowest incomes. Yet as analyzed in chapter 1, house remodeling has been insufficiently analyzed in the literature of housing reform (Figure 4.19). As a result, its impact, especially on common/vernacular house improvement, is not well known. Several factors help to explain this lack of recognition by journalists, academics, and housing authorities, principally involving an almost exclusive concentration on new house construction for the middle to upper classes.[32]

Remodeling existing common housing took many forms on a continuum from maintenance and repair to full-scale additions and even wholesale replacement. One of the most common forms of remodeling—and one widely criticized at the time—was the

Figure 4.19. *Difficult-to-document, continually remodeled and expanded houses.* Various working-class houses, Milwaukee, Wisconsin. When these houses were built in the early 1900s, the only modern improvements were piped water, kitchen stoves, and possibly electricity for lights.

practice of subdividing existing housing into multiple units, typically the dividing of existing single-family housing into two, or more, residences. These house-to-apartment conversions are difficult to identify in local and national estimates because they combine different types of housing classifications, such as owners and renters and original and converted building usage. For example, Figure 4.20 shows a two-story, side-hall house built in 1929 for my grandparents Anthony and Valerie Hubka in Perth Amboy, New Jersey. Although built as a two-story, single-family house at the beginning of the Depression, it was soon converted into a duplex, which it remains today. The remodeling conversion involved the construction of a basement bathroom for the first-floor apartment (where my grandparents and my father lived) and reconstructing the front entranceway by sealing off the second-floor apartment stairway from the first floor living room. Such conversions of single-family dwellings occur in all residential environments and

Figure 4.20. *House subdivision and conversion to multi-unit housing.* Single-family, Side-Hall house, subdivided into an up-and-down duplex (porch infilled with aluminum siding), Perth Amboy, New Jersey. Constructed 1929; subdivided 1932. Photograph by Nancy Hofmann.

eras but are most common in periods of economic downturn and depression within working-class neighborhoods.

Despite a general lack of interest and approval for similar early twentieth-century remodeling projects in the national literature and by financial and government institutions, significant housing reform by remodeling was accomplished through a largely unrecorded, bottom-up, incremental process conducted primarily by networks of local and regional builders, suppliers, and housing clients. Fortunately, several recent studies have greatly expanded the documentation of the popular domestic remodeling process. Particularly important is the work of Richard Harris and his analysis of the growth of a vast early twentieth-century construction supply industry.[33] This research has helped highlight the role of the small contractor-developer in the process of home construction and especially in remodeling existing homes. For example, in *Middletown,* their important study of Muncie, Indiana, the Lynds cite several instances of middle-majority, working-class housing remodeling, such as the installation of bathrooms. A local plumbing firm claimed that during the boom year of 1923, its staff installed 1½ times more bathrooms in remodeled houses than in all of Muncie's new houses built that year.[34]

In an unusually well-documented type of housing, the literature of New York's tenement reform provides extensive, detailed examples of apartment house or tenement remodeling. These projects, completed on a massive scale, account for the installation of modern conveniences and utilities, especially toilets, plumbing, and sewers.[35] The Lower East Side Tenement Museum provides a detailed examination of the stages in the tenement remodeling process for a building constructed in 1864 with only the most minimal utilities and technological improvements. The remodeling of existing tenements, however, was a controversial subject pitting owners and contractors against reformers and regulators, who frequently saw only the continuation of minimal housing conditions in efforts to reform older tenements, such as the Tenement Museum's building.[36]

Although there are no equivalent sources for documenting the improvement of average, common houses, a similar scale of domestic reform transformed much of America's early twentieth-century existing housing, particularly through bathroom and kitchen addition and remodeling, and the addition of bedrooms. The vast scale of this remodeling is evident when we consider that most pre-1910 common houses (and even many built into the 1930s) were originally constructed without modern improvements but were only later modernized. In 1910 there were approximately fourteen million households and of those surviving into the 1940s, I estimate that perhaps half of these structures (both single- and multifamily) were subsequently modernized and received some degree of remodeling improvement during this period. If we add all the homes that were remodeled for all the reasons houses are improved, we have a vast total of early twentieth-century remodeling improvement that warrants further intensive study.[37]

To demonstrate a typical remodeling improvement, we focus on the "Pyramid" house, a standard, national type of the "Four-Box" house plan analyzed in chapter 2 (see Figure 2.8). Ubiquitous and unheralded even in the western states, where it gained wide popularity, the Four-Box plan, often built with a "pyramid" roof, was probably one of America's most popular, small, single-family house types erected between 1890 and 1920. When constructed before about 1910, it was a boxy, working-class house with a simple four-room plan that included a living room, kitchen, and two bedrooms, but no bathroom. As the Fossil, Oregon, Pyramid in Figure 4.21 shows, this basic Four-Box plan was typically expanded and remodeled with a rear addition containing a new kitchen and bathroom.[38] (Alternatively, the new bathroom was often inserted between the two bedrooms within the existing house.) This common addition, accompanied by the conversion of the original kitchen into a dining room, produced a standard, middle-class-aspiring, five-room-with-bath house plan and thus transformed the household into a modest, condensed version of the Bungalow or Progressive Era plan. The Oregon house was also expanded with a "fruit room" on the back of the kitchen addition—an adaptation found in the fruit-growing regions of eastern Oregon. In most of the state's eastern towns, similar Pyramids, many with a conspicuous flattened peak and central chimney, surpassed the common bungalow as the most popu-

Figure 4.21. *Typical improvements to a popular house type.* The Pyramid, Four-Box plan, developed in the late nineteenth century and built into the 1920s, was frequently improved with a rear kitchen addition and a new bathroom. (a) Exterior photograph. (b) Four-Box plan showing additions, circa 1910, Fossil, Oregon.

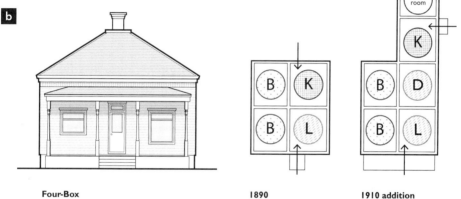

Four-Box   1890   1910 addition

lar type of early twentieth-century working-toward-middle-class house. Although not usually perceived as a "middle-class" house today, such modestly expanded and remodeled dwellings represented a significant path to housing improvement and middle-class status for working-class families with limited resources.

Even though there are no officially collected statistics on the extent of these various remodeling practices on a national scale, experience in fieldwork leads me to estimate that by 1940, nearly one-fourth of middle-majority households had obtained the basic standards of middle-class housing improvement through the remodeling of previously existing, minimally improved housing. Although national figures on the full extent of remodeling improvement might never be accurately calculated, or agreed upon, the home remodeling that I have recorded in every working-class community surveyed for this research represented a significant path to obtaining middle-class-quality housing, especially for a lower third of middle-majority Americans in the early twentieth century.[39]

Below the level of domestic improvement for small houses such as Four-Box-Pyramids and Early Bungalows, stand houses that received only partial or minimal improvement in the early twentieth century. In these dwellings of the least well off, the pace of domestic reform was incremental and long term and created patterns of domestic life different from those we have recorded throughout this book.[40] Such partial housing improvement has been documented by Paul Groth and Marta Gutman in groundbreaking studies of the working-class neighborhoods of San Francisco, Oakland, and Berkeley, California.[41] Here they explore a contested domestic terrain between minimally improved, "almost-polite houses" (the kind we have documented) and "informal workers' cottages," which by 1940 still lacked the standards of middle-class, middle-majority improvement. For example, Figure 4.22 shows the incremental improvement to a small late nineteenth-century Oakland workers' cottage, including minimally constructed additions. These remodeling changes expanded the kitchen and dining area and added a bathroom, but still produced a dwelling characterized by mixed

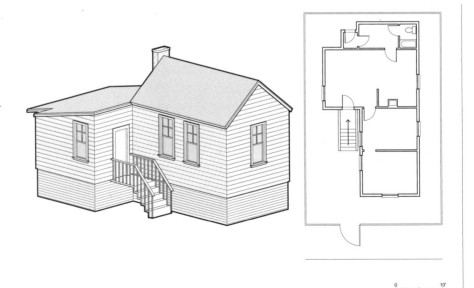

Figure 4.22. *Informal Workers' Cottage.* An example of the incremental expansion and improvement of an original two-room house (front-gable structure). Late nineteenth-century workers' cottage, 714 Pine Street, Oakland, California. Drawing adapted from Paul Groth and Marta Gutman, "Workers' Houses in West Oakland."

room usage, minimal construction standards, and pre-reform patterns of usage. In the interpretation of these types of dwellings, Groth and Gutman caution that the well-meaning housing reforms of the Progressive era not only brought tangible benefits but also raised the cost of dwellings beyond what many could afford and, in the process, challenged some of the values of working-class culture that set it apart from middle- and upper-class culture. Their studies remind us that housing reform for the middle majority was not applied uniformly to the least well off and that the glow of technological and social progress championed in this study did not extend to all households.

· · ·

Generally, the houses of America's least-well-off, 20–30 percent of residents have been the most difficult to analyze historically, especially because of their short-term occupancy and the short lifespans of these structures. An understudied issue is the process by which this marginal housing becomes worn down and is demolished so that it vanishes from the historical record.[42] These are dwellings in a constant state of remodeling transition in between "ruin and repair" as termed by architectural historian Dell Upton.[43] Here the common, hidden-from-the-street, unrecorded processes of existing house repair, expansion, partial demolition, subdividing, house moving, and continual remodeling are carried out. When added to an even more difficult-to-gauge housing stock of minimal multi-unit lodging, boardinghouses, and residential hotels and motels, these are the types of dwellings and residential processes that are not easily recorded or analyzed. Yet these types of houses were also remodeled and modestly "improved" during the early twentieth-century period of this study. Together their story provides insight into some of the complex factors that influence housing improvement for the least well off.

MAZUR HOUSE REMODELING

More than any other form of domestic improvement, remodeling was largely the product of local working-class agency—a kind of grassroots Progressive Era housing reform. That significant housing improvement could have been accomplished on a national scale with only minimal support from Progressive Era institutions, both public and private, demonstrates a remarkable collective determination to achieve domestic reform.

To summarize the ways different types of housing brought domestic reform to the middle majority, we conclude this chapter by analyzing the house construction history of the Mazurs, a working-class family from Milwaukee, Wisconsin. The changes they made to their house between 1894 and 1925 demonstrate how improvements in their standard of living were accomplished through home remodeling. Theirs is a case study of incremental steps toward domestic advancement that transformed and expanded their small, three-room Workers' Cottage with few amenities into an improved bungalow type of house with modern middle-class domestic standards. Although the steps the Mazurs took to expand their house were different and took longer than the ones involved in building the common bungalows highlighted in chapter 3, both households acquired similar major domestic enhancements.[44]

Figure 4.23 shows the street facade and floor plan of the Mazurs' well-built, turn-of-the-century Workers' Cottage. This dwelling was constructed in about 1889 and was slightly smaller than the typical Milwaukee cottage with its kitchen in a shed at the rear of the structure. Newly married Anton and Katarzyna Mazur bought this five-year-old, wood-frame cottage in 1894 for $800 from a German family in a South Milwaukee neighborhood that was increasingly being settled by immigrants from Poland's western provinces. The house had a standard nineteenth-century Workers' Cottage floor plan with two major rooms, an all-purpose living–bedroom and a kitchen, plus a small bedroom, entry, and storage room along the side wall. The price they paid indicates that, as the photo shows, it was well built and thus probably had the major technological features that had been acquired by the working classes during this period—an iron cookstove and piped running water. (Electricity service for lighting might not have been available for houses in this neighborhood in 1894.)

An arranged marriage brought together Anton, a twenty-six-

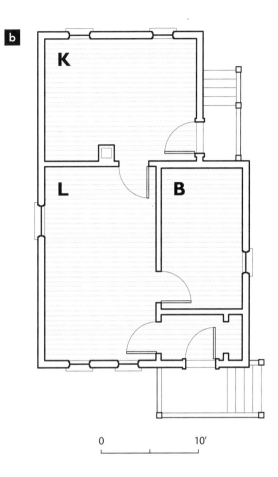

Figure 4.23. *Mazur house, Milwaukee, Wisconsin, circa 1900.* (a) Photograph of the Mazur family standing in front of their Workers' Cottage, circa 1900. (b) Mazur house floor plan, circa 1900. Photograph from and interviews with Bernice Mazur, Milwaukee, 1994.

year-old Austrian steelworker, and Katarzyna, a twenty-one-year-old recent arrival from the Poznan District of western Poland. The newlyweds moved into their new home along with Katarzyna's father, younger sister, and brother. A photograph of their house taken around 1900 shows Katarzyna's brother and sister and two of her children. By 1916 the Mazurs had added five more children in an extended family of twelve members with additional sleeping spaces created in the unfinished basement and attic. Finally, however, after twenty-three years of residence and the contributions of six wage earners, including working children, the Mazurs transformed their cottage by conducting a series of ambitious building improvements as illustrated in Figure 4.24.

First, they bought "Uncle" Joe Nisiewiecz's cottage, which was lifted off its foundation and moved one block down the street by

Figure 4.24. *Major remodeling and reconstruction, Mazur house, 1917–20.* The house was converted from an unimproved workers' cottage to an improved Bungalow plan in several stages. Interviews with Bernice Mazur, Milwaukee, 1994.

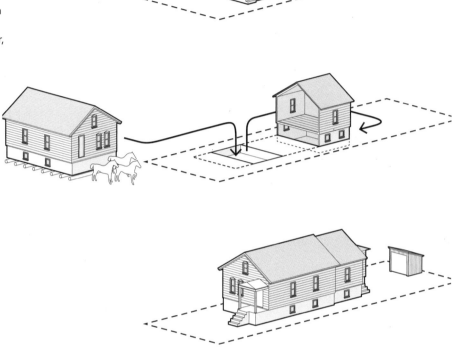

a team of horses to the Mazur house lot. As one observer of Milwaukee's Polish business community noted, there was a "blooming business" for Polish American house movers by the turn of the century.[45] Indeed, to a certain degree, a separate Polish American economy and building industry operated within their neighborhoods, providing skilled construction services, contractors, and architects. Prior to the move, a local builder had split the Mazurs' house apart and removed the rear shed containing the kitchen. He then turned the front portion of the house containing the original parlor–living room, and dragged it farther back on the lot. The Nisiewieczs' house was then moved into place at the front of the lot and attached to the original parlor–living room structure, which became the new rear facade of the house. The entire reconstructed house was then set atop a concrete block basement wall, which replaced a cedar-post foundation under the original cottage. Although local stories and popular legends frequently attribute this type of Polish Flat cellar excavation to the sweat equity of industrious Poles, projects such as this were almost always overseen and frequently performed by local contractors, perhaps with the help of resident owners.

The completed project expanded and remodeled the original three-room workers' cottage into a version of the bungalow plan (Figure 4.25). In the process, the Mazurs gained many of the important improvements of a middle-class lifestyle: a dining room, bathroom, expanded front porch, closets, bigger private bedrooms, and larger basement and attic spaces. During the next several years the quality of domestic life was incrementally enhanced by the addition of central heating, a hot water system, and a full three-fixture bathroom (electricity had been added previously). These

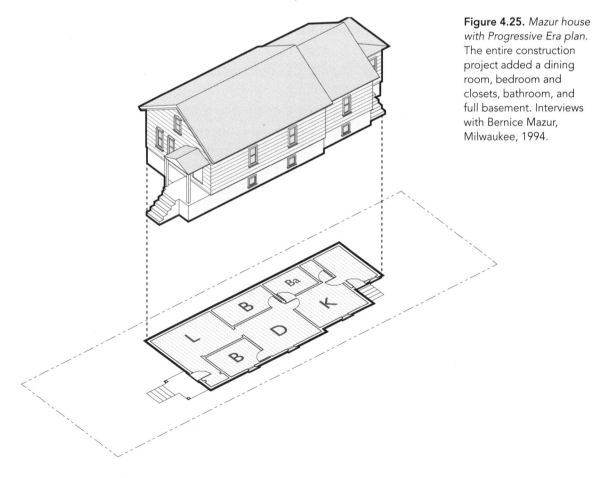

Figure 4.25. *Mazur house with Progressive Era plan.* The entire construction project added a dining room, bedroom and closets, bathroom, and full basement. Interviews with Bernice Mazur, Milwaukee, 1994.

improvements combined to radically transform the Mazurs' over-all quality of life and represented the incremental acquisition of the bungalow era's standard middle-class amenities highlighted in chapter 3. The Mazurs' remodeled plan arrangement, with three linked public rooms (living, dining, and kitchen) and two bedrooms and a bath, was a close variant of the most popular, one-story bunga-low or Progressive Era plan highlighted earlier.

If you drive the streets of South Milwaukee's older Polish neigh-borhood, as well as other ethnic neighborhoods, you can still find thousands of dwellings that were remodeled and improved like the Mazurs' house. In many of these neighborhoods, most houses were originally constructed without major twentieth-century domestic improvements and consequently were remodeled and modernized—many in an incremental process with results similar to the Mazurs. This is the same process that has shaped working-class neighbor-hoods in metropolitan and rural regions throughout the country.

Although the Mazurs completed their extensive project in a two-year period with the contribution of salaries from six family members, the home improvement projects of other working-class households might have extended over longer periods and often in-volved partial, incomplete, and longer-term incremental changes. These are more like the type of continual remodeling additions we have seen in the workers' cottages of West Oakland, California, re-corded by Paul Groth and Marta Gutman (see Figure 4.22).[46] This type of partial, long-term remodeling improvement, widely prac-ticed nationally, blurs the distinction between repair and remodel-ing/improvement projects and is difficult to assess in comparison with the more uniform standards of housing upgrades within the middle- and upper-class residential environments usually docu-mented. Nevertheless, projects like the Mazurs' probably tell a more typical story experienced by the lower third of the middle majority between 1900 and 1940. Despite significant urban–rural, ethnic–racial, and regional differences, case studies from across the country reveal similar types of incremental working-class home im-provement projects.[47]

. . .

Throughout this chapter, we have seen a variety of less well-documented housing types that many builders, owners, and residents used to achieve modern domestic improvement, including multi-family houses and renovated older houses not typically documented in the story of American housing reform. By examining the late nineteenth- and early twentieth-century emergence of these types, we also reveal the depths of pre-reform housing conditions experienced by the middle majority of Americans living in anonymous workers' cottages, tenement apartments, boardinghouses, and unimproved rural and farm environments. Despite the wide-ranging exterior variety of the improved housing we have examined, they are all linked by the same cluster of technological and spatial improvements characteristic of the common bungalow that came to characterize middle-class lifestyle during the early twentieth century.

CHAPTER 5

DOMESTIC LIFE TRANSFORMED

HOW THE WORKING CLASS BECAME MIDDLE CLASS IN HOUSING

Recasting *The Grand Domestic Revolution,* the title of Dolores Hayden's landmark study of feminist designs for American housing and domestic life, this book seeks to bring to light another type of domestic revolution—one that fundamentally transformed and improved the lives of many Americans.[1] Although the word "grand" rests uneasily upon the modest houses and households analyzed here, its meaning is still appropriate for describing the unprecedented scale of change experienced by a middle majority of the population. Economic historian Robert Gordon summarizes the revolutionary nature of these changes: "The revolution that re-made the American dwelling and the American standard of living occurred during a relatively small slice of human history, mainly between 1900 and 1940. Viewed from the perspective of millennia of economic stagnation, the networked modern conveniences arrived in a rush, from virtual invisibility in 1910 urban America to near pervasiveness in 1940."[2] This book confirms and extends Gordon's findings by analyzing the material and technological character of these houses and revealing the multiple paths Americans took in this process of improving their dwellings and transforming their domestic lives.

By revolutionary standards, this was a remarkably quiet transformation, little publicized at the time or documented later. We analyzed some of the reasons for this obscurity in the opening chapters, but an important contributing factor may also have been the hesitancy, shared by both analysts and participants, to acknowledge that the working classes were still only catching up and that most of the hard-won improvements they obtained in the early twentieth century had long been enjoyed in the households of the upper classes. Furthermore, these unprecedented gains were about to be engulfed and then bypassed by the largest domestic construction expansion in America's history, the celebrated post–World War II suburban boom, which built upon and further democratized the domestic improvements recorded here. Moreover, 20–30 percent of Americans still had not received significant domestic improvements by the eve of that war. Nonetheless, given the magnitude and rapidity of this early twentieth-century transformation, it was, indeed, a grand domestic revolution.

One of the leading symbols of this transformation was the common bungalow. As we have just seen, this modest dwelling became the widely recognized gold standard for a new type of modern middle-class domestic life (Figure 5.1). While this assessment is generally acknowledged in most architectural and housing literature (albeit not as enthusiastically), this book broadens and deepens the story of the bungalow's impact by revealing that even house types that did not look like bungalows nevertheless acted like them, in that they provided their middle-majority residents with long-sought-after domestic improvements. This was, I hope, one of the surprises of this book—that the benefits of early twentieth-century domestic improvement and modernization were obtained by so many Americans in such a wide assortment of unfamiliar and seldom considered houses and apartments. That a majority of Americans transformed their dwellings so substantially and so rapidly, moving from primitive to middle-class domestic conditions in less than a half century, was, I hope, another surprise.

These improved dwellings invite a reconsideration of the narratives often told about twentieth-century American houses. One widely cited interpretation surmises that during the first decades

Figure 5.1. *The bungalow—a symbol of modern middle-class living.* Four popular forms of the Craftsman Bungalow in early twentieth-century. (a) Front-Gable type with full recessed porch under gable, Portland, Oregon. (b) Front-Gable type with picturesque, nonsymmetrical porch and gable alignments, Portland, Oregon. (c) Wide-Porch Bungalow usually with a master bedroom and bathroom on the second floor, Portland, Oregon. (d) Standard Bungalow plan with porch/sunroom entry (also called a Sunroom Porch Bungalow in the Milwaukee, Wisconsin, area).

of the twentieth century, the overall size of houses (the number of rooms and the square footage) was reduced in comparison to houses in previous periods—or simply that most new houses got smaller and simpler in the early twentieth century (Figure 5.2). This house-size reduction theory was primarily derived from the observation that new patterns of domestic life in late nineteenth-century, upper-middle-class households resulted in calls for a reduction in the size and complexity of domestic space. Housing reformers advocated for the removal of elaborate stylistic detail, the elimination of extra rooms (such as nurseries and smoking rooms), and the reduction or elimination of servants. When linked to the production of smaller types of houses in the early 1900s, these reductions seemed to point to a general downsizing of the American house in the early modern period. Historians attentive to the houses and domestic life of the Victorian upper classes not illogically assumed that the production of smaller houses in this period was driven by changes taking place in these elite/upper-class households. For example, in his influential book *Home: A Short History of an Idea,* Witold Rybczynski focuses on changes in the availability of domestic help, noting that "the servantless household . . . required, above all, a reduction in the size of rooms."[3]

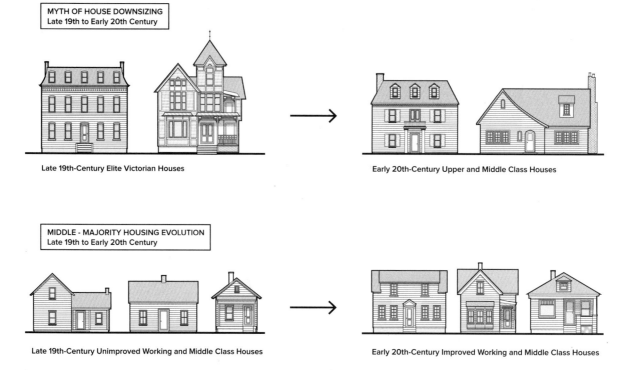

MYTH OF HOUSE DOWNSIZING
Late 19th to Early 20th Century

Late 19th-Century Elite Victorian Houses

Early 20th-Century Upper and Middle Class Houses

MIDDLE - MAJORITY HOUSING EVOLUTION
Late 19th to Early 20th Century

Late 19th-Century Unimproved Working and Middle Class Houses

Early 20th-Century Improved Working and Middle Class Houses

Figure 5.2. *"Shrinking-house theory."* Various studies have estimated that the average size of houses was reduced during the early twentieth century. This is a statistical anomaly based on a comparison of a smaller group of larger, late nineteenth-century, upper-class houses with the increasing production of smaller popular houses in the early 1900s. For the vast middle majority of the population, the average size of new and remodeled houses increased modestly but continuously (although slowed by depressions) from the 1870s to the 1970s.

This widely cited hypothesis, which we label "shrinking-house theory," is a cornerstone of both Victorian domestic and early modernist housing literatures. Yet for the vast majority of new twentieth-century homeowners and renters, most of whom came from the expanding working-toward-middle-classes, there was no reduction in the size of new houses. Instead, they experienced modest increases in domestic space having never lived in houses with formal parlors, back stairs, and servant spaces that required spatial reduction.[4]

One of the most authoritative sources for this house downsizing theory is Gwendolyn Wright, whose work on American housing and reform has been influential far beyond housing studies. In a section titled "Making the Most of Less Space," in *Moralism and the Model Home,* Wright contrasts new, reduced-sized houses of the early twentieth century with larger, more ornate Victorian houses of the late nineteenth century:

> Square-footage was cut back dramatically in these modern, simpler houses. The number and size of rooms declined. Extra or single-purpose rooms such as libraries, pantries, sewing rooms, and spare bedrooms had expressed the Victorian family's sense of uniqueness and its daily pastimes. By the late 1890s, these rooms had been discarded in most new middle-class homes. . . . Often the front hall, once a formal presentation area and a living space as well, was omitted. . . . The dining room was diminished in size.[5]

Here Wright links downsizing Victorian elites with the portion of the middle majority who were able to afford bungalows and other comparable early twentieth-century improved houses. Repeated in subsequent studies, this interpretation became a uniform narrative emphasizing early twentieth-century reductions in house size and complexity (see Figure 5.2).

This narrative has been difficult to dislodge, largely because there are no credible or official sources for house size and room usage data on a national scale in the late nineteenth and early twentieth century, especially for the lower 70 percent of households. One important exception is the wealth of Progressive Era statistical information on urban working-class housing in conditions of poverty within tenements and small apartment houses. These government-generated statistics, however, were rarely, if ever, added to estimates of national housing totals for the sizes and conditions of average housing. Had they been added, they would have further diminished the data supportive of house-size reduction.[6]

The wide acceptance of this shrinking-house theory can be attributed to an apples-to-oranges comparison of a small minority of upper-middle-class houses and households from the 1900s with the larger number of smaller, popular, middle-majority houses built in a later period. Given that few inquiries have considered both single-family houses and multifamily dwellings in the same study and that fewer still have attended to the remodeling process, it has been difficult to discern that most purchasers of improved bungalows and duplexes had moved from even smaller houses and apartments, not from large, middle-class houses (and certainly not from even larger nineteenth-century Victorian mansions). From the results of this study, it is estimated that for the middle majority of the population, more than half living in small, multi-unit rental houses and apartments, the average size of new and newly remodeled houses increased modestly from the 1870s to the 1970s, especially during the study period 1900–1940.[7]

In retrospect, the application of a shrinking-house theory to the houses of most Americans could only have occurred in an investigative context that focused on the emergence of newly built bungalows and duplexes without considering the social status of the majority of their new residents and without recognizing them as part of a larger trend that included multifamily dwellings and renovated houses. Yet a "shrinking-house theory" might have remained only a minor misinterpretation in the story of twentieth-century housing improvement, but instead, it has become an overarching interpretation of American middle-class housing development with unusual staying power. This is because it has dovetailed so seamlessly with several narratives of modernism in housing and domestic life. Chief among them is the architectural conception of functional and aesthetic minimalism as applied to housing. In this historic reading, the excesses of bloated Victorian dwellings and lifestyle were targeted for reduction according to new minimalist-abstract theories of modern architecture. The cumulative effect was to champion house size reduction and simplification toward smaller simpler houses.[8]

It is an epic story with a compelling linkage of art, architecture, and social theory, but it is not an accurate portrayal of early twentieth-century, middle-majority housing reform and its social development. As we have seen, the principal inhabitants of bungalows and other major types of improved housing were not well-to-do families downsizing from large Victorian mansions, but largely the middle majority expanding their residences from small workers' cottages, tenements, and average-sized dwellings into slightly larger, improved houses. Furthermore, modernist concepts of aesthetic minimalism had little to do with the production of mainstream common houses. Rather than being guided by a minimalist or abstract domestic aesthetic, the houses of the early twentieth-century middle majority generally followed modest traditional versions of architectural styles such as Arts and Crafts and Colonial Revival and added domestic complexity to their previously threadbare interior environments.[9] There is no reading of average early twentieth-century housing for the vast majority that supports claims of spatial reduction or aesthetic or functional minimalism.

· · ·

The extensive influence of these downsizing theories, repeated for almost a half century in the finest studies and in many disciplines outside architecture and housing, has skewed our understanding of common, vernacular, and working-class housing, especially during its most critical period of early twentieth-century development and expansion. Against this house-downsizing backdrop, we have told an alternative story of modest housing expansion and improvement, from small, unimproved houses to slightly larger, improved houses. Joseph Bigott has labeled this modest improvement as the move "from cottage to bungalow." We could also characterize it as a step from tenement flat to duplex, or from shanty to farm cottage, or simply from unimproved houses to improved houses in a process involving millions of households.[10] These were the modest, common house transformations that undergirded a grand domestic revolution.

COMFORTABLE MODERN HOMES

This book's praise for common bungalows highlights the introduction of technological conveniences, industrialized materials, and improved spaces that transformed the domestic lives of average Americans. These same material-technological improvements also created the conditions for entirely new experiences and attitudes about the conduct and quality of everyday domestic life. For its new middle-majority recipients, one distinctly new type of experience accompanying modern domestic improvement was comfort. Domestic comfort can simply mean physical contentment, well-being, or relief from the cares of daily life, but the term can also be used in a much broader, more profound sense related to the overall quality of domestic life, as we use it here. Comfort, however, is a subtle, difficult-to-define experience and the term has frequently invited scientific skepticism because of the difficulty of interpreting and measuring its conditions with precision—a "you know it when you feel it" type of experience. Despite these reservations, almost all books about the historical development of modern housing and domestic culture engage and emphasize the issue of comfort and its attainment within modern domestic life.

The beginning of this historical development of Western European bourgeois domestic comfort is usually located within seventeenth- and eighteenth-century Dutch and English traditions. The Dutch especially are often credited with establishing the fundamental functional, spatial, and experiential traditions underlying the development of modern American family life and its domestic comfort. In total development, it is a complex history uniting many cultures in a rich tapestry of domestic life and its comfort.[11] For example, living and dining room patterns of usage are typically traced from European royal traditions through house plans of the gentry and upper classes and eventually lead in gradual stages to more popular, middle-class lifestyles in the twentieth century.[12]

This elite telling of domestic history is well documented and often repeated, but it is not the story of the way most people gained comfortable dining rooms and bedrooms or received domestic comforts throughout their homes. For the middle majority, the comfort story is much shorter and far easier to tell. Before 1900 the average dwelling for over three-fourths of the population was almost completely lacking in domestic comfort however the term is defined. As described in chapter 2, typical middle-majority households lacked almost all comfort-producing amenities, such as furniture for relaxation, environmental controls, extra space for individual usage and recreation (not to mention basic comfort-producing amenities such as furnaces, servants, toilets). From the list of typical "constraints" in the same chapter, we can more fully appreciate that domestic comfort was not an accompaniment to turn-of-the-century middle-majority domestic life.

What makes the story of middle-majority domestic comfort easier to tell is that its arrival is quite sudden and recent, beginning for most at the turn of the twentieth century and crystallizing for many in the widely obtainable form of the common bungalow plan and its technological improvements during the first three decades of the century. Although we have emphasized its functional-technological achievements, the bungalow's package of standard domestic improvements also facilitated an entirely new world of domestic comfort never experienced by most of its initial residents from the working classes. This sudden arrival of domestic comfort is important to emphasize because the bungalow's typical working-class residents were not merely transitioning horizontally (as were the upper classes) from previously improved and comfortable domestic environments. Rather they were rocketing upward from small, unimproved working-class dwellings into an entirely new experience of domestic life—a world shaped by new materials, technologies, and domestic spaces but also new attitudes and experiences of domestic comfort—for the very first time.

We conclude this book in celebration of this great transformation in domestic life encapsulated within common bungalows and closely related houses with similar improvements. Although strikingly different in form, all the houses in Figure 5.3 contained

Figure 5.3. *Varied houses of American domestic reform.* (a) Two-up and Two-down houses, Cincinnati, Ohio.
(b) Brick fourplex, Cincinnati, Ohio. (c) One-over-one duplex, Cincinnati, Ohio. (d) Parlor-Bypass house, Cleveland, Ohio.
(e) Fourplex, Union, New Jersey. (f) Commercial below and residential units above and behind, Milwaukee, Wisconsin.

Figure 5.4. *Mill workers' multipurpose living room with furnishings for a future home.* Homestead, Pennsylvania, 1908. Margaret F. Byington, *Homestead: The Households of a Milltown* (New York: Russell Sage Foundation, Charities Publication Committee, 1910).

the same basic package of modern domestic technologies and spatial improvements we have emphasized throughout—all mass-produced for popular consumption and symbolized by the common bungalow.

Finally, to mark the bungalow's achievement and its important place within the story of working-class domestic history, we recall the family from Homestead, Pennsylvania, at the end of chapter 2 (Figure 5.4). This time, instead of concentrating on their lives of domestic toil, we might try to see them as poised on the threshold of a transformative, but rarely acknowledged, domestic journey as they contemplate leaving their crowded apartment, with their growing collection of fine furnishings, for a new dwelling containing all the technological improvements and comforts we have studied. This was the type of game-changing transition experienced by most of the working class in the early decades of the twentieth century.

Although we may have first assumed we were observing the blank stares resulting from working-class toil and exhaustion, we might actually be seeing a rare moment of reverie shared by wife and husband. To set the tone, we might even imagine that one of them is about to play the organ that sits in the corner on the other side of the room. Consequently, we might actually be witnessing a special moment of domestic repose when both wife and husband anticipate their approaching move into their new, comfortable bungalow. I hope they made it.

EPILOGUE

RESPONSE TO WORKING-CLASS IMPROVEMENT

The traumas of the Great Depression and the Second World War were quickly followed by twenty years of the largest housing construction boom in United States history. These great events have tended to overshadow the substantial housing accomplishments of the early twentieth century documented here. Nevertheless, the domestic improvements of the early 1900s had a significant impact on American social and cultural life. Three broad themes shed light on the way early twentieth-century middle-majority housing improvements were perceived both by observers and participants in a new world of midcentury, modern America: a broad unification of American culture as never before; a new type of criticism for this new popular culture; and the conflicting interpretations of domestic progress based on the status of women's work. Each theme sheds a different light on the consequences of massive early twentieth-century domestic improvement for America's middle majority.

UNIFORMITY IN DOMESTIC CULTURE

The domestic improvements obtained by middle-majority residents in early twentieth-century bungalows and bungalow equivalents were neither new inventions nor untested experiments in modern living. Most changes were close copies or modest variations of the technologies and spatial improvements already established in the households of the middle to upper classes. The narrowing of this gap by dramatic increases in the improvement of working-class domestic conditions, therefore, contributed to a greater uniformity in national domestic culture. An increasing uniformity, of course, does not imply a material-technological, one-to-one similarity, for vast differences in the basic size and quality of houses and domestic conditions continued to separate Americans of all classes, especially the Americans in the lowest quintile of economic distribution. Nevertheless, when considering the great chasm that once separated upper and working classes at the beginning of the twentieth century, the greater uniformity in domestic cultures in 1940s is an astounding material and social accomplishment.

An increasing homogeneity of American culture across historical class, ethnic, and regional divisions in the first half of the twentieth century is a theme cautiously articulated in American cultural studies. Most often portrayed as the popularization or democratization of American society, it typically references a long list of technological advances and shared cultural developments of the 1920s and 1930s that acted to enhance and consolidate an increasingly unified national culture. These improvements typically include mass communications (newspapers, radio, telephone, mail delivery, rural free delivery, and magazine distribution); medical advances (public hospitals, mass-produced medicines, scientific research, vaccinations); public education (high schools, libraries, and book publication); mass production of consumer goods; recreation opportunities (movies, phonographs, municipal parks); financial services and banking (consumer credit); and automobile culture (motels, modern highways, travel). Uniting many of these unprecedented improvements was the technological and symbolic web of electrification that acted irrevocably to integrate individuals, communities, and regions into a more cohesive national culture—increasingly referred to as middle class and expressive of a middle-class standard of living.[1] Architectural historian Peter Rowe characterizes this advent of societal improvements of the 1920s as "the time when most Americans crossed over into the modern era."[2] This book extends this thesis of cultural unification by emphasizing the effects of a range of important housing improvements that brought the middle majority into an American domestic culture formerly enjoyed only by the well-to-do—a trend that continued and broadened after World War II. Marina Moskowitz has noted: "As people across the country had access to the same goods, placed them in similar spaces, and arranged those spaces into similar communities, they shared more than taste or design sense; rather, they shared a way of organizing life. Taken together, the elements of the material environment, along with the values that these elements symbolized, made up a quality of life increasingly referred to as the standard of living."[3]

A central thesis of this study is that three-fixture bathrooms, kitchen technologies, and public utilities were a package of extraordinary, game-changing, one-time-only domestic improvements that contributed substantially to the creation of this more uniform domestic culture and standard of living on a national scale. This book adds to this improvement story by emphasizing both the extreme differences between historic upper- and working-class domestic cultures at the end of the nineteenth century and the rapidity with which new improvements narrowed these historic differences and contributed to a greater unification in the physical parameters of American domestic life. To demonstrate this increasing uniformity, we focused on the widespread introduction of the bungalow's standard formula of improved features as a strategic tipping point in the popularization of a modern domestic lifestyle increasingly shared by larger and larger segments of the population. While still recognizing wide differences in domestic conditions that continued to separate Americans of all classes, especially a 20–30 percent of Americans in conditions of poverty, a more uniform national domestic culture was facilitated by increasing similarities in the technological and spatial functions of improved homes for an increasing middle-majority, middle class during the first half of the twentieth century.[4]

CRITIQUE OF THE MASSES

Perhaps because of these increasing similarities in domestic cultures, there emerged in the national literature of the 1920s and 1930s an often-repeated "critique of the masses." To be sure, such criticisms had a long history in nineteenth-century English and American literature and journalism, when authors focused on the working classes and highlighted alcohol consumption, agrarian social traditions, religious and moral failings, and unfavorable domestic conditions, such as crowding, squalor, and uncleanliness. While these earlier criticisms were directed at the social and domestic traditions of a vastly different, subordinate working class, this new, twentieth-century critique was directed at a numerically expanding, new middle class whose members had begun to consume and act more like the upper classes.[5]

As this broad critique evolved in the national literature of the pre–World War II era, it typically projected a blind consumerism and conformist herd mentality onto this expanding middle class, a criticism that would continue to be deployed and intensified in a postwar critique of suburban lifestyle and culture.[6] Daniel Horowitz identifies the change in critical emphasis as critics "turned their attention from workers to the whole of society, especially the middle class. They argued that mass, commercial consumption threatened to dominate America. In their hands, the danger of conformity took the place of profligacy. Movies and automobiles succeeded saloons as the enemies of the good life."[7] Gradually, after the war and the rise of American suburban culture, this critique would evolve into a wholesale condemnation of middle-class suburban lifestyle and suburban sprawl in all its manifestations.

What originally drove and sharpened this critique for many analysts was the growing awareness that for the first time, these rising "masses" were purchasing domestic products and imitating domestic behaviors that were increasingly shared across previously fixed boundaries between upper- and working-class Americans. Although these new entrants to the middle class were often portrayed as lacking refinement and good taste as well as being self-indulgent consumers easily manipulated by advertisers and external forces, historians such as Horowitz and Lizabeth Cohen have emphasized their limited but real choices in a commercial market balanced between manipulation and collective self-interest.[8] With regard to the judgment of reckless consumption in others, perhaps it is best to consider the trenchant observation of English housing historian Judith Flanders who notes, "It is notable that most who indulged in this type of debate in Britain tended to see the desires of the groups below or above them as damaging; their own desires, generally, were assumed to be proportionate and reasonable."[9]

Just a few decades earlier, a similar criticism of the masses would have been unimaginable because the vast inequalities in domestic conditions between upper and working classes meant that the masses did not consume the same goods, or organize their homes, or inhabit them in a similar manner. But suddenly, in the early twentieth century and increasingly into the 1920s and 1930s, there were more and more comparisons to be made as a growing majority of Americans began to share more consumer goods, housing standards, and domestic behaviors with the upper classes. What makes this new twentieth-century critique of the masses so relevant to our story is how it reveals, by the rising intensity of its criticism, the establishment of a new type of middle-class majority, literally and demographically, in the middle of American culture. This had never happened before.[10]

MORE WORK FOR MOTHER?

Throughout this book, we have consistently emphasized the positive benefits that early twentieth-century industrial-technological domestic improvement brought to the lives of middle-majority American households. For example, in chapter 3, the new century's major laborsaving technological advances and spatial improvements for average households are celebrated with little reservation. In the process, we have generally assumed a near-universal acceptance and approval of the benefits of this process, especially when these improved conditions are compared to the primitive conditions typical of average households in the late nineteenth century.[11]

As many readers of current domestic literature are aware, however, modern architectural and social historians have cautioned that these twentieth-century domestic improvements had many unanticipated, long-term negative consequences, especially for women. Principally cited is a range of additional, unanticipated household tasks and domestic labors, such as escalating cycles of housecleaning chores that consigned homemakers to ever-expanding (although less strenuous) routines of housework. As Ruth Schwartz Cowan argued in her influential work *More Work for Mother*, the trade-off for modern household laborsaving efficiency can also be interpreted as an entangling commitment to uncompensated domestic labor.[12]

Cowan's critique, of course, has special significance for this study. It is important to ask what percentages of women or households were affected by the burden of additional work brought about by the process of domestic improvement in the late nineteenth and the early twentieth century. For example, as we have emphasized in chapter 2, this type of analysis was most often derived from the experiences of homemakers and writers from the upper classes, reflective of only 20–30 percent of households at the turn of the twentieth century. For many of these women, who were transitioning from households that had either included servants or that had already obtained earlier versions of twentieth-century laborsaving devices, this "more work" critique correctly reflects a changing household economy that balanced a shrinking supply of outside labor with the arrival of improved domestic conveniences, some requiring women to devote additional time to housework. For these women, the advent of domestic improvements we have championed may have done little to free a woman's time for social, cultural, or professional pursuits outside the home.

For the vast majority of women during the first half of the twentieth century, however, those whose lives had previously been almost entirely consumed by unrelenting routines of domestic hard labor, the major improvements we emphasized throughout this book brought substantial, unqualified relief in both time and effort. Furthermore, these labor-reducing improvements were, as far as limited sources reveal, nearly universally desired and, where possible, acquired by middle-majority consumers.[13]

Despite significant studies that consistently advance the claim that early twentieth-century domestic improvements added to the work of the homemaker—for example, that mid-twentieth-century daughters worked harder and longer than their early twentieth-century mothers—I believe these assessments can only be applied to a minority of upper-class homemakers and not primarily to a middle majority of households in any period before 1940. At the very least, we should acknowledge that vast differences existed between two different types of housewives: a minority from the middle to upper classes whose lives were already improved by new domestic technologies involving both losses and gains in labor savings, and a wide majority of women whose lives were profoundly altered and vastly improved upon receiving these technological improvements for the first time.[14]

Yet we should also recognize that for the working-class women who received the greatest laborsaving benefits, these new technological improvements did bring some additional work, albeit more work of a different kind. For middle-majority women, modern domestic improvement opened up entirely new possibilities for domestic life by slashing domestic labor and then permitting participation in entirely new categories of activities and housework in support of the newly elevated standards of middle-class domestic life.[15] These new tasks typically raised previously unobtainable standards of personal hygiene, clothes cleaning, food preparation and consumption, child care, personal educational development, and most of all, more time to devote to opportunities of their own selection outside of endless demands of preimprovement, domestic labor.

For example, one of the most laborious tasks of housework, the cleaning of clothes, was dramatically improved by the incremental development of better clothes-washing aids from early hand-powered mechanical devices to electrical washing machines in combination with a range of supportive improvements such as kerosene and electric irons, hot water storage, cheaper washable fabrics, and storage opportunities. For upper-class women who previously employed servants or laundry assistants, the arrival of the washing machine and the loss of servant assistance may certainly have required increased time and labor. But for most women, the technological improvements of clothes washing saved immense labor, and, unlike for upper-class women, this improvement literally opened entirely new worlds of domestic life, including employment and social opportunities. There were, however, new tasks that accompanied this improvement. New openings for office clerical work often required greater clothing care—more time needed for cleaning, ironing, and making finer clothes to achieve these new middle-class standards. These new categories of housework, however, were not merely make-work, domestic chores, but critical components in the attainment of new employment opportunities in support of a middle-class lifestyle.

Consequently, the major technological and architectural improvements we have highlighted throughout this book typically generated new kinds of middle-class opportunities and tasks for an ascendant middle majority. But rather than unleashing an endless spiral of escalating housework, the major technological enhancements we have emphasized (like the three-fixture bathroom, washing machine, and vacuum cleaner) were revolutionary, one-time changes that fundamentally transformed primitive domestic conditions into a modern domesticity.

After World War II, however, this "more work" critique became increasingly appropriate for all but the poorest households when the basic character of domestic life achieved broader technological and spatial consistency. Although improvements continued to be made in nearly every category of domestic function during the postwar era, they were not of the same order of magnitude as the one-time changes of a previous generation. Therefore, regarding domestic improvements of the postwar suburban era, the "more work" critique assumes far greater significance, as has been emphasized in most domestic studies.

· · ·

The three concluding themes—cultural unity; critique of the masses; and women's work—represent different outcomes to large-scale middle-majority domestic improvement in the early twentieth century. Chief among them, I believe, is the establishment by 1940 of America's expanding, more uniform, "middle class," including a far more unified, and technologically improved, domestic culture than the ones that existed in 1900.

Throughout this book we have attempted to maintain a focus on the houses and households in the middle; a middle-majority, economic 60 percent of the population, regardless of how it might be labeled, and specifically whether or not it was called "middle class." By maintaining this focus, we have been introduced to new and different types of houses not usually associated with the story of American housing reform. These are the types of houses, discussed in chapter 4, that brought significant domestic improvement to a new type of people in the middle—a new middle majority, middle class.

NOTES

PREFACE

1. Robert J. Gordon, *The Rise and Fall of American Growth: The U.S. Standard of Living since the Civil War* (Princeton, N.J.: Princeton University Press, 2016), 1–128, especially 113–28. Gordon's outer period of study for American growth is 1870–1970, but he emphasizes the same time frame as this book (1900–1940) for interpreting the most intensive period of economic growth (113). The second part of his work, emphasizing slower or negative growth after 1970, falls outside the study period of this book. Gordon's work was identified after much of this book had been written, but his primarily economic analysis so closely coincides with this study's housing analysis that his work is extensively cited.

   Gordon investigates the spectacular American economic growth in the late nineteenth and first half of the twentieth century generated by unprecedented technological and industrial advances that lifted the overall quality of domestic life. Similar themes are developed in a range of ideologically different works; for example, Gregory Clark, *A Farewell to Alms: A Brief Economic History of the World* (Princeton, N.J.: Princeton University Press, 2007); Angus Deaton, *The Great Escape: Health, Wealth, and the Origins of Inequality* (Princeton, N.J.: Princeton University Press, 2013); and Stanley Lebergott, *The Americans: An Economic Record* (New York: W. W. Norton, 1984). Deirdre N. McCloskey questions the emphasis on economics in these works; see *Bourgeois Dignity: Why Economics Can't Explain the Modern World* (Chicago: University of Chicago Press, 2010).

INTRODUCTION

1. For analyses of standard of living, see Clair Brown, *American Standards of Living, 1918–1988* (Hoboken, N.J.: Wiley-Blackwell, 1995), 1–39; Marina Moskowitz, *Standard of Living: The Measure of the Middle Class in Modern America* (Baltimore: The Johns Hopkins University Press, 2004), 1–18; Lee Rainwater, *What Money Buys: Inequality and the Social Meaning of Income* (New York: Basic Books, 1974), 41–63; Catherine Bauer and Jacob Crane, "What Every Family Should Have," *Survey Graphics* 29, no. 2 (February 1940): 64–139 (skipped pages); Lizabeth

Cohen, "Embellishing a Life of Labor: An Interpretation of the Material Culture of American Working-Class Homes, 1885–1915," in *Common Places: Readings in American Vernacular Architecture,* ed. Dell Upton and John Michael Vlach (Athens: University of Georgia Press, 1986), 261–80; Robert D. Johnston, "Conclusion: Historians and the American Middle Class," in *The Middling Sorts: Explorations in the History of the American Middle Class,* ed. Burton J. Bledstein and Robert D. Johnston (New York: Routledge, 2001), 296–306. The first English usage of the term "standard of living," 1903, *Oxford English Dictionary.*

Most analysts differentiate between standard of living (or economic criteria) and quality of life (or social welfare criteria). Gordon, *The Rise and Fall of American Growth,* 8–13, stresses that excessive focus on GDP distorts standard of living analysis.

2. See Paul Krugman, "The Undeserving Rich," *New York Times,* January 19, 2014. Citing "distaste for the implications of the numbers," Krugman repeatedly challenges his readers to pursue the consequences of public policy for larger constituencies, which often become marginalized in policy discussions reflective of smaller constituencies.

3. For analysis of the middle class, see Margo Anderson, "The Language of Class in Twentieth-Century America," in *Social Science History* 12, no. 4 (Winter 1988): 349–75; Robert D. Johnston, "Conclusion: Historians and the American Middle Class," and Burton J. Bledstein, "Introduction: Storytellers to the Middle Class," both in Bledstein and Johnston, *The Middling Sorts.* For an alternative view, see Andrew Levison, *The Working-Class Majority* (New York: Coward, McCann & Geoghegan, 1974), 17–52.

The debate about defining "middle class" extends from the mid-nineteenth century, escalates in the Progressive Era, and becomes a central topic for national examination during the post–World War II era of suburban housing development, as explored in an expansive literature and summarized in Kenneth T. Jackson, *Crabgrass Frontier: The Suburbanization of the United States* (New York: Oxford University Press, 1985), 116–71. For postwar analysis, see Levison, *Working-Class Majority,* 1–52. For a focused study of the working class, see Frank Stricker, "Affluence for Whom? Another Look at Prosperity and the Working Classes in the 1920s," *Labor History* 24, no. 1 (January 1983): 5–33. For distinctions within the nineteenth-century middle class, see Sven Beckert, "Propertied of a Different Kind: Bourgeoisie and Lower Middle Class in the Nineteenth-Century United States," in Bledstein and Johnston, *The Middling Sorts*; Johnston, "Conclusion: Historians and the American Middle Class," in Bledstein and Johnston, *The Middling Sorts*; and Elaine Lewinnek, *The Working Man's Reward: Chicago's*

Early Suburbs and the Roots of American Sprawl (New York: Oxford University Press, 2014), 85–86, 178–87.

4. Clifford Edward Clark Jr., *The American Family Home, 1800–1960* (Chapel Hill: University of North Carolina Press, 1986), 114.

5. For the problem of studying underdocumented vernacular housing, see Dell Upton, *Another City: Urban Life and Urban Spaces in the New American Spaces* (New Haven, Conn.: Yale University Press, 2008), 1–40; Henry Glassie, *Folk Housing in Middle Virginia: A Structural Analysis of Historic Artifacts* (Knoxville: University of Tennessee Press, 1976), 3–18; Dell Upton and Michael Vlach, introduction, Upton and Vlach, *Common Places*; Thomas Hubka, *Houses without Names: Architectural Nomenclature and the Classification of America's Common Houses* (Knoxville: University of Tennessee Press, 2013), 14–22.

   Various historical and geographical factors have limited the study of vernacular environments. For example, multi-unit apartments in single-family-house-rich Los Angeles have been understudied; see Todd Gish, "Building Los Angeles: Urban Housing in the Suburban Metropolis, 1900–1936" (PhD diss., University of Southern California, 2007), 117–24. In city, state, and federal historic preservation studies and surveys, under State Historic Preservation and U.S. Department of the Interior administrations, preservation recognition and study have historically been awarded to housing based on elite (nonvernacular) stylistic criteria; see Thomas Carter and Elizabeth Collins Cromley, *Introduction to Vernacular Architecture: A Guide to the Study of Ordinary Buildings* (Knoxville: University of Tennessee Press, 2005), 1–18; and Glassie, *Folk Housing in Middle Virginia*, 8–18.

6. There is no standard statistical percentage for "middle majority." For purposes of discussion in this book, 60 percent of the income distribution of housing or population was selected to represent a majority of Americans during the period of study (1900–1940). This construct was necessitated by the fluid, imprecise usage of "middle class" in the dominant housing literatures.

7. In twenty research investigations, the primary goal was to identify a region's most numerous or dominant types of housing in historic periods with an emphasis on the 1900–1940 period. These metropolitan regions were Pittsburgh, Pa.; Cincinnati, Ohio; Portland, Ore.; Portland, Maine; Boston, Mass.; Atlanta, Ga.; Los Angeles; Philadelphia; Chicago; Milwaukee, Wis.; Buffalo, N.Y.; Cleveland, Ohio; Eugene, Ore.; and suburban and rural regions, including southwestern Maine, central New Hampshire, western and eastern Oregon, central Pennsylvania, southeastern Wisconsin, and central New Jersey. Further reconnaissance surveys were conducted in San Francisco; Seattle;

Butte, Mont.; Portsmouth, N.H.; Columbus, Ohio; Baton Rouge, La.; Omaha, Neb.; Minneapolis, Minn.; Salt Lake City, Utah; Macon, Ga.; Providence, R.I.; St. Louis, Mo.; and Brooklyn and Staten Island, N.Y. Over a forty-year period, I have conducted detailed housing studies and taught and practiced architecture in three of these regions: southeastern Maine, concentrating on rural towns; south-central Wisconsin, concentrating on Milwaukee and its suburbs; and Oregon, concentrating on the metropolitan area of Portland and towns and rural areas throughout the state. In each of these regions, I have documented residential landscapes through books and articles, architectural tours, student surveys, academic and popular lectures, and consulting work with state and local preservation groups and historical societies.

While these case-study areas were intended to be broadly representative of American housing development, several regions are less well represented, particularly the South and especially Texas and Florida. I have attempted to compensate through literature survey and interviews with historians such as Carl Lounsbury and Pam Simpson. In a national summary of common house forms, the pre-1940 South differs substantially from other regions, as symbolized by the region's shotgun house. The South also remained somewhat isolated from the mainstream development of early twentieth-century pattern books and housing literature that are explored in this book.

The research program for assessing housing types within selected investigative areas typically included three-to-five-day study tours preceded by preliminary background housing and historical research including the establishment of all-important contacts with local historians and housing authorities to facilitate the selection of neighborhood districts for survey and individual house documentation. During each study tour, neighborhood reconnaissance was conducted with local experts to identify the major types of common housing within sample districts representative of a region's overall pattern of housing development. The goal was to compile both a representative housing census of the dominant house types in successive historic periods and a listing of a range of the most popular local houses. These surveys were followed by individual house inspections of the region's dominant house types, including photographic documentation and, where possible, measured plan drawings.

Subsequent follow-up visits tested initial hypotheses through interviews with local historians and housing experts to assess preliminary findings, leading to subsequent presentations and lectures to neighborhood groups, schools, and historical societies. Hypotheses were further tested through the presentation of housing lectures and national conference papers—principally to the Society of Architecture Historians (SAH); Vernacular Architecture Forum (VAF); Society of American City and Regional Planning History (SACRPH); and American Association of Geographers (AAG) to further test and disseminate research findings.

This atypical research strategy was structured by the lack of accurate and complete house-type data during the study period (1900–1940), plus inadequate data for assessing historic house plans and room usage. Future research techniques may well make this information available; for example, Google Search holds great potential for interpreting all houses. Current photographs, however, limit historical research, especially for locating previous houses and discovering remodeling changes.

8. The localized character of vernacular architecture is recognized in most vernacular scholarship; see Glassie, *Material Culture,* 257–312; Paul Oliver, *Dwellings: The Vernacular House World Wide* (New York: Phaidon Press, 2007), 9–19; and Amos Rapoport, *House Form and Culture* (Englewood Cliffs, N.J.: Prentice Hall, 1969), 46–82. Most studies, however, interpret a preindustrial folk architecture whereas this study evaluates the localized nature of an industrialized, post–Civil War era vernacular housing. See, for example, Hubka, *Houses without Names,* 40–45; Kingston Wm. Heath, *Vernacular Architecture and Regional Design: Cultural Process and Environmental Response* (Burlington, Mass.: Elsevier, 2009), 3–36, 49–60; Kingston Wm. Heath, "Assessing Regional Identity amidst Change: The Role of Vernacular Studies," *Perspectives in Vernacular Architecture* 13, no. 2 (January 2006): 76–94. The localized nature of vernacular housing is a theme developed in different ways throughout this book; see especially chapter 4.

9. Hubka, *Houses without Names,* 6–29.

10. "U.S. Census Bureau, American Housing Survey for the United States," 2016, Housing statistics for historic periods, throughout, taken from Mason C. Doan, *American Housing Production, 1880–2000: A Concise History* (Lanham, Md.: University Press of America, 1997), xiii–xv, 143–57.

11. For an overview of housing demographics, see Dowell Myers, "Introduction: The Emerging Concept of Housing Demography," in *Housing Demography: Linking Demographic Structure and Housing Markets,* ed. Dowell Myers (Madison: University of Wisconsin Press, 1990), 3–31, especially 13, emphasizing, "housing demography or the statistical study of dwellings uniting housing stock and resident populations or households." For a proposal for developing house-type typology on a national scale, see Hubka, *Houses without Names,* 47–63; and Howard Wight Marshall, "Vernacular Housing and American Culture," in

Popular American Housing: A Reference Guide, ed. Ruth Brent and Benyamin Schwarz (Westport, Conn.: Greenwood Press, 1995), 5–8. For a comparison to a building typology from a standard architecture historical perspective, see Nikolaus Pevsner, *A History of Building Types* (Princeton, N.J.: Princeton University Press, 1976).

12. For architectural modernism, see Nikolaus Pevsner, *Pioneers of Modern Design* (New York: Museum of Modern Art, 1949), 7–19, 109–35; Marvin Trachtenberg and Isabelle Hyman, *Architecture: From Prehistory to Postmodernity,* 2d ed. (New York: Pearson, 2003), 464–507; Le Corbusier, *Towards a New Architecture* (New York: Brewer & Warren, 1927), 9–20, 85–104. For architectural modernism in the social science literature of housing, see Gail Radford, *Modern Housing for America: Policy Struggles in the New Deal Era* (Chicago: University of Chicago Press, 1996), 7–109; and H. Peter Oberlander and Eva Newbrun, *Houser: The Life and Work of Catherine Bauer* (Vancouver: University of British Columbia Press, 2002), 48–172.

    How the Working-Class Home Became Modern challenges standard definitions of architectural modernism by interpreting common houses like the bungalow as representative of domestic modernity without the aesthetics of minimal, abstract expressionism typically associated with avant-garde architecture. Despite the overwhelming consensus of professional and academic scholarship about modern aesthetics, there is also a large volume of literature criticizing the limitations of aesthetically focused, avant-garde modernism; for example, Witold Rybczynski, *Home: A Short History of an Idea* (New York: Viking Penguin, 1986); Andres Duany, Elizabeth Plater-Zyberk, and Robert Alminana, *The New Civic Art: Elements of Town Planning* (New York: Rizzoli, 2003), 75, 191, 277, 353; Peter Blake, *Form Follows Fiasco: Why Modern Architecture Hasn't Worked* (Boston: Little, Brown, 1977); and Tom Wolfe, *From Bauhaus to Our House* (New York: Pocket Books, 1982).

13. In a detailed publication about turn-of-the-century poverty, Robert Hunter estimated that 20 percent of Americans existed in conditions of poverty; *Poverty* (New York: Macmillan, 1904), 60. Clair Brown, *American Standard of Living, 1918–1988* (Oxford: Blackwell, 1994), 79–83, estimates 40 percent poverty in 1909, and 30 percent in 1919; James T. Patterson, *America's Struggle against Poverty, 1900–1980* (Cambridge, Mass.: Harvard University Press, 1995), 13, estimates that 40 percent of Americans were considered to be living in poverty in 1900 and approximately 30 percent following the Depression in 1940. Edith Elmer Wood, "That 'One Third of a Nation,'" in *Survey Graphic* 29, no. 2 (February 1940): 83–84, echoes Franklin D. Roosevelt's Second Inaugural Address in 1937 assessing that one-third of households were

in poverty during the Depression. For other assessments of poverty in the first half of the twentieth century, see David Ward, *Poverty, Ethnicity and the American City, 1840–1925* (Cambridge: Cambridge University Press, 1989), 94–150; Paul Boyer, *Urban Masses and Moral Order in America, 1820–1920* (Cambridge, Mass.: Harvard University Press, 1978), 189–232.

Basic definitions for the conditions of poverty vary and are compounded by incomplete data for the pre–World War II period and especially for minority populations. For pre-1940 African American housing poverty, see President's Conference on Home Building and Home Ownership [1931], *Negro Housing: Report of the Committee on Negro Housing,* ed. John M. Gries and James Ford (Washington, D.C., 1932), 4–34, 79–91. For an excellent summary of African American housing conditions in Baltimore's row houses, see Mary Ellen Hayward, *Baltimore's Alley Houses: Homes for the Working People since the 1780s* (Baltimore: Johns Hopkins University Press, 2008), 179–211. For a summary of African American housing conditions on the eve of World War II, see Radford, *Modern Housing for America,* 26–27.

1. HEADWINDS TO RESEARCHING COMMON HOUSES

1. There is no scholarly or popular agreement about what to call most common houses analyzed in this book, either individually or as a type or classification of houses. The many contributing factors are analyzed by Glassie, *Folk Housing in Middle Virginia,* 19–40; Carter and Cromley, *Invitation to Vernacular Architecture,* 65–81; Heath, *Vernacular Architecture and Regional Design,* 2–21; Hubka, *Houses without Names,* 1–30. For overviews, see Howard Davis, *The Culture of Building* (New York: Oxford University Press, 2006), 3–21; Peirce Lewis, "Axioms for Reading the Landscape," in *The Interpretation of Ordinary Landscapes,* ed. D. W. Meinig (New York: Oxford University Press, 1979), 11–32; Rapoport, *House Form and Culture,* 1–17. For nomenclature of common houses today, see Richard Harris, "Tulips in Winter: A Sales Job for the Tract House," in *Buildings & Landscapes: Journal of the Vernacular Architecture Forum* 15 (Fall 2008): 1–10.

2. For a comprehensive visual survey of various housing literatures that consistently display larger, upper-class houses (both photographs and drawings) as the dominant house types representative of American domestic reform, see Richard Cheek, *Selling the Dwellings: The Books That Built America's Houses, 1775–2000* (New York: Grolier Club, 2013); Alan Gowans, *The Comfortable House: North American Suburban Architecture, 1890–1930* (Cambridge, Mass.: MIT Press, 1986); Daniel D.

Reiff, *Houses from Books: The Influence of Treatises, Pattern Books, and Catalogs in American Architecture, 1738–1950; A History and Guide* (University Park: Penn State University Press, 2000). These major studies and other standard works also display modest houses similar to the types emphasized in this book, but they are greatly outnumbered by the larger, middle-to-upper-class dwellings.

This broad assertion about upper-middle-class housing dominance encompasses many different early twentieth-century literatures, including architectural histories, magazines, builders' pattern books, manufacturing catalogs, and novels (as outlined in Cheek, Reiff, and Gowans). In my research involving hundreds of publications for this book, the overwhelming majority of illustrated material showed middle-to-upper-class housing reflective of an upper 20–30 percent of economic distribution in their era or region of origin. While there is a small, diverse, and difficult-to-locate literature about more common houses, it has not generally been used by current researchers when depicting "average," "middle-class" houses. See, for example, Richard Harris's groundbreaking use of obscure builder catalogs and product literature to illuminate common houses and building practices in *Building a Market: The Rise of the Home Improvement Industry, 1914–1960* (Chicago: University of Chicago Press, 2012).

3. Kristina Borrman, "One Standardized House for All: America's Little House," in *Buildings and Landscapes* 24, no. 2 (Fall 2017): 37–57.

4. Janet Hutchison, "The Cure of Domestic Neglect: Better Homes in America, 1922–1935," in *Perspectives in Vernacular Architecture* 2 (1986): 168–78. Hutchison analyzes similar "ideal suburban homes" in "Building for Babbitt: The State and the Suburban Ideal," *Journal of Policy History* 9, no. 2 (1997): 184–210.

5. See the introduction, note 5.

6. In chapter 2, nine seldom-documented turn-of-the-century house types will be identified as some of the most popular of their era. Because there is no accurate documentation of most early twentieth-century house types, especially on a national level, this selection, similar to those identifying house types throughout this book, is largely an estimate based on metropolitan area case studies (see the introduction, note 7), local and regional literature review, and interviews with local and regional scholars.

Adding to the problems of house type identification, many of the most popular houses of the late nineteenth- and early twentieth-century period were built in older, industrial ring suburbs that have received far less study than the post–World War II suburbs; see, for example, articles in *Manufacturing Suburbs: Building Work and Home on the*

Metropolitan Fringe, ed. Robert Lewis (Philadelphia: Temple University Press, 2004), especially the introduction. The gradual destruction of this housing, coupled with the unprecedented rates of postwar housing production and the doubling of the housing stock between 1950 and 1970 (Doan, *American Housing Production, 1880–2000,* 186), has increased the difficulty of documenting the types and densities of the most common houses in the early twentieth century that are key to supporting the conclusions of this book. For estimates of 1900–1940 housing production, I have used Doan, *American Housing Production,* 182–87.

7. Philip Dole analyzes the housing of the early settlement era in *Space, Style, and Structure: Building in Northwest America,* vol. 1, ed. Thomas Vaughan (Portland: Oregon Historical Society, 1974); see "Farmhouses and Barns of the Willamette Valley," 78–129; "The Rural Landscape," 130–40; and "The Aurora Colony," 141–49. Although these are some of the finest studies of the region's early architecture, Dole emphasizes large, upper-middle-class farmsteads and not far more numerous, one-story, two-to-four-room houses.

8. Abbott Lowell Cummings, *The Framed Houses of Massachusetts Bay, 1625–1725* (Cambridge, Mass.: Harvard University Press, 1979), 22–39 and throughout. The vast majority of early settlement house histories (exclusive of pioneering or temporary log cabin structures) have frequently emphasized large, well-documented, upper-middle-class houses. This "first period" problem—the absence of early period popular houses and the emphasis on larger surviving houses—is analyzed in Judith Flanders, *The Making of Home* (London: Atlantic Books, 2015), 58–62, and Hubka, *Houses without Names,* 22–23.

   A recent book that attempts to correct the dominance of larger-house histories in a region well known for its studies of elite dwellings is Cary Carson and Carl R. Lounsbury, eds., *The Chesapeake House: Architectural Investigation by Colonial Williamsburg* (Chapel Hill: University of North Carolina Press, 2013), which addresses a wide range of houses from manor houses to middle-class houses to common houses and slave quarters.

9. Jacob Riis, *How the Other Half Lives* (1890; reprint, Mineola, N.Y.: Dover, 1971). The extraordinary impact and importance of Riis's work on Progressive Era housing and social reform movements are continuously cited in every major study. For example, Boyer, *Urban Masses and Moral Order in America, 1820–1920,* 168 and throughout; Richard Plunz, *A History of Housing in New York City* (New York: Columbia University Press, 1990), 34–36, 50–55.

10. For a focus on wealthy New Yorkers, see David Hammack, *Power and*

Society: Greater New York at the Turn of the Century (New York: Russell Sage Foundation, 1982); and upper-class housing in Elizabeth Collins Cromley, *Alone Together: A History of New York's Early Apartments* (Ithaca, N.Y.: Cornell University Press, 1990), 128–71.

11. Zachary J. Violette, *The Decorated Tenement: How Immigrant Builders and Architects Transformed the Slum in the Gilded Age* (Minneapolis: University of Minnesota Press, 2019), 1–86. Violette's groundbreaking research makes clear that throughout the late nineteenth century a range of working-class-to-middle-class apartment tenements existed in between the extremes of rich and poor that are usually cited. For an excellent analysis of the range of multi-unit housing beyond the tenements, see Plunz, *A History of Housing in New York City,* 88–121. See also Robert G. Barrows, "Beyond the Tenement: Patterns of American Urban Housing, 1870–1930," *Journal of Urban History* 9 (1983): 395–420; Diane Jacobsohn, "Boston's 'Three-Decker Menace': The Buildings, the Builders and the Dwellers, 1870s–1930" (PhD diss., Boston University, 2004), 7–64; Cromley, *Alone Together,* 1–31. The Tenement House Museum in New York City consistently depicts the lives of average tenement families in three-room apartments; those "average" families were not the destitute families Riis documented, as presented in Andrew S. Dolkart, *Biography of a Tenement House in New York City: An Architectural History of 97 Orchard Street* (Charlottesville: University of Virginia Press, 2006).

12. Gordon, *The Rise and Fall of American Growth,* emphasizes that "Riis's title, *How the Other Half Lives,* greatly exaggerates the misery of the working class for the nation taken as a whole" (97). Most turn-of-the-century tenement studies did not attempt to rank or differentiate between domestic conditions of poverty and those from different economic levels of the lower working classes, as shown in Violette, *The Decorated Tenement,* 1–34. Also see Robert W. DeForest and Lawrence Veiller, eds., *The Tenement House Problem,* vols. 1 and 2 (1903; repr., New York: Arno Press and New York Times, 1970), 1:3–43, 193–213, 243–57. The report was first published by the New York State Tenement House Commission. See also the introduction, note 13.

13. Contributing to this dialectic assessment was the practice of calling multi-unit residential buildings either "apartments" or "tenements." Consequently, "tenement," despite its historic application to all scales of multi-unit housing, has been associated with urban slums. See Cromley, *Alone Together,* 12–20. Adding to the complexity of this issue is the problem of how to positively identify middle-to-working-class multi-unit accommodations without the stigma of "tenement" poverty. This problem is compounded because the term "apartment"

is often reserved for upper-class residences of the Progressive Era (see Cromley, 1–31), so that there is no neutral or positive term for the residences of the middle majority not living in conditions of poverty.

Emphasizing the longevity of this problem, Wendy Gamber, in *The Boardinghouse in Nineteenth-Century America* (Baltimore: The Johns Hopkins University Press, 2007), writes that "working-class families had always lived in 'apartments'; indeed, one of the key challenges early apartment builders faced was to distinguish themselves from the crowded tenements that packed urban slums" (165–66).

14. This classic division between the working classes and a bourgeois upper class is shared by most observers of nineteenth-century social and economic conditions; see, for example, Olivier Zunz, *The Changing Face of Inequality: Urbanization, Industrial Development, and Immigrants in Detroit, 1880–1920* (Chicago: University of Chicago Press, 1982), 129–76; Lebergott, *The Americans,* 366–87. Others, such as Stuart M. Blumin, *The Emergence of the Middle Class: Social Experience in the American City, 1760–1900* (Cambridge: Cambridge University Press, 1991), 258–310, analyze the emergence of an enlarged white-collar, nonmanual labor, middle class in the post–Civil War period, an idea developed by Burton J. Bledstein, introduction, Bledstein and Johnston, *The Middling Sorts*; and Gordon, *The Rise and Fall of American Growth,* 46–47, 52–61. For an analysis of the tensions between these two cultures, see Boyer, *Urban Masses and Moral Order in America,* 132–42.

The dramatic late nineteenth- and early twentieth-century social and economic progress in altering these seemingly intractable human conditions is analyzed by Deaton, *The Great Escape*; Clark, *A Farewell to Alms*; Thomas Piketty, *Capital in the Twenty-First Century,* trans. Arthur Goldhammer (Cambridge, Mass.: Harvard University Press, 2014); Lebergott, *The Americans,* and especially, Gordon, *The Rise and Fall of American Growth,* 46–47, 52–61. Although these books vary widely, they are united by the story they present of unprecedented industrial-technological-scientific progress leading to unprecedented Western European and American economic and social development in the late nineteenth and early twentieth century.

15. Robert G. Barrows highlights the statistical marginality of large-scale, masonry tenement apartments and the dominance of small wooden buildings even in urban-metropolitan areas up until the 1920s; see "Beyond the Tenement: Patterns of American Urban Housing, 1870–1930," *Journal of Urban History* 9, no. 4 (August 1983): 395–420. For example, Detroit in 1903 was 87 percent single-family houses; see Zunz, *The Changing Face of Inequality,* 156. DeForest and Veiller described the city as "having no housing problem at all and tenement houses are

unknown" in *The Tenement House Problem,* 1:146–47. For the evolution of the term "tenement," see Jacobsohn's dissertation, "Boston's 'Three-Decker Menace,'" 30–36.

Concentrations of multistory, masonry tenements, although rare, occur in other American cities. For example, Cincinnati contains a smaller, indigenous type of late nineteenth-century three- and four-story, urban tenement concentrated in the Over-the-Rhine district that parallels New York City's development, although at a much smaller scale. See Robert J. Wimberg, *Cincinnati: Over-the-Rhine; A Historical Guide to 19th Century Buildings and Their Residents* (Cincinnati: Ohio Book Store Publishers, 1987); and Thomas Hubka, "Cincinnati's Housing for the Working Class, 1865–1930" (paper presented at Society of Architectural Historians annual meeting, Cincinnati, April 2008).

16. For "cult of domesticity" literature, see Clark, *The American Family Home, 1860–1960,* 3–71; and Gwendolyn Wright, *Moralism and the Model Home: Domestic Architecture and Cultural Conflict in Chicago, 1873–1913* (Chicago: University of Chicago Press, 1980), 9–20. Many writers acknowledge the writings of Andrew Jackson Downing as an important source for the popularization of the "cult of domesticity," especially his *The Architecture of Country Houses* (1859; repr., Mineola, N.Y.: Dover, 1969); see also Jackson, *Crabgrass Frontier,* 45–52.

17. This journalistic criticism of existing vernacular housing is an assessment of broad trends in national literature during the late nineteenth and early twentieth century, for example, as reviewed in hundreds of articles assessing housing in New England's agricultural journals and magazines between 1850 and 1920; see Thomas C. Hubka, *Big House, Little House, Back House, Barn: The Connected Farm Buildings of New England* (Lebanon, N.H.: University Press of New England, 1984), 134–38, 181–86, 196–98. See also Richard Harris, *Building a Market: The Rise of the Home Improvement Industry* (Chicago: University of Chicago Press, 2012), 1–10; Joseph Bigott, *From Cottage to Bungalow: Houses and the Working Class in Metropolitan Chicago 1869–1929* (Chicago: University of Chicago Press, 2001), 1–16; Wright, *Moralism and the Model Home,* 199–227; and Clark, *American Family Home,* 73–102.

Late nineteenth-century housing reform literature rarely analyzed or illustrated existing common vernacular houses as sources for housing ideas (except to caricature and condemn); see Hubka, *Big House, Little House, Back House, Barn*; and Herbert Gottfried and Jan Jennings, *American Vernacular: Buildings and Interiors, 1870–1940* (New York: W. W. Norton, 2000), 1–16.

18. Harris, *Building a Market,* documents the absence of home remodeling studies; see also Richard Harris, *Unplanned Suburbs: Toronto's American*

Tragedy, 1900–1950 (Baltimore: Johns Hopkins University Press, 1999), 200–232. For home remodeling in New Deal studies, see President's Conference on Home Building and Home Ownership [1931], *Reconditioning, Remodeling, and Modernizing Home,* ed. John M. Gries and James Ford (Washington, D.C., 1932).

19. Chad Garrett Randl, "'Live Better Where You Are': Home Improvement and the Rhetoric of Renewal in the Postwar United States" (PhD diss., Cornell University, 2014), 29–36 and throughout. See also Harris, *Building a Market,* 229–346; Lizabeth Cohen, *A Consumers' Republic: The Politics of Mass Consumption in Postwar America* (New York: Vintage Books, 2004), 112–65. See note 61 in this chapter.

20. Gordon, *Rise and Fall of American Growth,* 128.

21. Merritt Ierley, *The Comforts of Home: The American House and the Evolution of Modern Convenience* (New York: Clarkson Potter, 1999), 172, provides a comprehensive review of nineteenth-century domestic technological development while recognizing that by 1900 most inventions had not been widely distributed. Similarly, most studies of domestic technologies concentrate on the date or era of first invention or usage. Unavoidably, this strategy imprints a single date or era associated with an invention or technological development, as Edison's first lightbulb experiment reinforces a 1880s interpretation of electrification. For the purposes of this book, however, the dates and circumstances of invention are secondary to understanding the demographics of usage and distribution—when various percentages of Americans received improvements or utilities. For example, the mid-1920s was the tipping point when more than half of American families gained electricity; see Lebergott, *The Americans,* 352.

22. For a comprehensive review of the factors of wealth and class that structured the distribution of utilities, see S. J. Kleinberg, *The Shadow of the Mills: Working-Class Families in Pittsburgh, 1870–1907* (Pittsburgh: University of Pittsburgh Press, 1991), 84–93; also see Ierley, *Comforts of Home,* 142–50.

23. Because small private companies generally controlled the production of gas, it is extremely difficult to determine the national demographics of late nineteenth- and early twentieth-century popular gas installation and usage. See various studies for differing assessments of gas usage and installation: Ierley, *Comforts of Home,* 56–61, 136–40; Kleinberg, *Shadow of the Mills,* 214.

In 1900 there is little evidence of gas lighting on a national scale in the homes of the middle-to-working classes just as the increasing availability of electric lighting reduced the use of gas lighting for all classes; Ierley, *Comforts of Home,* 139–40. Rybczynski's *Home,* 138–43, cites the development and popularity of gas lighting in urban areas and "middle class" users, but this probably included no more than 30 percent of urban residences in the studies he cites.

24. For experimentations in plumbing development before the standardization of the three-fixture bath, see Maureen Ogle, *All the Modern Conveniences: American Household Plumbing, 1840–1890* (Baltimore: The Johns Hopkins University Press, 1996), 119–52; Ierley, *Comforts of Home,* 65–72, 85–91, 98–103, 141–50; and Moskowitz, *Standard of Living,* 64–77. Most sources emphasize the long period of nineteenth-century experimentation in various methods of plumbing and waste removal before settling upon flush water systems with gas traps and vent piping at the turn of the twentieth century; see Ierley, *Comforts of Home,* 141–50.

25. Margaret Byington, *Homestead: The Households of a Mill Town* (New York: Russell Sage Foundation, 1910), 60.

26. Paul Groth, "Workers'-Cottage and Minimal-Bungalow Districts," *Urban Morphology* 8, no. 1 (2004): 17. During the Depression my grandfather Anthony Hubka with uncle Andrew Mazurek, an experienced plumber-builder, installed a basement toilet in my family's two-story, side-hall house in Perth Amboy, New Jersey, to convert the home into a duplex. Information obtained from family interviews.

27. Bernard Waites, "The Language and Imagery of 'Class' in Early Twentieth-Century England (circa 1900–1925)," *Literature and History* 4, no. 4 (1976): 30–55. For an excellent overview of English influences on "middle class" traditions in American domestic development, see John Archer, *Architecture and Suburbia: From English Villa to American Dream House, 1690–2000* (Minneapolis: University of Minnesota Press, 2005), 45–92, 173–202. Archer also emphasized English influences on American suburban housing development. See also Peirce Lewis, "Common Houses, Cultural Spoor," in *Re-Reading Cultural Geography,* ed. Kenneth Foote et al. (Austin: University of Texas Press, 1994), 85–86.

   English judgments of American architectural and domestic traditions by critics as different as Frances Trollope, Charles Dickens, and Oscar Wilde have had extraordinary influence on American domestic tastes and manners; see, for example, Richard L. Bushman, *The Refinement of America: Persons, Houses, Cities* (New York: Alfred A. Knopf, 1992), 402–20. For the British books that shaped America's architecture, see Reiff, *Houses from Books,* 5–22. On the persistence of English culture as a primary shaper of American culture, see David Hackett Fischer, *Albion's Seed: Four British Folkways in America* (New York: Oxford University Press, 1989).

The English influence on American architectural development is profound and ubiquitous, including common housing, from the earliest colonial periods until the advent of modernism. Anti-English attitudes following the revolution briefly interrupted British architectural influence, but English sources and building traditions were never relinquished. English influences are assumed by most historians to such an extent that they are sometimes insufficiently mentioned or analyzed. The intertwining nature of this influence is evident, for example, in the study and appreciation of American colonial architecture and the Queen Anne style in England and America. For a comprehensive summary, see Reiff, *Houses from Book,* 1–78 and throughout.

28. See, for example, "inexpensive bungalows," in Richard Cheek, *Selling the Dwelling,* 201.

29. Candace M. Volz, "The Modern Look of the Early Twentieth-Century House: A Mirror of Changing Lifestyles," in *American Home Life, 1880–1930: A Social History of Spaces and Services,* ed. Jessica H. Foy and Thomas J. Schlereth (Knoxville: University of Tennessee Press, 1994), 26.

30. Gordon, *Rise and Fall of American Growth,* 53, 276.

31. The emergence of the twentieth-century middle class is treated by many authors; see the introduction, note 3. For an excellent account of a growing white-collar, nonmanual labor component of the nineteenth-century middle class, see Blumin, *Emergence of the Middle Class,* 258–97; and Moskowitz, *Standard of Living,* 220–38.

    In addition to "middle-class creep," there is a tendency for many authors, myself included, to enlarge the boundaries of their housing topics, often by stating or implying that an observation or characteristic about housing is common or widespread (or is becoming so), when, in fact, the reference has a more limited application—to a smaller-than-majority portion of the population. About this tendency to exaggerate, I have found few authors writing about the "middle class" who would err in the opposite direction, except, of course, for elite studies that wish to confirm the uniqueness or rarity of a building or characteristic. Similar traditions are present in English housing history, but there is generally a collective realization that the pre-1900 "middle class" refers to a very small economic upper class of the population, never a majority constituency. American sensibilities and traditions, however, have generally erred in the opposite direction by enlarging constituencies of the implied "middle class."

32. The classic works of architecture history have long relegated topics of vernacular architecture to a separate, marginal place, often as a topic of prehistoric studies, as in Trachtenberg and Hyman, *Architecture,*

57–62, or as a subject of global (or foreign) architectural analysis, as in Nezar AlSayyad, *Cairo: Histories of a City* (Cambridge, Mass.: Belknap Press, 2011). These tendencies have, unfortunately, been reinforced by vernacular scholars who have treated common, vernacular architecture as standing outside the larger traditions of common architecture and culture, particularly modern industrialized cultures. These themes have also been exaggerated in popular picture books such as Bernard Rudofsky's *Architecture without Architects: A Short Introduction to Non-Pedigreed Architecture* (1964; repr., Albuquerque: University of New Mexico Press, 1987), which typically romanticize and distort the design traditions of vernacular builders. The study of modern, everyday, industrialized vernacular architecture has attracted less scholarship, as analyzed in Gwendolyn Wright's critique of traditional vernacular scholarship, "On Modern Vernaculars and J. B. Jackson," in *Everyday America: Cultural Landscape Studies after J. B. Jackson,* ed. Chris Wilson and Paul Erling Groth (Berkeley: University of California Press, 2003), 163–98.

33. E. P. Thompson, *The Making of the English Working Class* (London: Penguin, 2013).

34. David E. Nye, *Electrifying America: Social Meaning of a New Technology* (Cambridge, Mass.: MIT Press, 1991), 254.

35. For example, Rybczynski's *Home* is an outstanding work based largely on the history of upper-middle-class domestic conditions. His analysis follows a consensus of major historians who emphasize the foundations of American domestic customs in sixteenth-to-eighteenth-century English and Dutch traditions. See Simon Schama, *The Embarrassment of Riches: An Interpretation of Dutch Culture in the Golden Age* (New York: Alfred A. Knopf, 1987), 373–480. (Schama does not treat the subsequent influence of Dutch domestic culture on English and American traditions.)

36. See Flanders, *The Making of Home,* an excellent work consistently emphasizing the domestic history of common people.

37. Estimates of the total number of kit houses vary considerably and rely principally on the records of the top five-to-ten major manufacturers, such as Sears, Roebuck, Montgomery Ward, Aladdin, Gordon–Van Tine, as outlined in Robert Schweitzer and Michael W. R. Davis, *America's Favorite Homes: Mail-Order Catalogues as a Guide to Popular Early 20th-Century Houses* (Detroit, Mich.: Wayne State University Press, 1990), 61–75; and Katherine Cole and H. Ward Jandl, *Houses by Mail: A Guide to Houses from Sears, Roebuck, and Company* (New York: Wiley, 1986), 19–43. Dozens of smaller companies also produced kits; see *California's Kit Homes: A Reprint of the 1925 Pacific Ready-Cut Homes*

Catalog, intro. Rosemary Thornton and Dale Patrick Wolicki (Alton, Ill.: Gentle Beam Publications, 2004), i–xvii. For a review of individual kit houses companies, see Reiff, *Houses from Books,* 149–206; Schweitzer and Davis, *America's Favorite Homes.*

Combining these sources, 400,000 kit house units may have been constructed during the thirty-year period of major construction, 1900–1930, averaging almost 14,000 per year, or approximately .03 percent of the total of new house construction (14 million units) during this period. Yet even this total of kit houses may have been significantly smaller because of widely acknowledged discrepancies resulting from partial kit house orders and plan-only and specialized orders, as recognized in Schweitzer and Davis, *America's Favorite Homes,* 65–66. In addition, some kit house research has been compiled by stated advocates and boosters of kit houses with perhaps less incentive to critically examine manufacturing totals from product literature for partial or catalog-only sales.

For an alternative view, see Richard Harris, who estimates that less than .05 percent were kit houses in their major period of development, "The Rise of Filtering Down: The American Housing Market Transformed, 1915–1929," *Social Science History* 37, no. 4 (Winter 2013): 525.

Over a fifteen-year period of research for this book in hundreds of survey neighborhoods from throughout the country, the presence of documented kit houses was rarely recorded in sufficient numbers to warrant mention as a significant factor in the production of early twentieth-century housing. It is important to add "documented" kit houses because the recent newfound recognition and popularity of "kit houses" by the general public has increased the number of small, common houses that are incorrectly identified as "kit houses" without any documentary evidence merely because they are small and common. This is an observation compiled in housing research, publication, and dissemination in public lectures over a forty-year period. See the introduction, note 7.

38. Bigott, *From Cottage to Bungalow,* 228, note 81.
39. The design and construction methods of vernacular builder-developers are analyzed in Hubka, *Houses without Names,* 37–40; and "Just Folks Designing: Vernacular Designers and the Generation of Form," in Upton and Vlach, *Common Places,* 426–32 (originally published in *Journal of Architectural Education* 32, no. 3 [1979]: 27–29). Henry Glassie has analyzed vernacular builder methods, especially from preindustrial communities, in many works, e.g., *Folk Housing in Middle Virginia,* 19–40 and throughout; *Passing the Time in Ballymenone* (Philadelphia:

University of Pennsylvania Press, 1982), 315–424. Also see Wright, *Moralism and the Model Home*, 14–21; and Reiff, *Houses from Books*, 149–251, especially 244–51. For an excellent analysis of the design methods of brick row house builders in Washington, D.C., see Melissa McLoud, "Craftsmen and Entrepreneurs: Builders of the Red Brick City, 1880–1900," in *Housing Washington: Two Centuries of Residential Development and Planning in the National Capital Area*, ed. Richard Longstreth (Chicago: Center for American Places, 2010), 23–39.

New methods of post–Civil War, industrial-vernacular methods used by small-scale builders have not received adequate historical analysis but can be gleaned from the collective record of common house production, as outlined, for example, in Mary Ellen Hayward's *Baltimore's Alley Houses*. In his influential *Streetcar Suburbs: The Process of Growth in Boston (1870–1900)* (Cambridge, Mass.: Harvard University Press, 1962), 126–29, Sam Bass Warner Jr. credits the massive building of Boston's suburbs to nine thousand small-scale "suburban builders" between 1872 and 1901, working speculatively, without architects and typically producing fewer than four houses per year. Diane Jacobsohn also analyzed Boston's common builders in her dissertation, "Boston's 'Three-Decker Menace,'" 144–53. See also Donna J. Rilling, *Making Houses, Crafting Capitalism: Builders in Philadelphia, 1790–1850* (Philadelphia: University of Pennsylvania Press, 2001). Although Rilling analyzes an earlier period, *Making Houses* is one of the finest histories of small-scale builders and speculative building practices. Although she does not address the production of housing, Lizabeth A. Cohen, *Making a New Deal: Industrial Workers in Chicago, 1919–1939* (Cambridge: Cambridge University Press, 1990), 99–158, provides a useful framework, in the chapter titled "Encountering Mass Culture," for interpreting popular consumption that has informed the production of common houses.

The speculative practices of large scale, post–World War II builder-developers are more frequently analyzed, such as the Levitt family, in Richard Longstreth, "The Levitts, Mass-Produced Houses, and Community Planning in the Mid-Twentieth Century," in *Second Suburb: Levittown, Pennsylvania*, ed. Dianne Harris (Pittsburgh: University of Pittsburgh Press, 2010), 123–74. Ann Durkin Keating analyzes a late nineteenth-century speculative builder-developer, S. E. Gross of Chicago, in *Building Chicago: Suburban Developers and the Creation of a Divided Metropolis* (1988; reprint, Champaign: University of Illinois Press, 2002), 70–88; and Marc A. Weiss assesses the developer profession in *The Rise of the Community Builders: The American Real Estate Industry and Urban Land Planning* (New York: Columbia University Press, 1987), 1–90.

For an in-depth analysis of suburban house builders and their design and construction methods in the postwar suburban period, see Barbara Miller Lane, *Houses for a New World: Builders and Buyers in American Suburbs, 1945–1965* (Princeton, N.J.: Princeton University Press, 2015), 47–186. Similar house-builder studies have generally concentrated on builders with the largest volume of well-documented housing construction. Such builders, however, were responsible only for a small percentage of pre-1940s housing construction. Small-scale builders, who have built the vast majority of America's housing, are much more difficult to document and their design and construction methods remain relatively unexplored. See Bigott, *From Cottage to Bungalow*; Carolyn S. Loeb, *Entrepreneurial Vernacular: Developers' Subdivisions in the 1920s* (Baltimore: The Johns Hopkins University Press, 2001); and Reiff, *Houses from Books*, 256–67, for analysis of common builder methods and insights into the difficulties of recording their design-building process. For an overview of the parallel development of speculative building traditions in England in the nineteenth century, see John Burnett, *A Social History of Housing, 1815–1985* (London: Methuen, 1986), 20–29.

When assessing the speculative methods of common house builders, it is important to distinguish between the pre–Civil War era (as defined by Glassie in *Folk Housing*) and the post–Civil War era industrial vernacular methods (as defined by Hubka, *Houses without Names*). For an overview of vernacular methods, see Carter and Cromley, *Introduction to Vernacular Architecture,* 13–18. Howard Davis provides an excellent analysis of the design decision-making process for common buildings in a broader global cultural context; see "Rules and Knowledge about Building," chapter 3 of *The Culture of Building* (New York: Oxford University Press, 2006), 85–218. Rapoport provides a classic interpretation of environmental design in premodern societies in *House Form and Culture*, 18–45, 104–25. For a rare, in-depth analysis of the complete developmental process behind the production of a post–World War II developer subdivision, see Witold Rybczynski, *Last Harvest: How a Cornfield Became New Daleville* (New York: Scribner, 2007). Rybczynski's analysis reminds the reader that builder-contractors continue to follow basic patterns of marketing and production similar to those of early twentieth-century builders.

40. See the last paragraph of the immediately preceding note.
41. In every metropolitan and rural region investigated for this study,

builder data were consistently investigated, (see the introduction, note 7). While owner-builders were mentioned in interviews with local housing experts and residents, in no metropolitan area or region was their presence identified as a significant factor. In only a few of the hundreds of books and articles investigated for this book was the presence of owner-builders a significant factor (those sources will be cited in the following notes).

The literature about owner-builders is dominated by the groundbreaking scholarship of Richard Harris in several works, among them, *Building a Market*, 23–53, 229–63, and throughout; Harris, *Unplanned Suburbs*, 177–99. Also see Nicolaides, *My Blue Heaven*, 27–35, 205–19; and "'Where the Working Man Is Welcome': Working-Class Suburbs in Los Angeles, 1900–1940," *Pacific Historical Review* 68 (November 1999): 517–59.

Except in the specific, limited areas and depression eras, as cited in Harris and Nicolaides, there is little documented evidence that owner-builders made up significant percentages of housing construction in any American metropolitan area's or region's total housing stock. See my analysis of Milwaukee in note 49, this chapter.

42. Beginning in the early twentieth century, it is important to distinguish between rapidly increasing owner-remodelers (Harris, *Building a Market*, 229–63) and the specialized skills of rare owner-builders capable of constructing an entire house. Similarly, it is important to distinguish between an owner's or buyer's partial contribution and the fundamental role of the often uncredited professional builder or technical tradesperson in the overall construction process. For an excellent review of the complexities of builder-contractor nomenclature and definitions, such as a small scale, "owner-builder contractor," see *Structure of the Residential Building Industry in 1949*, U.S. Department of Labor Bulletin no. 1170 (November 1954): 1–10. (In *Streetcar Suburbs*, Warner uses multiple meanings of the term builder: developer, financer, speculator, and owner; 37.) When considering these complexities, it is not hard to appreciate how differences in assessing and counting owner-builders might occur. Good scholars might, of course, differ about the basic definitions. Here owner-builder means the total, multifaceted expertise it takes to build a complete home in any era—and this typically applies to rare individuals and not to the contributions of house remodelers, no matter how extensive their contribution.

Zunz, in *The Changing Face of Inequality*, 129–76, makes an extensive analysis of the differentiation between professional builders and independent ethnic-local builders with informal, localized, catch-as-catch-can building practices without the aid of realtors, architects, or government agencies. Though unlicensed, these "local professionals" contractors are still professional builders and not owner-builders; Zunz, 172, 173. This is the type of complex housing data most readily obtained in detailed fieldwork studies, the type continually cited in this book, notably in studies by Paul Groth, Kim Hoagland, Joseph Bigott, and Daniel Reiff.

43. According to building permit records for Portland, Oregon's Eastmoreland neighborhood, it was common for small-scale builders to establish first ownership of new housing before selling. Data collected for the Eastmoreland Neighborhood, Historic District nomination process, City of Portland, Development Services Department. See also *Structure of the Residential Building Industry in 1949,* which defines several categories of builder-contractors, such as "operative builders," that build houses on a small scale and are sometimes listed as owner-builders. Partial and incomplete documentation of building permits and practices outside municipal boundaries makes this a confusing, difficult-to-research topic; see Harris, *Building a Market,* 1–19.

44. Zunz, *Changing Face of Inequality,* 170–76.

45. The record of professional assistance is consistently cited in agricultural building histories nationwide, for example, Glassie, *Folk Housing in Middle Virginia,* 19–40. During a twenty-year period, I researched and interviewed farmers from all parts of the country, particularly in New England, Wisconsin, and Oregon to understand the history and construction of their farm buildings. When farmers had detailed knowledge of the construction history of their buildings, they consistently credited an experienced builder (often a local farmer with special skills) as the primary designer-builder for their houses and barns. Most of these informants also emphasized how they, or their ancestors, assisted in the construction process. For a historical analysis of farm buildings and their builders in northern New England, see Hubka, *Big House, Little House, Back House, Barn,* including the contribution of farmers to the building of their own houses and barns.

46. Margaret Garb, *City of American Dreams: A History of Home Ownership and Housing Reform in Chicago, 1871–1919* (Chicago: University of Chicago Press, 2005), 43.

47. Nicolaides, *My Blue Heaven,* 26–38, emphasizes the limited financial resources of owner-builders in urban fringe conditions of Los Angeles in the early twentieth century. About the use and reuse of existing buildings, see Richard U. Ratcliff, "Filtering Down and the Elimination of Substandard Housing," *Journal of Land & Public Utility Economics* 21, no. 4 (November 1945): 322–30; Richard Harris, "The Rise of Filtering Down: The American Housing Market Transformed, 1915–1929,"

Social Science History 37, no. 4 (Winter 2013): 515–49; and David Ward, *Poverty, Ethnicity and the American City,* 94–147. For minimal and temporary housing conditions during the Depression Era, see Edith Elmer Wood, "That 'One Third of a Nation,'" *Survey Graphic* 29, no. 2 (February 1940): 83–84. For an overview, see Nancy Isenberg, *White Trash: The 400-Year Untold Story of Class in America* (New York: Viking, 2016), 175–230.

48. In the twenty metropolitan and rural regions surveyed for this book (see the introduction, note 7) and the investigation of housing studies and builder interviews over forty years, I never found owner-builders in concentrations that would warrant mention in articles and books about housing. Based on these studies, I would estimate that no more than .03 percent of the total number of American houses built between 1900 and 1940 were substantially owner-built and not just the contribution of the owner to the building process. Also see chapter 1, notes 43 and 45.

49. Most estimates of owner-builders in Milwaukee are drawn from the work of Craig Thomas Reisser, "Immigrants and House Form in Northeast Milwaukee" (MA thesis, University of Wisconsin–Milwaukee, 1977), 35–45 and throughout; and Roger Simon, "Houses and Services in an Immigrant Neighborhood," *Journal of Urban History* 2, no. 4 (1976): 435–58; and "City Building Process: Housing Services in New Milwaukee Neighborhoods, 1880–1910," *Transactions of the American Philosophical Society* 65 (1978): 39–40. Both authors based their owner-builder analyses on limited interviews of descendants of the residents described as owner-builders. In similar interviews, I discovered that by inquiring about the details of construction, for example, "When granddad built your Polish Flat," it would often be explained that the family provided limited actual labor and that they relied on (Polish) community builders. An inspection of the city's directories from the late nineteenth and early twentieth century provides evidence of the many firms serving the building needs of various ethnic communities. See Judith T. Kenny, Deanna Benson, and David Bump, "Beyond 'the Zone of Workingmen's Homes': Locating Industrial Neighborhoods in Milwaukee's Real Estate Market, 1880–1930," *Wisconsin Geographer* 21 (2006): 15–40.

For analyses of builders and their building practices for Milwaukee's late nineteenth- and early twentieth-century Polish working classes, see Thomas Hubka and Judith Kenny, "The Workers' Cottage in Milwaukee's Polish Community," *Perspectives in Vernacular Architecture* 8 (2000): 33–52; Hubka and Kenny, "Examining the American Dream:

Housing Standards and the Emergence of a National Housing Culture, 1900–1930," *Perspectives in Vernacular Architecture* 13, no. 1 (2006): 49–69. See also Judith T. Kenny, "Polish Routes to Americanization: House Form and Landscape on Milwaukee's Polish South Side," *Wisconsin Land and Life,* ed. R. Ostergren and T. Vale (Madison: University of Wisconsin Press, 1996), 263–81; "The Homebuilders: The Residential Landscape of Milwaukee's Polonia, 1870–1920," *Milwaukee History* 22, no. 2 (Summer 1999): 99–116; "Americanizing Milwaukee's Polish South Side, 1900–1925," *Wisconsin Geographer* 10 (March 1994): 41–50. Research for these articles included detailed documentation of common Polish housing and extensive interviews with residents. Results were corroborated by University of Wisconsin–Milwaukee student research projects for Kenny and Hubka, including detailed interviews and building analysis.

Similar to the way in which additive construction or irregular setbacks cannot be assumed to be the mark of owner-builders (see the following note), so too the presence of an "incidence of unique dwellings," the "distinctive character" of the owner, and "low assessed value" do not automatically indicate the presence of owner-builders as cited by Reisser and Simon and emphasized in Harris, *Unplanned Suburbs,* 224–25. Furthermore, in the conclusion to *Unplanned Suburbs,* Harris strongly links the existence of U.S. working-class industrial suburbs to the widespread presence of owner-builders, but this assertion cannot be assumed from studies of industrial suburbs except to note the presence of owners who contributed to their building projects. In a detailed study of working-class housing in the Calumet-Hammond region, Bigott's detailed analysis of workers' cottages and bungalows did not reveal the presence of owner-builders although owner contributions to the building process were widely observed; see Bigott *From Cottage to Bungalow,* 1–16.

50. Nicolaides, *My Blue Heaven,* 31. I would argue that the presence of irregular setbacks and other house grid irregularities strongly suggests evidence for an informal housing market as described by Zunz and Kenny and often the presence of owner-builder-contributors in this irregular market and not necessarily the presence of owner-builders who executed the entire project. See notes 47 and 49, this chapter.

51. See chapter 1, note 39.

52. Archer, *Architecture and Suburbia,* 423, note 2.

53. On immigrant "hunger" for home ownership, see, for example, Elaine Lewinnek, *The Working Man's Reward: Chicago's Early Suburbs and the Roots of Suburban Sprawl* (Oxford: Oxford University Press, 2014), 33–112, esp. 108–12; and Hubka and Kenny, "The Workers' Cottage

in Milwaukee's Polish Community." See also this chapter, notes 49 and 56. For the pros and cons of home ownership, see Garb, *City of American Dreams*, 148–207.

54. Doan, *American Housing Production, 1880–2000*, 186. Many housing studies frequently cite the rise in the attainment of home ownership to record 60 percent levels in the post–World War II period of suburban development. In this study, however, during the 1900–1940 period of study, 55 percent of households on average did not own their dwellings. Also see Albert Chevan, "The Growth of Home Ownership: 1940–1980," *Demography* 26, no. 2 (May 1989): 249–66; and Gordon, *Rise and Fall of American Growth*, 105–7.

55. President's Conference on Home Building and Home Ownership [1931], *Negro Housing*, 35–48, 79–91; Patterson, *America's Struggle against Poverty*, 9–19; and Harvey Green, *The Uncertainty of Everyday Life, 1915–1945* (New York: HarperCollins, 1992), 98–104.

    For the complex issues surrounding Black acceptance or accommodation with new housing construction and the issue of its white symbolism, see Barbara Burlison Mooney, "The Comfortable Tasty Framed Cottage: An African American Architectural Iconography," in *Journal of the Society of Architectural Historians* 61, no. 1 (March 2002): 48–67.

56. Bigott, *From Cottage to Bungalow*, 7; and Hubka and Kenny, "The Workers' Cottage in Milwaukee's Polish Community."

57. Radford, *Modern Housing for America*, 26–27.

58. For the rebound in late 1930s housing production, see Doan, *American Housing Production, 1880–2000*, 183; Harris, *Building a Market*, 127–89; and as recorded in Joseph B. Mason, *History of Housing in the U.S., 1930–1980* (Houston: Gulf Publishing, 1982), 25–30. For the improvements in rural electrification during the 1930s, see Nye, *Electrifying America*, 23–25, 286–335. For increases in utility distribution after the early years of the depression, see Gordon, *Rise and Fall of American Growth*, 113–28. For an overall assessment of the rebounding consumer economy, see Cohen, *Consumers' Republic*, 18–41.

59. For the 1940 Census of Housing, see Gordon, *Rise and Fall of American Growth*, 120–22; Doan, *American Housing Production*, 46–48; Howard G. Brunsman, "The Housing Census of 1940," *Journal of the American Statistical Association* 36, no. 215 (September 1941): 393–400. Many of the 1940 census statistics documenting widespread domestic improvements are foreshadowed in Robert S. Lynd and Helen M. Lynd, *Middletown: A Study in American Culture* (New York: Harcourt, Brace, 1929), 93–109, 167–78; and Lynd and Lynd, *Middletown in Transition: A Study in Cultural Conflicts* (New York: Mariner, 1982), 144–203.

60. Frank Coffey and Joseph Layden, *America on Wheels: The First One Hundred Years, 1896–1996* (Los Angeles: General Publishing Group, 1996), 35–120.

61. For a list of the most significant new building products in 1933, see Mason, *History of Housing in the U.S., 1930–1980,* 27. For an analysis of pre-1940 tract developments that documents many of the practices of post–World War II construction, see Loeb, *Entrepreneurial Vernacular,* 1–15 and throughout. For a detailed analysis of the status of 1930s house construction materials and methods, see The President's Conference on Home Building and Home Ownership, Washington, D.C. [1931], *House Design, Construction and Equipment,* ed. John M. Gries and James Ford (Washington, D.C., 1932), 1–325; Harris, *Building a Market,* 161–85; and Gordon, *Rise and Fall of American Growth,* 113–28. Also see this chapter, notes 18 and 19.

    The literature of modern architecture consistently emphasizes pre–World War II technological development in housing construction, as summarized in Trachtenberg and Hyman, *Architecture,* 491–517. In an ironic twist, the Levitt brothers built larger, higher-quality houses before the war than in their widely studied postwar suburban tract developments; Longstreth, "The Levitts, Mass-Produced Houses, and Community Planning in the Mid-twentieth Century," 126–33.

62. In surveys of Portland, Oregon's "Eastside" neighborhoods with high concentrations of post–World War II dwellings, the vast majority of houses lacked modernist features such as plate glass walls, prominent roof-beam extensions, and open plans as featured in avant-garde literature, for example, in Joseph Eichler–inspired houses. Most houses were constructed in styles uniting historic Colonial Revival features with modest modern details, such as glass block, corner windows, and small, flat-roofed porch canopies. Similar examples were constructed throughout the country as surveyed in all metropolitan and rural areas investigated for this book (see the introduction, note 7). These traditional-looking, nonmodernist houses are confirmed in most common housing studies, for example, Loeb, *Entrepreneurial Vernacular,* 34–37 and throughout, and continued into the postwar era; as shown in Lane, *Houses for a New World,* 8–20 and throughout; and Jamie A. Jacobs, *Detached America: Building Houses in Postwar Suburbs* (Charlottesville: University of Virginia Press, 2015), illustrations throughout. Also see the introduction, note 12.

    Modern architectural literature has consistently exaggerated the impact and presence of avant-garde influences on popular housing, as satirized in the work of Tom Wolfe, especially *From Bauhaus to Our House.*

2. TWO WORLDS APART

1. On the partial successes of late nineteenth-century reforms see Gordon, *The Rise and Fall of American Growth*, 27–61; Kleinberg, *The Shadow of the Mills*, 65–99. For example, the founders of utopian, experimental industrial villages, Titus Salt of Saltaire, England, and George Pullman of Pullman, Illinois, experienced considerable difficulties in achieving long-term domestic improvements for even small segments of the working classes. The limits of late nineteenth-century economic and social progress to eliminate inequities and scarcities for the general public were the basis for theorists like Karl Marx to advocate for class struggle in *Das Kapital* (*Capital: Critique of Political Economy*). For the foundations of twentieth-century economic progress to overcome these inequities, see Piketty's introduction to *Capital in the Twenty-First Century*, 7–13.

2. See chapter 1, note 14.

3. Doan, *American Housing Production*, 182; Barrows, "Beyond the Tenement."

4. There are no reliable national statistics for identifying the basic types of housing (such as bungalows, ranches, and Four-Squares) in any period, as well as statistics for their house size and number of rooms until the 1940 census. Furthermore, although there is general agreement about how to identify a few common houses (such as bungalows and Four-Squares), there is no agreement about names and classifications for most common houses, nor is there agreement about the basic definitions of "house type." See Hubka, *Houses without Names*, 1–30. Also see chapter 1, note 6.

   Lacking this information, the selection of nine of America's most common houses types in 1900 is, therefore, a hypothesis based on a limited sample of city and regional case studies from around the country (see Introduction, note 7). Certainly, others may identify different houses, but the important underlying principle is that American housing in all periods and regions can be distilled into demographically dominant types of houses identifiable by both house plan and exterior style.

5. For architectural histories of housing that primarily use architectural style and exterior form to classify housing, see Virginia and Lee McAlester, *A Field Guide to American Houses* (New York: Knopf, 1992); Lester Walker, *American Shelter: An Illustrated Encyclopedia of the American Home* (Woodstock, N.Y.: Overlook Press, 1981); David P. Handlin, *The American Home: Architecture and Society, 1815–1915* (Boston: Little, Brown, 1979); Gerald Foster, *American Houses: A Field Guide to the Architecture of the Home* (New York: Houghton Mifflin, 2004). For

efforts to widen current analysis, see Barbara Wyatt, "Surveying and Evaluating Vernacular Architecture," *National Register Bulletin,* no. 31 (Washington, D.C.: U.S. Department of the Interior, n.d.), 1–32.

Also influential are listings of housing nomenclature contained in National Park Service, Historic Preservation guidelines interpreted by State Historic Preservation Offices (SHPOs), which are primarily based on traditional categories of exterior stylistic classification (although there are currently efforts to reform these practices). For a parallel assessment of the major types of houses for the English working classes, see Burnett, *Social History of Housing,* 140–87.

Over the past twenty-five years, I have addressed the issue of housing nomenclature and problems of stylistic classification for common houses in books and articles, college courses, and more than one hundred lectures at town meetings, neighborhood groups, schools, and historical societies throughout the country. Through audience communication, I have had the opportunity to inquire about local housing and nomenclature, especially the difficulties of using academic, exterior-stylistic terms to describe local or regional vernacular housing. Following the principal themes of this book, I encourage the use of house plan analysis coupled with exterior stylistic analysis (integrated with local–regional nomenclatures) to modify and define the variations of national common housing types. See chapter 1, note 1.

6. Bigott, *From Cottage to Bungalow,* 1–56.
7. Paul Groth, "Workers'-Cottage and Minimal-Bungalow Districts," 15.
8. In national comparison, similarly scaled, one-room-deep I-Houses have multiple names and origins, often simply identified as small vernacular houses or cabins. For the historical development of "I-Houses," see Glassie, "Eighteenth-Century Cultural Process in Delaware Valley Folk Building," in Upton and Vlach, *Common Places,* 407–25; Lewis, "Common Houses, Cultural Spoor," 92–94; Fred Kniffen, "Folk Housing: Key to Diffusion," in Upton and Vlach, *Common Places,* 4–17; Cummings, *Framed Houses of Massachusetts Bay,* 22–39; Dell Upton, "Vernacular Domestic Architecture in Eighteenth-Century Virginia," in Upton and Vlach, *Common Places,* 315–35; Alison K. Hoagland, *Mine Towns: Buildings for Workers in Michigan's Copper Country* (Minneapolis: University of Minnesota Press, 2010), 3–5, 11–12; Gowans, *Comfortable House,* 156–58; Virginia Savage McAlester, *Field Guide to American Houses,* 140–43; Fred Peterson, *Homes in the Heartland: Balloon Frame Farmhouses of the Upper Midwest, 1850–1920* (Lawrence: University Press of Kansas, 1992), 61–95; and summarized in Henry Glassie, *Vernacular Architecture* (Bloomington: Indiana University Press, 2000), 138–45.
9. Glassie, *Folk Housing in Middle Virginia,* 120–22.

10. Alison K. Hoagland, *The Log Cabin: An American Icon* (Charlottesville: University of Virginia Press, 2018), 32, estimates that in 1800, one-half of America's houses, including many I-Houses, were built of logs.

11. This estimate is based on the sources listed in note 8, which represent wide geographic distribution and some of the finest studies of house form in eighteenth- and nineteenth-century America. In most cases the I-House is the most dominant or one of the most dominant houses in the region covered by these studies.

12. Lewis, "Common Houses, Cultural Spoor," 96–101; Peterson, *Homes in the Heartland,* 96–135; Fred Peterson, "Vernacular Building and Victorian Architecture: Midwestern American Farm Houses," in Upton and Vlach, *Common Places,* 433–46; Alison K. Hoagland, *Mine Towns,* 8–10; Gowans, *Comfortable House,* 94–98; Virginia Savage McAlester, *Field Guide to American Houses,* 138–39. As expressed in these studies, there is no standard name for this extremely popular house, built nationally in large numbers from the 1820s until the early twentieth century.

13. Peterson, *Homes in the Heartland,* 96–135; Peterson, "Vernacular Building and Victorian Architecture," 433–46. These estimates of Side-Gable houses in rural Wisconsin and Oregon towns have been complied in research conducted over a fifteen-year period through student surveys and individual housing documentation.

14. Groth, "Workers'-Cottage and Minimal-Bungalow Districts," 15; Barrows, "Beyond the Tenement"; Hubka and Kenny, "The Workers' Cottage in Milwaukee's Polish Community," 33–52; Thomas Hubka and Judith Kenny, "Examining the American Dream: Housing Standards and the Emergence of a National Housing Culture, 1900–1930," *Perspectives in Vernacular Architecture* 13, no. 1 (2006): 49–69; Bigott, *From Cottage to Bungalow,* 41–53 and throughout; Hoagland, *Mine Towns,* 1–54.

15. Jay D. Edwards, "Shotgun: The Most Contested House in America," *Building and Landscapes: Journal of the Vernacular Architecture Forum* 16, no. 1 (Spring 2009): 62–96; and John Michael Vlach, "An African Architectural Legacy," in Upton and Vlach, *Common Places,* 58–78. Current analysis assesses the combined cultural influences of African, Creole, and French traditions.

16. Earlier versions of Side-Hall houses are analyzed in Bernard L. Herman, *Town House: Architecture and Material Life in the Early American City, 1780–1830* (Chapel Hill: University of North Carolina Press, 2005), throughout. Standard versions are analyzed by Hoagland, *Mine Towns,* 10–18, 42–48. Also see Glassie, *Vernacular Architecture,* 116–31. For an analysis of the Side-Hall tradition in upper-class row housing of the nineteenth and early twentieth centuries, see Charles Lockwood,

Bricks and Brownstone: The New York Row House, 1783–1929 (New York: Rizzoli, 2003), throughout; and Virginia Savage McAlester, *Field Guide to American Houses,* 136–38.

17. Row house sources include Mary Ellen Hayward and Charles Belfoure, *The Baltimore Row House* (New York: Princeton Architectural Press, 2001); Hayward, *Baltimore's Alley Houses,* 147–211; McLoud, "Craftsman and Entrepreneurs," 23–40; Caroline Mesrobian Hickman and Sally Lichtenstein Berk, "Harry Wardman's Row House Development in Early Twentieth-Century Washington," in Longstreth, *Housing Washington,* 41–60; Anne Vernez Moudon, *Built for Change: Neighborhood Architecture in San Francisco* (Cambridge, Mass.: MIT Press, 1986), 41–96; for English housing sources, see Stefan Muthesius, *The English Terraced House* (New Haven, Conn.: Yale University Press, 1982).

18. Sources for the Two-up and Two-down house were cited by Thomas Hubka in "The Common Houses of the Pittsburgh Region" (lecture presented at the Society of Architectural Historians Annual Meeting, Pittsburgh, 2007). The name "Two-up and Two-down" was occasionally used by residents and local historians in the Pittsburgh and Cincinnati regions but was not commonly cited. This inconsistency of nomenclature for the most common houses is typical throughout the country. See chapter 1, note 1, and chapter 2, note 8.

19. Hoagland, *The Log Cabin,* 11–48.

20. The Four-Box plan appeared simultaneously in several regional builder catalogs and pattern book publications at the turn of the twentieth century. This usually indicates a widespread, simultaneous vernacular builder development similar to the multisourced origins of the bungalow plan and other popular vernacular house forms. See Peterson, *Homes in the Heartland,* 174–82; Gowans, *The Comfortable House,* 90–93; Virginia Savage McAlester, *A Field Guide to American Houses,* 146–47. Individual Four-Box houses were documented for this study in three eastern Oregon towns, Fossil, Condon, and Heppner. The house is sometimes called a "Pyramid" because of its typical, four-sided pyramidal roof covering a square floor plan.

21. The Parlor-Bypass plan is not documented or named in traditional vernacular research, but it is added here because its plan was consistently found in most of the case-study research areas for this study (see the introduction, note 7). It was one of the most popular house plans of Cleveland, Ohio, in the first decades of the twentieth century as determined in selected case-study neighborhood estimates and frequently seen, for example, in *Residential Vernacular Architecture in Cleveland, 1870–1940* (Cleveland: Cleveland Landmarks Commission, 1992), 17–19 (Cleveland 1991 Preservation Program). In Portland, Oregon,

this popular house plan is most often found in a small, late nineteenth-century house, called the Queen Anne cottage because of its typical ornamental detail.

22. Because of the lack of data for small apartment houses on a national scale, my estimates are hypotheses based on limited apartment surveys in each of the fourteen metropolitan areas investigated for this study. A 1901 study of Chicago tenements, Robert Hunter, *Tenement Conditions in Chicago* (Chicago: City Homes Association, 1901), 60, cited a slightly more than three-room average size for tenement apartments, similar to New York City tenements shown in research and highlighted in the Tenement Museum's typical three-room plan apartments, as analyzed by Dolkart, *Biography of a Tenement House in New York City*. Several regional studies offer glimpses of the range of small, multi-unit apartments and boardinghouses, such as Paul Groth, *Living Downtown: The History of Residential Hotels in the United States* (Berkeley: University of California Press, 1994), 90–200 and throughout. Also see Howard Davis, *Living over the Store* (Hoboken, N.J.: Taylor and Francis, 2012), 67–84, 141–70, for small apartments over commercial establishments in historic and international perspective.

23. The bungalow's most popular one-story floor plan appears to have been developed simultaneously throughout middle America in the late nineteenth-century; see Bigott, *From Cottage to Bungalow*, 41–53, and discussed from various perspectives in Gowans, *The Comfortable House*, 74–83; Anthony D. King, *The Bungalow: The Production of a Global Culture* (London: Routledge and Kegan Paul, 1984), 127–55; and Hubka, *Houses without Names*, 63–68. The American bungalow's standard plan has no specific ethnic or regional origins but combines many strains of elite and vernacular housing traditions.

    Less well documented was the simultaneous development of smaller versions of the popular bungalow that were typically constructed in working-class neighborhoods. These smaller bungalows included many features of the larger bungalows but in smaller, compact floor plans. See Michael P. McCulloch, "Building the Working City: Designs on Home and Life in Boomtown Detroit, 1914–1932" (PhD diss., University of Michigan, 2015), 96–104.

24. Bigott, *From Cottage to Bungalow*, 43–53.

25. It is rare to find accurate statistics about the dominant types of houses in any region or metropolitan area. Even the knowledge of a region's most numerous houses is rare. For example, in small towns and rural areas of southwestern Maine and southern New Hampshire, the Side-Hall plan house in one-and-one-half-to-two-story versions accounted for 50–60 percent of houses built or remodeled between

around 1880 and 1930—an extraordinary percentage for one house form. Local residents and historians are, however, surprised when this house and its density are described. Similarly, in Portland, Oregon, a little-recognized 1910–1930, "Colonial Bungalow" (combining Colonial Revival and bungalow details) is still one of the city's most popular, pre-1950s houses. Similarly, throughout the country, numerically dominant houses are not widely recognized.

26. For the social centrality of the kitchen and the work of the kitchen comparing working-class with upper-middle-class lifestyles, see Ruth Schwartz Cowan, *More Work for Mother: The Ironies of Household Technology from the Open Hearth to the Microwave* (New York: Basic Books, 1983), 151–91. Also see Elizabeth Collins Cromley, *The Food Axis: Cooking, Eating, and the Architecture of American Houses* (Charlottesville: University of Virginia Press, 2011), 133–76.

27. For development of the stove, see Ierley, *Comforts of Home*, 129–31, 160–64; Peterson, *Homes in the Heartland*; Cowan, *More Work for Mother*, 53–62; Susan Strasser, *Never Done: A History of American Housework* (New York: Henry Holt, 1982), 36–41, 50–57. On gas for stoves and lighting, see Strasser, *Never Done*, 68–73; Ierley, *Comforts of Home*, 160–64; Jack Larkin, *The Reshaping of Everyday Life, 1790–1840* (New York: Harper & Row, 1988), 50–53; Hubka, *Big House, Little House, Back House, Barn*, 125–28. Lebergott, *Americans*, 71, estimates that two-thirds of American households had stoves in 1860.

28. For toilet installation percentages see Gordon, *Rise and Fall of American Growth*, 114; for water delivery, 122–25; see also Ierley, *Comforts of Home*, 104–20 and throughout. The arrival of mechanically facilitated running water in a variety of prepiped water mechanisms is extremely difficult to evaluate for the lower 50 percent of households, especially in rural areas before electrical pumps became available, often after the 1920s and 1930s. See Hubka, *Big House, Little House, Back House, Barn*, 99, 129, 176; Flanders, *Making of Home*, 246–50.

29. Gordon, *Rise and Fall of American Growth*, 128.

30. Doan, *American Housing Production*, 35, 64.

31. Except for conditions of pioneer settlement, most historical domestic scholarship has assumed the separation of domestic functions into separate rooms; for example, Clark, *The American Family Home*; Rybczynski, *Home*; Archer, *Architecture and Suburbia*. For a critique of this assumption in working-class and pre-1900 houses, see Flanders, *Making of Home*, 78–93; Hubka, *Houses without Names*, 63–68.

32. Most Progressive Era housing and tenement reform studies used the ratio of family size to the number of rooms in an apartment as a major determinant of economic and social prosperity or "congestion," as, for

example, in a study of Milwaukee's urban housing; Reports of the Immigration Commission, *Immigrants in Cities* (Washington, D.C.: Government Printing Office, 1911), 703–15 ("Living Conditions").

33. Patty Dean, "Home Furnishings in the Mining City of Butte," *Drumlummon Views* 3, no. 1 (2009): 177–201; Cohen, "Embellishing a Life of Labor," 268–276; and Cowan, *More Work for Mother,* 31–39.

34. Progressive Era photographers and reformers frequently published photographs of some of the most severely impoverished residential conditions. Often these photographs came to stand for average domestic conditions of the working classes. This assessment is based on a review of the photographic collections in municipal libraries from the cities surveyed for this book (see the introduction, note 7).

35. For example, Karin Calvert, "Children in the House, 1890 to 1930," in Foy and Schlereth, *American Home Life, 1880–1930,* 75–93.

36. Cohen, "Embellishing a Life of Labor," 261–280; Gordon, *The Rise and Fall of American Growth,* 97–108; Kleinberg, *The Shadow of the Mills,* 78–81; Hoagland, *Mine Towns,* 41–54.

37. Bigott, *From Cottage to Bungalow,* 28–41; Herbert Gottfried and Jan Jennings, *American Vernacular,* 33–44 and throughout; William Cronon, *Nature's Metropolis: Chicago and the Great West* (New York: W. W. Norton, 1991), 148–82.

38. Susan Estabrook Kennedy, *If All We Did Was to Weep at Home* (Bloomington: Indiana University Press, 1979), 93, finds 20 percent of women employed outside the home in 1900. Cowan, *More Work for Mother,* 160–61, 168–72, reviews the difficulties of estimating paid labor for housewives in the early twentieth century, and although citing 10 percent employed, adds that this might leave out many working-class women; 169.

39. Lebergott, *The American Economy,* 93–94; Harvey M. Choldin, "Kinship Networks in the Migration Process," in *Immigrant Family Patterns: Demography, Fertility, Housing, Kinship, and Urban Life,* ed. George E. Pozzetta (New York: Garland, 1991), 61–73.

40. Gamber, *The Boardinghouse in Nineteenth-Century America,* 3.

41. S. P. Breckinridge, *New Homes for Old* (New York: Harper and Brothers, 1921), 25.

42. Gamber, *The Boardinghouse in Nineteenth-Century America,* 1–10 and throughout. See also John Modell and Tamara K. Hareven, "Urbanization and the Malleable Household: An Examination of Boarding and Lodging in American Families," *Journal of Marriage and the Family* 35 (1973): 467–79; Strasser, *Never Done,* 145–61; Cowan, *More Work for Mother,* 160–62; Lebergott, *The American Economy,* 250–55. For case

studies of boarder issues within working-class families, see Alison K. Hoagland, "The Boardinghouse Murders: Housing and American Ideals in Michigan's Copper Country in 1913," in *Perspectives in Vernacular Architecture* 11 (2004): 1–18; Kleinberg, *The Shadow of the Mills*, 81–84; Hoagland, *Mine Towns*, 48–54; Strasser, *Never Done*, 145–61; Gordon, *The Rise and Fall of American Growth*, 106, estimates that in 1900, 23 percent of urban households took in boarders.

43. Kleinberg cites several studies that estimate 40–60 percent of urban households experienced displacement in the last decades of the nineteenth century, in *The Shadow of the Mills*, 52–64. Also see Howard P. Chudacoff, *Mobile Americans: Residential and Social Mobility in Omaha, 1880–1920* (New York: Oxford University Press, 1973), 25; Choldin, "Kinship Networks in the Migration Process," 64–67. Movement brought about by eviction through unemployment and job loss was a major contributor, as outlined in Hunter, *Poverty*, 24–34. Lynd and Lynd, *Middletown in Transition*, 186–90, emphasize the mobility of the larger working classes and permanence of the smaller upper, business classes.

44. Social historians have emphasized the negative consequences of population turnover in urban and rural working-class communities of the least wealthy; e.g., Zunz, *Changing Face of Inequality*, 178–83. Zunz documents a stable core of permanent ethnic-entrepreneurial families and a transient working class. Kleinberg, *The Shadow of the Mills*, 64, emphasizes a transient urban working class and a stable suburban middle class at the urban periphery.

45. Richard Harris, "The Rise of Filtering Down: The American Housing Market Transformed, 1915–1929," *Social Science History* 37, no. 4 (Winter 2013): 515–49, traces the historical development of this filtering-down process and its complex implication for the production of twentieth-century common housing. The filtering down of housing stock in Los Angeles is analyzed in Gish, "Building Los Angeles," 87–94.

46. Wright, "On Modern Vernaculars and J. B. Jackson," 170.

47. Byington, *Homestead*, 145. Note that the photograph was probably taken at a different time of day than the interview because of the presence of the husband in the photo. Similar interior photos of working-class home interiors are rare, often because of poor lighting conditions (so that the interview and the photography may not have occurred on the same day).

48. This subdivided Two-up and Two-down house is a form of the Side-Hall house with a central stair paralleling the front facade. Common to the Pittsburgh region, it was analyzed by Thomas Hubka, "Pittsburgh's

Housing for the Working Class: Improvement and Reform, 1880–1930" (lecture presented at the Society of Architectural Historians Annual Meeting, April 2007, Pittsburgh).

49. Byington frequently described similar patterns of working-class families acquiring parlor furnishings while living in cramped quarters to provide a semblance of parlor formality. This was also done in anticipation of a future parlor; see *Homestead*, 55–56.

50. Ibid.

3. MODERN HOUSES FOR A NEW MIDDLE CLASS

1. See chapter 2, note 29.

2. Ruth Schwartz Cowan uses the term "Industrial Revolution" to describe late nineteenth- and early twentieth-century domestic reforms in common housework; see "Coal Stoves and Clean Sinks: Housework between 1890 and 1930," in Foy and Schlereth, *American Home Life*, 211.

3. See the introduction, note 13, and chapter 1, note 55. Also see Patterson, *America's Struggle against Poverty in the Twentieth Century*, 19–33.

4. Moskowitz, *Standard of Living*, 1–18; Gordon, *Rise and Fall of American Growth*, 9–13; Bauer and Crane, "What Every Family Should Have," 64–65, 136–39; Lawrence Glickman, "Inventing the 'American Standard of Living': Gender, Race and Working Class Identity, 1880–1925," in *Labor History* 34, no. 2–3 (1993): 221–35; Cohen, "Embellishing a Life of Labor"; Rainwater, *What Money Buys*, 41–63; Peter R. Shergold, *Working Class Life: The "American Standard" in Comparative Perspective, 1899–1913* (Pittsburgh: University of Pittsburgh Press, 1982), 207–32; Newel Howland Comish, *The Standard of Living: Elements of Consumption* (New York: Macmillan, 1923), 93–107.

5. Moskowitz, *Standard of Living*, 3; also see 1–15.

6. Karl Polanyi, *The Great Transformation: The Political and Economic Origins of Our Time* (Boston: Beacon, 1957), 43–67; Schama, *Embarrassment of Riches*, 288–371; Moskowitz, *Standard of Living*, 1–13; Piketty, *Capital in the Twenty-First Century*, 1–20.

7. Garb, *City of Dreams*, 97.

8. Gordon, *Rise and Fall of American Growth*, 115–32; Joseph C. Bigott, "Bungalows and the Complex Origin of the Modern House," in *The Chicago Bungalow*, ed. Dominic A. Pacyga and Charles Shanabruch (Chicago: Chicago Architecture Foundation, 2001), 45–52.

9. Bigott provides an excellent summary of the popular development of the bathroom and plumbing fixtures in common bungalows, in "Bungalows and the Complex Origin of the Modern House."

The influence of hotels, department stores, and modern urban apartment houses on the popular domestic adoption of bathroom fixtures is emphasized by Marina Moskowitz, "Public Exposure: Middle-Class Material Culture at the Turn of the Twentieth Century," in Bledstein and Johnston, *The Middling Sorts,* 170–84. See the development of the toilet in the nineteenth century, in Ierley, *Comforts of Home,* 65–72, 141–50, 220–28.

Although the absence of bathrooms in new, post-1900 working-class housing is rarely described, these conditions are revealed, for example, in builders' catalogs and pattern books, in which small or older-styled houses are shown lacking bathrooms, as for example in *Aladdin Houses, "Built in a Day,"* catalog no. 26 (Bay City, Mich.: North American Construction Company, 1915), 23–29, 55, 106–9. (After 1900, most pattern books and professional house-building literature pictured houses with bathrooms.)

10. Newel Howland Cornish, *The Standard of Living: Elements of Consumption* (New York: Macmillan, 1923), 97. (From Moskowitz, *Standard of Living,* 253, note 2.)

11. Gordon, *Rise and Fall of American Growth,* 1–7 and throughout.

12. The consensus selection of bathrooms does not eliminate the possibility of rejections by unrecorded individuals and especially antiprogressive technological or religious groups. This type of limited rejection does not, however, negate the overwhelming acceptance of the three-fixture bathroom formula. Similarly, this popular consensus should not be interpreted as an unthinking "herd mentality" of the "masses" type of popular consumer selection. See the epilogue, notes 5–8. Nothing about the bathroom's expense and constant long-term usage suggests rash or commercially influenced decision making regarding its selection and installation.

13. Gordon, *Rise and Fall of American Growth,* 114–15.

14. Ierley, *Comforts of Home,* 151–55; Cowan, *More Work for Mother,* 165–68; Gordon, *Rise and Fall of American Growth,* 52–60. Strasser stresses that washing clothes was by far the most time-consuming, difficult housework task for most women in an extended analysis, *Never Done,* 85–124; Ierley, *Comforts of Home,* 151–55; Nye, *Electrifying America,* 319. In interviews over thirty years with female farm residents about pre–World War II domestic conditions, many emphasized the importance of obtaining a washing machine, often as the first or most important purchased appliance or home improvement. For rural and small-town households, the acquisition of washing technology is linked to the installation of water-pumping devices and power generation; Ierley, *Comforts of Home,* 104–20.

15. For refrigerators, Gordon, *Rise and Fall of American Growth,* 114, 120–21; Ierley, *Comforts of Home,* 167–71; Cowan, *More Work for Mother,* 128–31; Strasser, *Never Done,* 15–22; Nye, *Electrifying America,* 356–57.

    The expansion of ice production by the mid-nineteenth century allowed widespread availability in the eastern United States. Yet, ice for iceboxes, because of erratic seasonal delivery and the concentration of customers in urban areas, never achieved popular distribution, especially in the rural areas and for the lower economic half of the population. In any case there are no accurate statistics of the percentages of popular ice distributions, which were frequently seasonal.

16. Ierley, *Comforts of Home,* 181–82, 233–34.

17. Nye, *Electrifying America,* 287–335.

18. See chapter 1, note 22.

19. For electrification percentages, see Nye, *Electrifying America,* 16. Also Lebergott, *Americans,* 352; Gordon, *Rise and Fall of American Growth,* 120.

20. Garb, *A City of American Dreams,* 86–96.

21. Cowan, *More Work for Mother,* 89–95; Nye, *Electrifying America,* 1–28, 138–84; Flanders, *Making of Home,* 251–53; Strasser, *Never Done,* 74–84. There were great variations in the distribution of utilities to various portions of the population; rich–poor, urban–suburban–rural, north–south, various geographies. Overall there is a lack of distribution statistics for the final 50 percent of the population for all utilities.

22. Kleinberg, *Shadow of the Mills,* 84–93.

23. For an overview of utilities and public service development, see Gordon, *Rise and Fall of American Growth,* 94–128. For urban garbage disposal, see Martin V. Melosi, *Garbage in the Cities: Refuse, Reform, and the Environment* (Pittsburgh: University of Pittsburgh Press, 2005), 1–167.

24. Gordon, *Rise and Fall of American Growth,* 95.

25. Ierley, *Comforts of Home,* 172.

26. Ibid., 172–77.

27. Lynd and Lynd, *Middletown,* 174–75.

28. Gordon, *Rise and Fall of American Growth,* 114–15.

29. There are no credible pre-1940 statistics for determining the number of rooms in average housing nor for identifying their name or usage. Based on estimates in selected neighborhoods from twenty metropolitan areas (see the introduction, note 7) and fieldwork-based studies, such as those by Kim Hoagland, Paul Groth, and Joseph Bigott, cited throughout, I estimate that in 1900, within a three-to-four-room, average working-class household, the presence of separate, single-usage dining rooms would have been extraordinarily rare.

Also see typical pre-1900 houses analyzed in chapter 2, in the section titled "Nine Common Houses," where a separate room used exclusively for dining would have been unusual. The likelihood of multifunctional rooms allowing occasional or seasonal dining is analyzed by Roger Roper, "Homemakers in Transition: Women in Salt Lake City Apartments, 1910–1940," *Utah Historical Quarterly* 67, no. 4 (Fall 1999): 349–56. For an alternative interpretation that estimates a majority of households had dining rooms as early as the middle of the nineteenth century, see Cromley, *The Food Axis,* 92.

30. Cohen, "Embellishing a Life of Labor," 264–73; Thomas Bell, *Out of this Furnace: A Novel of Immigrant Labor in America* (Pittsburgh: University of Pittsburgh Press, 1994), 62, 136, 152.

31. Byington, *Homestead,* 56.

32. Ibid., 55.

33. Roper analyzes the physical and social issues within new multi-unit apartments in Salt Lake City in "Homemakers in Transition."

34. Cohen, "Embellishing a Life of Labor," 261–78, situates the working-class decision making for interior furnishing within a context explaining both the constraints and choices. Glassie, *Folk Housing in Middle Virginia,* 19–24, provides a classic summary of vernacular design and decision making emphasizing creativity within tradition. It is also important to recognize that all architectural traditions borrow selectively from other sources and cultures, even isolated vernacular cultures. Nevertheless, the multisourced borrowing within late nineteenth-century, industrially influenced modern vernaculars was unprecedented. See Hubka, *Houses without Names,* 37–40.

35. Ethnic studies and research from nearly all American immigrant cultures have emphasized the persistence of "old world" patterns of material culture (as well as patterns of language, dress, food ways, etc.). Typically deemphasized is the massive abandonment of the largest portions of these material culture traditions in the face of relentless American industrialization and modernization of housing and house furnishings. For the methods and principles underlying retention or change in preindustrial vernacular architectural expression, see Glassie, *Passing the Time in Ballymenone,* 327–424. For an analysis of the subtle retention of ethnic Lithuanian cultural traditions (largely patterns of landscape) within a larger context of Americanization, see Gerald L. Pocius, "Lithuanian Landscapes in America: Houses, Yards, and Gardens in Scranton, Pennsylvania," in *New York Folklore* 22, no. 1–4 (1996): 49–87. Few American immigrant studies, however, have attempted a demographic analysis of their ethnic communities to determine the material cultural choices of larger percentages of their

population through time. With regard to the material culture development of American housing and interior furnishing, the vast majority
of ethnic communities have largely abandoned the architectural expression of their original cultures and adopted new forms of American
industrial-vernacular expression.

36. The functional simplicity of vernacular architectural and decorative expression is interpreted from various perspectives: Glassie, *Vernacular
Architecture*, 79–96; Rudofsky, *Architecture without Architects*; Le Corbusier, *Towards a New Architecture*, 9–20; E. H. Gombrich, *The Sense
of Order: A Study in the Psychology of Decorative Art* (London: Phaidon
Press, 1994), 3–62; Oliver, *Dwellings*, 64–84.

37. There are no standard, commonly accepted names for the multifunctional rooms within small common houses with four rooms or less.
In publications showing house plans, these rooms are given either
no names or inadequate names, such as parlor and dining room, borrowed from the domestic traditions of the middle to upper classes. See
Hubka, *Houses without Names*, 10–22. Further research is needed to assign meaningful names to the multipurpose rooms of small vernacular
houses, for example, as shown in chapter 2, "Nine Common Houses."
Also see chapter 1, note 1.

38. The importance of a bed and its purchase from a working-class perspective is described in Dean, "Home Furnishings in the Mining City
of Butte," 182–85; Flanders, *The Making of Home*, 79–80, 141; Cohen,
"Embellishing a Life of Labor," 272.

39. Flanders, *The Making of Home*, 65–93. The obtainment of bedroom
privacy is analyzed or assumed in middle-to-upper-class housing
literature; see Archer, *Architecture and Suburbia*, 140–44, 308, 357,
and throughout; Elizabeth Collins Cromley, "A History of American
Beds and Bedrooms," in *Perspectives in Vernacular Architecture*, vol. 4,
ed. Thomas Carter and Bernard L. Herman (Columbia: University of
Missouri Press, 1991), 177–87. Bedroom privacy is only discussed in
working-class literature to note its absence.

40. See chapter 5, notes 4 and 8.

41. Bigott, *From Cottage to Bungalow*, 28–53; Herbert Gottfried, "The Machine and the Cottage: Building Technology, and the Single-Family
House, 1870–1910," *Journal of the Society for Industrial Archeology* 21,
no. 2 (1995): 47–68; Cronon, *Nature's Metropolis*, 148–82; Pamela
H. Simpson, *Cheap, Quick, and Easy: Imitative Architectural Materials,
1870–1930* (Knoxville: University of Tennessee Press, 1999), 75–100;
Robert M. Cour, *The Plywood Age: A History of the Fir Plywood Industry's First Fifty Years* (Portland, Ore.: Binfords and Mort, 1955), 1–35,
94–165. Also see chapter 2, note 37.

42. Dean, "Home Furnishings in the Mining City of Butte," 185.

43. Stanley Lebergott, *Pursuing Happiness: American Consumers in the Twentieth Century* (Princeton, N.J.: Princeton University Press, 1993), 69–76; Cohen, *A Consumers' Republic*, 1–56; Cowan, *More Work for Mother*, 162–63. For an elite summary, see Harvey Molotch, *Where Stuff Comes From: How Toasters, Toilets, Cars, Computers, and Many Other Things Came to Be as They Are* (New York: Routledge, 2003), 1–22.

44. Clay Lancaster, *The American Bungalow, 1880–1930* (New York: Abbeville Press, 1985), 112–52; King, *The Bungalow*, 128–37. Social customs related to the bungalow porch are explored in Sue Bridwell Beckham, "The American Front Porch: Women's Liminal Space," in *Housing and Dwelling: Perspectives on Modern Domestic Architecture,* ed. Barbara Miller Lane (London: Routledge, 2007), 86–93.

45. Andres Duany, Elizabeth Plater-Zyberk, and Jeff Speck, *Suburban Nation: The Rise of Sprawl and the Decline of the American Dream* (New York: North Point, 2010), 1–30.

46. Gordon, *Rise and Fall of American Growth,* 106, 114–15.

47. The absence of stables and carriage houses in nonfarm working-class environments is distilled from case-study research for this book in metropolitan areas nationally. Unless transported by horse cars or electric streetcars, the largest numbers of nonfarm citizens walked. See Jackson, *Crabgrass Frontier,* 39–44, 103–20. For early twentieth-century, upper-class garages, see W. H. K. and J. C. H. Architects, *Garages Country and Suburban* (New York: American Architect, 1911). John Brinckerhoff Jackson, *The Necessity for Ruins* (Amherst: University of Massachusetts Press, 1980), 103–12, describes the evolution of the detached stable and garage into the attached garage after World War II. In the Lynds' study of Muncie, Indiana, only .05 percent of households had a horse and carriage in the late 1890s and these families were described as "practically all of them business class folk." In Lynd and Lynd, *Middletown,* 251.

48. Leslie G. Goat, "Housing the Horseless Carriage: America's Early Private Garages," in *Perspectives in Vernacular Architecture,* vol. 3, edited by Thomas Carter and Bernard L. Herman (Columbia: University of Missouri Press, 1989), 62–72.

49. Kleinberg, *Shadow of the Mills,* 48–49, and Nye, *Electrifying America,* 96–97. In a similar way, the initial layout and distribution of major utilities also followed white-collar middle-class expansion into the suburbs, often bypassing unserved or underserved blue-collar communities.

50. Major studies of the bungalow include Lancaster, *The American Bungalow, 1880–1930*; Lancaster, "The American Bungalow," in Upton and Vlach, *Common Places,* 79–106; Robert Winter, *The California Bungalow*

(Los Angeles: Hennessey and Ingalls, 1980), and King, *The Bungalow*, 127–55. Also see chapter 2, note 23.

Many popular books provide high-quality photographic documentation and detailed research analysis of the bungalow; for example, Paul Duchscherer and Linda Svendsen, *Beyond the Bungalow: Grand Homes in the Arts and Crafts Tradition* (Salt Lake City: Gibbs Smith, 2005).

51. National housing statistics: Doan, *American Housing Production*, 182–83, 186. Bungalow estimates were distilled from case-study research for this book in twenty metropolitan and regional studies nationally (see the introduction, note 7).

52. Schweitzer and Davis, *America's Favorite Homes*, 61–63.

53. Rybczynski, *Home*, 193.

54. Henry Glassie frequently emphasizes the primacy of plan and the subordination of exterior stylistic expression in vernacular architecture, "Artifact and Culture, Architecture and Society," in *American Material Culture and Folklore*, ed. Simon Bronner (Ann Arbor: University of Michigan Press, 1985), 53. Also see Rapaport, *House Form and Culture*, where plan diagrams are the dominant form of social and spatial analysis; 46–82. For a summary of methods of floor plan analysis to inform vernacular and housing studies, see Carter and Cromley, *Invitation to Vernacular Architecture*, 83–95; and Hubka, *Houses without Names*, 47–68; Bigott, "Bungalows and the Complex Origin of the Modern House," 35–38.

55. While leading bungalow analysts such as Lancaster, King, Winter, and Gowans describe the bungalow plan in general terms, they do not provide demographic analysis of its various popular plan types showing their distribution; nor do they analyze the bungalow plan's complex development by late nineteenth-century vernacular builders, as analyzed by Bigott, *From Cottage to Bungalow*, 41–53, and Hubka, *Houses without Names*, 46–68. Also see chapter 2, note 23.

56. Ierley, *Comforts of Home*, 160–64; Gowans, *The Comfortable House*, 1–13; Rybczynski, *Home*, 213–15; Flanders, *The Making of Home*, 207–9.

57. See Glassie, *Folk Housing in Middle Virginia*, 114–22. For an excellent summary of the evolution of turn-of-the-century vernacular (or working-class) material culture and inherent contradictions between its traditional aesthetic values and new industrial-commercial values (or between functional simplicity and Victorian excess), see Cohen, "Embellishing a Life of Labor." Also see chapter 2, notes 35 and 36.

58. Bigott, *From Cottage to Bungalow*, 206, emphasizes the same change from nineteenth-century workers' cottage to twentieth-century bungalow. Also Gordon, *Rise and Fall of American Growth*, 108.

59. For underlying unity in the bungalow's basic plan and technological

improvements, see Gowans, *The Comfortable House,* 74–83; Bigott, "Bungalows and the Complex Origin of the Modern House," 31–40. King, *The Bungalow,* 1–13, 244–63, synthesizes the bungalow's historical development and cultural meaning in global perspective.

60. Hubka, *Houses without Names,* 47–51.

61. For national housing statistics, see Doan, *American Housing Production,* 182–83, 186. Bungalow estimates were distilled from case-study research for this book in twenty metropolitan and regional studies; see the introduction, note 7. Because this is an estimate based on a limited number of case studies, I invite others to test and develop these preliminary conclusions.

4. THE DWELLINGS OF MODERN DOMESTIC REFORM

1. Heath, *Vernacular Architecture and Regional Design,* 1–21, interprets the persistence of vernacular patterns amidst modern or current cultural change. This challenging topic of innovation within tradition is examined by Glassie, *Folk Housing,* 66–75; Davis addresses this relationship as "tradition and innovation" in building form, in *The Culture of Building,* 131–58. Also see chapter 3, note 35.

2. Scott Sonoc, "Defining the Chicago Bungalow," in Pacyga and Shanabruch, *The Chicago Bungalow,* 9–30.

3. Based on the research of Jim Heuer, Portland, Oregon, historian, through inventory and census records in combination with detailed analysis of the Irvington neighborhood and other Eastside Portland neighborhoods. Also see note 8.

4. *A Book of Redimade Homes,* catalog (Los Angeles and Portland, Ore.: Redimade Building Company, 1924), 7.

5. See chapter 1, note 39.

6. Hubka, *Houses without Names,* 88–93.

7. For example, in Portland, Oregon, popular smaller versions of standard, early twentieth-century bungalows and other common houses are rarely included in architectural surveys and historical documentation. Smaller versions of Portland's standard popular houses are, however, shown in builders' plan catalogs, pattern books, and "kit house" catalogs. See, e.g., *A Book of Redimade Homes,* 22–33. The Redimade Building Company had a factory in Portland, and many of its smaller houses can be recognized throughout the city.

   Also see small versions of bungalows and "minimal bungalows" in Groth, "Workers'-Cottage and Minimal-Bungalow Districts," 20; James Borchert, "Alley Landscapes of Washington," in Upton and Vlach, *Common Places,* 281–91; and Hubka, *Big House, Little House, Back House,*

Barn, 42–47 and throughout (large and small versions of the same Side-Hall house plan are shown and analyzed).

8. Estimates were gathered from Portland housing authorities and evaluated through ten years of teaching architecture and housing courses at three Portland colleges, conducting neighborhood housing tours throughout Portland, and preparing for a book on Portland's common housing. Also see the introduction, note 7.

9. Ibid.

10. These partially improved houses were found in every case-study region (see note 8) and are described in Groth, "Workers'-Cottage and Minimal-Bungalow Districts in Oakland and Berkeley, California"; Bigott, *From Cottage to Bungalow,* pp. 117–48.

11. Older late nineteenth-century houses are shown, for example, in *Aladdin Houses, "Built in a Day,"* catalog no. 26, 28–29, 55–62, 105–8.

12. Doan, *American Housing Production, 1880–2000,* 29–33; Gish, "Building Los Angeles," 99–104.

13. Matthew Lasner, *High Life: Condo Living in the Suburban Century* (New Haven, Conn.: Yale University Press, 2012), 57.

14. Doan, *American Housing Production, 1880–2000,"* 30–33, 51; and Lasner, *High Life,* 57–61.

15. For example, Borchert, "Alley Landscapes of Washington."

16. *Annual Reports of the Building Inspector of the City of Milwaukee* (Reports for years 1910–14). Milwaukee Office of Inspector of Buildings, Report to the Common Council Committee on Buildings-Grounds-Bridges (May 9, 1938), 3–4. Also see chapter 1, note 49.

17. For the undercounting of multi-unit housing in Los Angeles, see Gish, "Building Los Angeles," 83–126. The frequent subdivision and reformulation of small, working-class housing in Milwaukee's immigrant neighborhood are outlined in *Public Documents of the State of Wisconsin, 1914,* vol. 10 (Madison: Department of Public Instruction, 1915), 172–86. Although the purpose of this documentation was to record the poorest conditions in immigrant neighborhoods, average conditions may be discerned. Unrecorded doubling-up of immigrant and migrant families and the accommodation of families due to sudden changes are summarized in Choldin, "Kinship Networks in the Migration Process," 61–73.

   In Detroit's Polish communities in 1900, 69 percent of the Polish families lived in multiple-unit dwellings, most of them in two-family duplexes. Forty percent of the Poles living in two-family dwellings were owners living in the same house. Zunz, *Changing Face of Inequality,* 157–58. Lynd and Lynd, *Middletown in Transition,* 193, recognize the frequency of doubling-up, especially during the Depression.

In national reviews, duplex housing statistics do not typically include houses modified or remodeled to become duplexes. These difficult-to-assess multi-family houses stand in a statistical middle ground, often combining homeowner and renter data.

18. Davis, *Living over the Store,* 73–84.

19. Disguised duplexes are, by their nature, difficult to identify; see, e.g., Gish, "Building Los Angeles," 91–94. In Milwaukee, Wisconsin, and Portland, Oregon, I have led neighborhood walking tours and organized student surveys where disguised duplexes were frequently difficult for participants to identify in pre-World War II neighborhoods (see note 3). Current twenty-first-century planning theorists and New Urbanists have revived patterns of concealed higher-density housing, such as the disguised duplex; see Duany, Plater-Zyberk, and Alminana, *The New Civic Art,* 298–99, 360–63.

    The social advantages of duplex and Three-Decker living arrangements to promote group cohesion and social support for immigrant families are outlined in Jacobsohn, "Boston's 'Three-Decker Menace,'" 299–325. This research stands in stark contrast to massive, post–Depression Era, government and private, anti-multihousing and tenement literature in support of single-family, suburban residential environments.

20. President's Conference on Home Building and Home Ownership [1931], *Home Ownership, Income and Types of Dwellings: Reports of the Committees on Home Ownership and Leasing,* ed. John M. Gries and James Ford (Washington, D.C., 1932), appendix I, "Family Types and Housing Trends," 192–99; duplex percentages, 193. For multi-unit housing totals in the 1920s, see Lasner, *High Life,* 58; and Doan, *American Housing Production,* 30–32.

    For duplex production in Detroit, see Zunz, *The Changing Face of Inequality,* 157–58; and McCulloch, "Building the Working City," 96–105.

    For recent totals, see *Historical Statistics of the United States: Colonial Times to 1970,* part 1, "Historical Census of Housing Tables, Units in Structure," 1/5.

21. Kingston William Heath, *The Patina of Place: The Cultural Weathering of a New England Industrial Landscape* (Knoxville: University of Tennessee Press, 2001), and Jacobsohn, "Boston's 'Three-Decker Menace.'"

22. Heath, *Patina of Place,* xvii–xxiii, 119–33; Jacobsohn, "Boston's 'Three-Decker Menace,'" 1–6, 65–70. Although individual examples of wood-frame, three-story apartment houses can be found in most cities, no urban area has recorded concentrations of this building type like those commonly found throughout New England's major urban-industrial centers.

23. Heath, *Patina of Place,* and Jacobsohn, "Boston's 'Three-Decker Menace'"; summarized in Hubka, *Houses without Names,* 40–45.

24. For a variety of cluster types, see, e.g., Stefanos Polyzoides, Roger Sherwood, and James Tice, *Courtyard Housing in Los Angeles: A Typological Analysis* (New York: Princeton Architectural Press, 1992).

25. For example, Plunz, *History of Housing in New York City*; Cromley, *Alone Together*; Neil Harris, *Chicago Apartments: A Century of Lakefront Luxury* (New York: Acanthus Press, 2004); Lasner, *High Life*.

26. Betsy Klimasmith, *At Home in the City: Urban Domesticity in American Literature and Culture, 1850–1930* (Durham: University of New Hampshire Press, 2005), 128–60.

27. This estimate is based on case-study fieldwork in twenty metropolitan areas; see Introduction, note 7. There are no pre-1940 historical census data for the number of apartment units within specific types of large, multi-unit buildings, or any other type of large apartment houses. The estimate is based on detailed studies of Shorewood, Wisconsin, housing types conducted by students of the University of Wisconsin–Milwaukee. This research determined that, on the eve of the Depression, large two-story, multi-unit apartment houses accounted for an estimated 15 percent of the population—a high proportion in a suburban community dominated by single-family houses.

28. Doan, *American Housing Production, 1880–2000,* 31.

29. Roper, "Homemakers in Transition," 352.

30. Groth, *Living Downtown,* esp. 19; also 1–25, 90–167.

31. Buchman Neighborhood walking tour field notes. Compiled by the Architecture Heritage Center staff, Portland, Oregon. Additional research of the Buchman Neighborhood's late nineteenth-century multi-unit and boardinghouses conducted during preparation for Historic District nomination process, 2012–14.

32. See chapter 1, note 18.

33. Harris, *Building a Market,* 1–19, 54–74. Although focused on the houses of a company town, Hoagland, *Mine Towns,* chapter 4, "Acquiring Conveniences," is one of the finest studies of the incremental nature of the home-remodeling improvement process in working-class housing.

34. Lynd and Lynd, *Middletown,* 97.

35. On tenement sanitation reform, see Plunz, *History of Housing in New York City,* 1–49; Dolkart, *Biography of a Tenement House in New York City,* 53–64. For a turn-of-the-twentieth-century summation, see De Forest and Veiller, *Tenement House Problem,* 1:301–38 and throughout.

36. Dolkart, *Biography of a Tenement House in New York City,* 74–114; Plunz, *History of Housing in New York City,* 126–28. The context for tenement

reform and remodeling is provided by Violette, *Decorated Tenement,* 139–71.

37. Doan, *American Housing Production 1880–2000,* 64–66, 183, 186.

38. The house in Fossil, Oregon, was documented in 2013 and later destroyed.

39. Estimate based on fieldwork summaries; see the introduction, note 7. For related investigations, see Harris, *Building a Market,* 1–19; Harris, "The Rise of Filtering Down." Radford, *Modern Housing for America,* 25, documents a large volume of existing house remodeling, specifically toilet and bathroom additions in the 1920s.

40. Groth and Gutman, "Workers' Houses in West Oakland"; Hoagland, "Boardinghouse Murders"; Ratcliff, "Filtering Down and the Elimination of Substandard Housing"; Harris, "The Rise of Filtering Down." High percentages of the most impoverished rural families have always lived in unimproved single-family housing whether owned or rented, often single-room and log structures; see Hoagland, *Log Cabin,* 78–114.

41. Groth and Gutman, "Workers' Houses in West Oakland," and Groth, "Workers'-Cottage and Minimal-Bungalow Districts in Oakland and Berkeley, California, 1870–1945."

42. Most studies of the domestic conditions of those in poverty touch upon the subject of housing abandonment and demolition, but it is difficult to quantify pre-1940 conditions on regional or national scales. One of the finest summaries of these marginal housing conditions is Richard Harris, *Unplanned Suburbs,* 233–63. Also see Harris, "The Rise of Filtering Down," and William C. Baer, "Aging of the Housing Stock and Component of Inventory Change," in Myers, *Housing Demography,* 249–73. For the social meaning of house change and abandonment, see Michael Ann Williams, *Homeplace: The Social Meaning of the Folk Dwelling in Southwestern North Carolina* (Charlottesville: University of Virginia Press, 1991), 115–36. For conditions of small rural housing, see Hoagland, *Log Cabin,* 78–114. Also see the introduction, note 13, and chapter 4, note 35.

43. Upton, *Another City,* 20.

44. The Mazur family housing history was obtained through interviews with Bernice Mazur and subsequent house documentation and architectural drawings. The house and family history are analyzed in Hubka and Kenny, "The Workers' Cottage in Milwaukee's Polish Community"; "Examining the American Dream," 49–69. See also Kenny, "Polish Routes to Americanization"; "The Homebuilders"; and "Americanizing Milwaukee's Polish South Side, 1900–1925."

Housing and resident documentation within the surrounding Polish neighborhoods was collected over a ten-year period that contributed to the preceding five publications. The most extensive project was funded by the Urban Research Initiatives Program, University of Wisconsin–Milwaukee Center for Urban Initiatives and Research resulting in Hubka and Kenny, "The Workers' Cottage in Milwaukee's Polish Community." Documentation included case studies of twenty-five households with architectural drawings of seventeen structures. These records complemented contemporary inventories and descriptions of the housing stock reported in the State of Wisconsin Public Documents. Oral histories with current and former residents within the study area assisted in compiling building documentation.

45. Bayrd Still, *Milwaukee: The History of a City* (Madison: State Historical Society of Wisconsin, 1993), 273.

46. Groth and Gutman, "Workers' Houses in West Oakland"; and Groth, "Workers'-Cottage and Minimal-Bungalow Districts in Oakland and Berkeley, California, 1870–1945."

47. For example, Groth and Gutman, "Workers' Houses in West Oakland"; Bigott, *From Cottage to Bungalow*, 1–18; Hoagland, "Boardinghouse Murders"; Zunz, *The Changing Face of Inequity*, 129–75.

5. DOMESTIC LIFE TRANSFORMED

1. Dolores Hayden, *The Grand Domestic Revolution: A History of Feminist Designs for American Homes, Neighborhoods, and Cities* (Cambridge, Mass.: MIT Press, 1982).

2. Gordon, *Rise and Fall of American Growth*, 113.

3. Rybczynski, *Home*, 176. Less than 10 percent of households between 1880 and 1910 had servants; Gordon, *Rise and Fall of American Growth*, 107. Rybczynski, *Home*, 154–78, is typical of many authors in linking the reduction in large Victorian house size, for example, by the elimination of specialized rooms (such as libraries, extra bedrooms, nurseries, smoking and playrooms), to the smaller size of typical houses in the early twentieth century.

4. The theory of early twentieth-century house shrinkage is stated or implied in many of the major and minor works of late nineteenth- and early twentieth-century housing and social reform. There are many sources for this theory, but the dominant referenced citations are two major works by Gwendolyn Wright: *Building the Dream: A Social History of Housing in America* (Cambridge, Mass.: MIT Press, 1983), 171 and 154–76; and *Moralism and the Model Home*, 244–46.

    A short list of some of the books that reference this theory includes Janet D. Ore, *The Seattle Bungalow: People and Houses, 1900–1940*

(Seattle: University of Washington Press, 2006), 56; Radford, *Modern Housing for America*, 10–12; Clark, *The American Family Home, 1800–1960*, 162–63; Nye, *Electrifying America*, 254; Peter Ward, *A History of Domestic Space: Privacy and the Canadian Home* (Vancouver: University of British Columbia Press, 1999), 19–22; Bigott, *From Cottage to Bungalow*, 9; Annmarie Adams, *Architecture in the Family Way: Doctors, Houses, and Women, 1870–1900* (Montreal: McGill-Queen's University Press, 1996), 163; King, *The Bungalow*, 150–51; Lane, *Houses for a New World*, 6–7; Sandy Isenstadt, "The Small House Era," in *The Modern American House: Spaciousness and Middle-Class Identity* (Cambridge: Cambridge University Press, 2006), 14–58. Gordon, *Rise and Fall of American Growth*, 102, 108–9, cites the theory but expresses doubts.

One of the key references for this house reduction theory appears to be Michael J. Doucet and John C. Weaver, "Material Culture and the North American House: The Era of the Common Man, 1870–1920," *Journal of American History* 72, no. 3 (December 1985): 583, Table 5, "Estimated Range of Interior Area of Inexpensive and Expensive Houses by Ten-Year Intervals, 1870–1920." This table demonstrates that the average size of both inexpensive and expensive houses was reduced between 1870 and 1920, often by as much as one-third to one-half. To substantiate these estimates, the authors include an extensive list of architectural and builder journals and catalogs from the period. Instead of a census of actual buildings, this is a list of architect-builder-merchant publication series of current and future houses. These lists are useful for identifying future trends of middle-to-upper-class house construction, but they are inadequate for identifying house sizes for the entire population. Furthermore, there are no credible statistics estimating house size development for a lower 50 percent of the housing population (except tenement studies for the very poor).

What appears to support these unsubstantiated estimates are individual house construction totals from selected years, especially from the 1920s (see Doan, *American Housing Production*, 182–83). House production in this era more than doubled compared with any previous era for all categories of house construction, including small houses. Therefore, citing these statistics in comparison with hypothetical totals of house sizes in the late nineteenth century does not substantiate house size reduction theories for the early twentieth century. (The average size of typical late 1800s and early 1900s working-class housing for two-thirds of the population has not been the subject of systematic national analysis.)

Since there are no credible pre-1940 house size statistics (square footage or number of rooms) on a national scale, previous estimates have relied on small sample surveys in city or metropolitan area studies with considerable variation in estimates. In no study analyzed for this research was there an attempt to survey and compare the size of all households for an entire population of a metropolitan area or region and none that came close to evaluating these estimates over time in order to evaluate the expansion or reduction of house size—the basis for testing a shrinking-house theory on local, regional, or national scales.

From case-study fieldwork and the review of existing research on common vernacular housing, this study records a slight but steady increase in house size and number of rooms (although halted during periods of economic depression) for the vast majority of working-to-middle-class households between 1870 and 1970, and especially during the period of this study, 1900 to 1940. Whether significant percentages of upper-class families actually experienced real spatial reduction is a debatable topic. In any case, during the first half of the twentieth century, for a vast majority of Americans leaving small, unimproved houses for slightly larger, improved houses, there was no shrinkage of house size, only modest but significant improvement and expansion.

5. Wright, *Moralism and the Model Home*, 244.

6. See chapter 2, note 22.

7. See note 4 of this chapter.

8. The desire for house size reduction is rooted in mid-nineteenth-century domestic reform literature such as the writings of Catharine Beecher, who offered unprecedented recommendations for the reduction of house size based on functional planning efficiency as well as the desire to reduce women's domestic labor and increase family comfort. While Beecher's progressive ideas were not widely followed, the impulse for house reduction remained and resurfaced in early twentieth-century reforms.

See Catherine E. Beecher and Harriet Beecher Stowe, *The American Women's Home* (Hartford, Conn.: Stowe-Day Foundation, 1869), 13 (plan); as analyzed by Hayden, *Grand Domestic Revolution,* 54–63; and Wright, *Building the Dream,* 37.

Though widely cited today and in the housing reform literature of its period, Beecher and Stowe's radical reformulation of the house, especially the reduction of house and room size, was not widely influential on the construction of nineteenth-century houses, elite or common.

9. Hubka, *Houses without Names*, 40–45. Also see chapter 3, note 34.

10. Bigott, *From Cottage to Bungalow*, 1–16.

11. Rybczynski, *Home*, 101–22, 217–32, and throughout, develops an outstanding review of the development of domestic comfort, which he

emphasizes is the outcome of technological advances, largely of the early twentieth century, as this study concurs. He ends his book with a spirited defense of bourgeois domestic comfort and its "implicit criticism of modernity," 224. See also the introduction to Gowans, *The Comfortable House,* xiv–xv, where he advances a similar thesis of comfort to summarize the broad-based development of a middle class of American housing. Gowans elevates domestic comfort as a crowning achievement of American housing production, similar to the emphasis in this book. See also Flanders, *The Making of Home,* 150–51, 167–68.

　　Authors from various disciplines have interpreted everyday domestic life and its comforts from different perspectives: Tony Judt, *Ill Fares the Land* (New York: Penguin, 2010), 21–25; Deirdre N. McCloskey, *The Bourgeois Virtues* (Chicago: University of Chicago Press, 2006), 1–90; Henri Lefebvre, *A Critique of Everyday Life,* trans. John Moore (London: Verso, 1991); Michel de Certeau, Luce Giard, and Pierre Mayol, *The Practice of Everyday Life,* vol. 2, trans. Timothy J. Tomasik (Minneapolis: University of Minnesota Press, 1998), 251–56; Glassie, *Passing the Time in Ballymenone*; Gaston Bachelard, *The Poetics of Space* (New York: Penguin, 2014).

12. See Rybczynski, *Home,* 108–12 and throughout.

EPILOGUE

1. Nye, *Electrifying America,* 26–28.
2. Peter G. Rowe, *Making a Middle Landscape* (Cambridge, Mass.: MIT Press, 1991), 3.
3. Moskowitz, *Standard of Living,* 3. Others have described this unity of American culture in economic terms stressing the consumption of goods and services; see especially Cohen, *A Consumers' Republic,* 1–20; and Stephanie Dyer, review essay, "The Moral Economy of Shopping," *Journal of Planning History* 6, no. 4 (2007): 353–61. In *Middletown,* Lynd and Lynd emphasize widespread unity in consumer culture; the "tools and services" of the domestic economy, a unity they noted was entirely absent in 1890, 82; see also 21–24.
4. See chapter 4, note 42.
5. For an excellent summary of how criticisms of America's middle classes evolved from the late nineteenth into the consumer-oriented, culturally deficient criticisms of the twentieth century, see Bledstein, "Introduction: Storytellers to the Middle Class." For another view of the evolution of the nineteenth-century middle class, see Blumin, *Emergence of the Middle Class,* 259–97.

6. See John Carey, *The Intellectuals and the Masses: Pride and Prejudice among the Literary Intelligentsia, 1880–1939* (New York: St. Martin's Press, 1992), 3–70. The economic and moral critique of mass culture is analyzed by Daniel Horowitz, *The Morality of Spending: Attitudes toward the Consumer Society in America, 1875–1940* (Chicago: Ivan R. Dee, 1985), xi–xxxi, 134–65; John R. Stilgoe, *Borderland: Origins of the American Suburb, 1820–1939* (New Haven, Conn.: Yale University Press, 1988), 2–10; and Cohen, *Making a New Deal* and *Consumers' Republic,* 99–158.

This "masses" critique was continued and broadened after World War II into a criticism of suburban development, lifestyle, and culture. Continuing also was the critique of blind consumerism and shallow intellectualism, as outlined in James Howard Kunstler, *The Geography of Nowhere: The Rise and Decline of America's Man-Made Landscape* (New York: Simon and Schuster, 1993). More balanced assessments were given by Rosalyn Baxandall and Elizabeth Ewen, *Picture Windows: How the Suburbs Happened* (New York: Basic Books, 2000); and Robert A. Beauregard, *When American Became Suburban* (Minneapolis: University of Minnesota Press, 2006), 138–43.

The classic objective depiction of the suburbs is Herbert J. Gans, *The Levittowners: Ways of Life and Politics in a New Suburban Community* (New York: Columbia University Press, 1967), which stood out against the criticisms of urbanists and intellectuals such as Lewis Mumford, *The City in History* (New York: Harcourt, 1961), 486 and throughout; and Vincent J. Scully, *American Architecture and Urbanism* (New York: Praeger, 1969), 165 and throughout. The urban intellectual skepticism and hostility to the domestic sphere and popular culture, often referred to as "kitsch," is summarized by Christopher Reed, *Not at Home: The Suppression of Domesticity in Modern Art and Architecture* (London: Thames and Hudson, 1996), 7–17. Fundamental criticisms of postwar suburban environment and lifestyle are numerous; see, e.g., John Keats, *The Crack in the Picture Window* (Boston: Houghton Mifflin, 1957); Kunstler, *Geography of Nowhere*; Dolores Hayden, *Redesigning the American Dream: The Future of Housing, Work, and Family Life* (New York: W. W. Norton, 2002), 19–139.

In their reevaluation, *Middletown in Transition,* the Lynds blame the rise of 1920s consumer culture for a decline in overall popular culture, as analyzed in Richard Wightman Fox, "Epitaph for Middletown: Robert S. Lynd and the Analysis of Consumer Culture," in *The Culture of Consumption: Critical Essays in American History, 1880–1980* (New York: Pantheon Books, 1983), 101–42.

7. Horowitz, *The Morality of Spending,* xxxi.

8. Cohen, *Consumers' Republic,* 5–15; Horowitz, *The Morality of Spending,* xi–xxxi. Also see Flanders, *The Making of Home,* 53.

9. Flanders, *The Making of Home,* 145.

10. Horowitz, *The Morality of Spending,* xxv–xxxi, 68–69.

11. See Cowan, *More Work for Mother,* 151–71. Also see Moskowitz, *Standard of Living,* 15–18.

12. Almost all major works analyzing domestic labor emphasize this criticism; for example, Hayden, *The Grand Domestic Revolution*; Cowan, *More Work for Mother*; Strasser, *Never Done*; and Gwendolyn Wright, *Building the Dream.*

13. Historical sources have rarely recorded the voices and opinions of the majority of working-class women who received these improvements. Often their consumer selections have been interpreted as unthinking or motivated almost entirely by outside commercial interests. For interpretations giving voice to a working-class constituency, see Moskowitz: *Standard of Living,* 7–18; Cohen, "Embellishing a Life of Labor," Upton and Vlach, *Common Places,* 261–78; Bledstein, "Introduction"; Johnston, "Conclusion," Bledstein and Johnston, *The Middling Sorts,* 296–306; and Cohen, *Making a New Deal,* 99–120.

14. Many sources advance the general theme that women's work of domestic labor in the mid-1900s was longer and harder than domestic labor earlier in the century. These conclusions, however, are principally based on the experiences of early twentieth-century middle-to-upper-class housewives or sources that were then applied to the experiences of a broad middle-to-working class in a cross-cultural comparison. For example, both S. J. Kleinberg, *Women in the United States, 1830–1945* (New Brunswick, N.J.: Rutgers University Press, 1999), 237–42; and Strasser, *Never Done,* 82–84, 67–84, criticize kitchen improvements largely from the perspective of upper-middle-class domestic experience and give less importance to the elimination of physical labor provided by domestic technology. In a typical analysis, Flanders, *The Making of Home,* 115, advances the theme that in 1940 English housewives spent more time on housework than their mothers in 1900. But we learn that servants and commercial (laundry) services aided housework in 1900. See also Jean Gordon and Jan McArthur, "American Women and Domestic Consumption, 1800–1920: Four Interpretive Themes," in *Making the American Home: Middle-Class Women and Domestic Material Culture, 1840–1940,* ed. Marilyn Ferris Motz and Pat Browne (Bowling Green, Ohio: Popular Press, 1988), 27–47. In another standard assessment, Thomas Schlereth, citing Ruth Schwartz Cowan, estimates that housewives spent more time doing housework in 1930 than their mothers spent in 1890; introduction, *American Home Life,* 13. See also

Cowan, "Coal Stoves and Clean Sinks," 214–15. For alternative views from the perspective of working-class women, see Kennedy, *If All We Did Was to Weep at Home,* 93–156.

15. Cowan, *More Work for Mother,* 151–90, constructs an excellent, groundbreaking, chapter-length comparison between two types of housewives and housework in the 1900 to 1940 period: "those who were struggling to make ends meet" and "those who lived comfortably." By comparing these two experiences, the reader can vividly appreciate the gulf in domestic experience that the working classes were attempting to bridge by gaining technological and social improvements.

INDEX

Thomas C. Hubka is professor emeritus in the Department of Architecture at the School of Architecture, University of Wisconsin–Milwaukee. He is the author of *Resplendent Synagogue: Architecture and Worship in an Eighteenth-Century Polish Community*; *Big House, Little House, Back House, Barn: The Connected Farm Buildings of New England*; and *Houses without Names: Architectural Nomenclature and the Classification of America's Common Houses.*